Tough Guy : The American Movie Macho

TOUGH GUY

The American Movie Macho

by

James L. Neibaur

McFarland & Company, Inc., Publishers

Jefferson, North Carolina, and London

Frontispiece: James Cagney in Lady Killer *(Warner Bros., 1933).*

British Library Cataloguing-in-Publication data available

Library of Congress Cataloguing-in-Publication Data

Neibaur, James L., 1958–
  Tough guy.

  Bibliography: p. 219.
  Includes filmographies.
  Includes index.
  1. Men in motion pictures. 2. Machismo in motion
pictures. 3. Motion picture actors and actresses —
United States. 4. Men actors — United States. I. Title.
PN1995.9.M46N45 1989   791.43′09′09353   88-27309

ISBN 0-89950-382-9 (lib. bdg.; 50# acid-free natural paper) ∞

Printed in the United States of America.

McFarland & Company, Inc., Publishers
  Box 611, Jefferson, North Carolina 28640

This book is dedicated with love to my son Max: my very own "Little Tough Guy";

and to the memory of my beloved wife Diana (1961–1987).

Acknowledgments

For various methods of assistance including research, photos, or just plain old encouragement, the author wishes to express his deepest appreciation to the following:

Ted Okuda, Peter Jackel, Dr. Andrew McLean, Donald Key, Lionel Stander, Pineapple Jackson, Greg Andregg, Gary Schneeberger, *The Big Reel*, Leon Smith, Metro Goldwyn Memories, the University of Wisconsin–Parkside, and the Racine Public Library.

Table of Contents

Introduction

The term "tough guy," when used to describe a film characterization, describes more than just one standard character. It could describe a good guy, a bad guy, a staple of masculinity, a presentation of youthful rebellion, a level of insanity or a bluntly visceral image. Tough guys are men who don't back down, no matter how intimidating the circumstances may be. They are omnipotent, all-powerful. They are the winners in a world of losers; in fact they are often losers from society's perspective who prove to the audience that they are indeed winners within the context of the film's narrative.

Silent pictures presented different characters who could be considered tough from the perspective of a movie audience. Western heroes, hard military men, shady gangster types—all with their own firmness of character—were the portents to tough-guy personas which were firmly established during the thirties. In silent films, the actors who played tough guys were not essentially movie tough guys, per se. In their next picture they could be playing a wimpy, pretentious fop. However, once talking pictures manifested themselves, actors like Edward G. Robinson, James Cagney and Clark Gable immediately presented a strong, masculine image which they carried with them from picture to picture and honed to perfection. These were the true tough guys, beginning a tradition that continues.

Once these tough guys were firmly established they gave the meek a vicarious thrill, while all moviegoers admired their gall, their unshaken demeanor despite the odds. Americans measured their masculinity against movie tough guys to such a degree that even today John Wayne is considered in many quarters to be the prototypical American male. But over the years tough guys changed. The traditionalism of a Wayne character was challenged by different types of tough guys who exuded many qualities which were the antithesis of the archetypal male in films up to that time. James Dean epitomized the rebellious adolescent during the fifties, when the youthful wholesomeness of the forties films evolved into the presentation of alienated teenagers trapped in a materialistic society. Dean's form of tough guy was as a trapped young boy who had the guts to rebel and take

1

charge of his followers despite opposition from a suppressive adult society. Elvis Presley personified the rebellious spirit of period rock and roll or rhythm and blues music, which stemmed from the collective unconscious of the American working class.

While the term "tough" immediately calls forth images of strength and defiance, it does not always mean a still, stoic demeanor any more than it always must mean that which is stereotypically labeled as masculine by society. It is a very complex term which is capable of taking on a variety of different forms. This text will attempt to present the most important operators of each of the varied styles of movie toughness and the influences of every presentation.

Each actor profiled in this study has been chosen due to his originality, popularity and influence in the realm of the American movie tough guy. Each is unique, and all these performers put their own indelible stamp on every role they essayed. Not all of these actors are great practitioners of their art. Clint Eastwood, for instance, does not have the acting versatility of James Cagney. And this is a very diverse group despite their all being tough guys. John Wayne, Elvis Presley and George Raft have nothing in common as far as their screen personas are concerned except for the fact that they all are noted for their own individual presentations of a certain, select toughness.

In each chapter we will look at the actor's persona and how it was utilized over the years in different contexts. James Cagney, for instance, managed to use his tough-guy persona as a New York gangster, as a Broadway showman, as a conniving promotions expert, even as a war coward. We will also examine how moviegoers reacted to each image, and how they influenced the other, lesser tough-guy actors as well as how Americans regarded masculinity and determined through film characters just which characteristics were typically male. The most important films will be discussed for each performer as well as the actors they most closely influenced (Eastwood's influencing Charles Bronson for instance).

What we are trying to accomplish in this study is to better understand the true complexities of this very popular and pivotal motion picture subgenre. We will discover that toughness does not only come in forms of what is traditionally and stereotypically tough. We will find out just what it is that makes us call each of these performers tough. And in the end we will be able to better understand and appreciate the American movie tough guy's purpose in motion pictures.

The First Movie Tough Guys

As the tough guy was a pivotal screen characterization in the overall development of American film, it is important to examine the first uses of this persona. The silent era boasted very little in the way of major tough-guy "stars" (like Edward G. Robinson or John Wayne) but were instrumental in presenting the foundation of many assorted tough-guy traits through a handful of actors from this period.

The very first tough guys were not genuine screen characters at all. Early Edison films from the late nineteenth century and early twentieth century afforded our first glimpse of the tough guy, but through a film's setting and overall production. For instance, *Cripple Creek Barroom* (1898) was a Western that featured no plot or substance other than a Western-style setting. Thus those who inhabited the screen presented traits of the Western movie tough guy before the fact. *A Desperate Encounter Between Burglars and Police* (1905) was an action drama that preceded the detective and gangster films.

Some of the earliest movie stars were also among the first screen toughs as well. While it wasn't until the talkie era that performers actually created tough-guy personas which they were to play over and over again, movie toughs continued to develop, albeit very gradually, from the early Edison films until these tough-guy leads were established. Perhaps the best way to examine the impact of the early tough guys on those which came later is to study the silent era according to its relative genres.

The Gangster Films

Gangsters and badmen have always been glamorized in the media. Motion pictures are certainly no exception, as some of the screen's most colorful characters have come from the gangster films. While this is especially true during the thirties (when Prohibition and the Depression caused real-life gang activity that ultimately evolved into several film studies on the gangster), the silent era did present the foundations of at least the style of plot utilized in later gang dramas. Characterizations were not those that were expected to be presented again and again in a series of films with similar bases (as the Bogart or Cagney characters were used). Actors played these roles once and could very well be seen as a romantic lead in their next picture. Yet the characterizations laid down in these early gang sagas presented us with at least the basic character traits that would be used in the coming decades.

Perhaps the very first substantial gangster film was D. W. Griffith's one-reeler *The Musketeers of Pig Alley* (1912) which starred Lillian Gish as the heroine while Elmer Booth and Harry Carey, Sr., appeared as the tough gangsters. Carey was soon to become an interesting Western star whose style was influenced by William S. Hart and subsequently helped influence John Wayne's legendary characterization. In this film he acts as the large, brutal sidekick of tenacious antihero Booth. Carey's big, tough, ugly appearance is the prototype to such character roles as those played by the likes of Allen Jenkins or Lionel Stander years later. That his very appearance is intimidating makes good use of what was genuinely a visual medium at that time. Elmer Booth, however, is closer to the James Cagney–type character in his role of an energetic, engaging young tough with fast, deliberate gestures and a two-fisted, swaggering approach to all situations. Booth could very well have developed this into a genuinely important characterization if he had lived long enough to extend these personality traits into something with true substance (he died in 1915). These little mannerisms do form what was soon to become a collection of stock gestures employed by the more hyperactive tough guys in later films (a direct antithesis to the quiet cool of a Bogart type; hence the teaming of Bogart with Cagney in a number of films).

William Selig's *The Making of Crooks* (1914) was a study of period juvenile delinquency (young criminal types) featuring Jack Pickford in the leading role. Not unlike Samuel Goldwyn's *Dead End* (1937, based on a play by Sidney Kingsley), this Selig film was so titled due to its attempt at showing the development of gangsters by presenting them as stemming from the exploits of alienated youths of the period. Pickford, like Booth in *Musketeers*, portrayed an antihero who is endearing in retrospect (after countless endearing baddies from thirties filmmaking onward), but audiences of this period weren't inclined to accept a bad guy as a hero, no matter how attractively he was presented. While the toughs of *Musketeers* were allowed to survive for the duration of the film, the ultimate message in *The Making of Crooks* was apparently the utter futility of juvenile delinquency, as the ending serves just desserts to the young toughs (they are imprisoned), correlating the confines of the jail cell to the confines of the pool room, shown as the portion of society that victimizes the youths and fosters their delinquency. This underlying theme has far less substance than *Dead End*, and instead could be considered a very early harbinger to the teenage exploitation pictures of the thirties (e.g., *Are These Our Children*) which relied on pathos to develop emotion from a lackluster narrative that was very calculated in its preachiness.

One of the most important portents to the gangster films that become firmly established during the thirties was the 1913 George Loane Tucker feature *Traffic in Souls*. While very primitive in retrospect, it does present a grimness and harsh realism that was to be a staple of the Warner Bros. social dramas of the thirties, which gave us some of film's most important screen toughs. Dealing with white slavery, or prostitution, *Traffic in Souls* is very melodramatic, but still important, in that it shows the seedy underworld which was soon to become the backdrop of several prototypical tough-guy adventures. This film can also be considered a lead-in to the most important gangster picture of the silent era, that being Joseph Von Sternberg's 1927 feature *Underworld*, which was the first gangster feature to rely solely on characterization for its impact.

Underworld was a prohibition drama set in Chicago with George Bancroft portraying gangleader and bootlegger Bull Weed. Von Sternberg allowed the film's narrative to work through Bancroft's characterization, the basis of the work being Bull Weed's potent force in the prohibition racket. Bancroft plays the character with all key elements of tough-guy characterization intact, borrowing from a variety of preceding styles to create Bull Weed as a textured, tormented, tragic figure whose hard edge is augmented by his circumstances. This film and its leading character are precursors for Edward G. Robinson's Rico Bandello character in *Little Caesar* and James Cagney's Tom Powers character in *Public Enemy* a few short years later. What Bull Weed lacks is a voice to fit his characterization (unlike monsters, gangsters just don't seem as terrifying in silent pictures, despite Bancroft's wide range of facial expressions). Yet this business of a narrative depending solely on the exploits of its leading character is what makes *Underworld* a most effective example in the earliest presentations of screen toughness. Bancroft did not define this role, but he did serve as the most essential early practitioner, presenting elements that further manifested themselves in subsequent portrayals by men who became masters at this sort of art form.

Another important aspect of *Underworld* is that it performed very well at the box office, ensuring further Hollywood gangster sagas, even if only to cash in on a financially established idea. But *Underworld* was released the same year as *The Jazz Singer*, a movie milestone that introduced sound to this visual art form. The success, then, that *Underworld* enjoyed had to be presented in a talking picture, and, thus, a talking actor was sought. While Bancroft later proved his mettle in character roles throughout the thirties, Bull Weed was his last movie role of such stature. And in their quest to repeat the box office success of this gangland saga, Hollywood filmmakers needed to find methods to present established visuals as well as the proper use of sound, including both dialogue and nonverbal effects, to create a work that not only utilized a gangland premise (as was proven popular with moviegoers) but also exhibited the substance found in the earlier work. Filmmakers of this period realized the importance of not doing a film that only boasted sound as an asset over the previous effort.

The result was *Little Caesar* (1930), with Edward G. Robinson portraying gangster Rico Bandello. Rico, however, was an even greater character than Bull Weed; he was more intimidating, meaner, more tormented and, ultimately, more tragic. And it also established the tough guy in American film, bringing forth a subgenre that was to remain in motion pictures as one of its most popular and representative characterizations.

The Western

The screen depiction of the West has always been one of awe. What with the large, vast scenic settings and the bigger-than-life heroes and villains found in Western pictures, it could be stated that the Western is the archetypical film genre as far as the medium's visuals are concerned. Westerns have been accused of racism, sexism, and unattractive right-wing sensibilities as well as depicting a false notion as to how people of Western days looked upon death (killing without remorse was a staple of Western movies and television shows for many years). Out of this genre, though, many of the most decided traits of screen toughness emerged (all of them culminating in the John Wayne character subsequently honed to perfection by his last films). In an effort to understand many of the qualities that constituted the most standard and natural elements of screen toughness, the Western must be examined from the beginning.

One of the first films to utilize a fluid narrative through its visuals was Edwin S. Porter's *The Great Train Robbery* (1903). That the film was a Western makes Westerns central to the development of film. Most of the importance of *The Great Train Robbery* is in the presentation of its narrative structure (contrary to popular belief, this was *not* the first film to tell a story, but *was* the first to use a variety of important editing techniques that were later mastered by D. W. Griffith and thus introduced to the future of American filmmaking). The film crosscuts from good guys to bad guys, and initiates action sequences at a pace that caused (and still causes) as much exhilaration as fascination on the part of the viewer (Griffith developed crosscutting into a true art form with his epics *Intolerance* and *The Birth of a Nation* some years later). There is little character development in the film;

the players are merely going through the motions as good guys, bad guys, or innocents within the framework of the narrative, never exuding any outstanding character qualities. The bad guys grimace while the good guys project overt heroism with shoulders back and chins held high. But this little milestone did form the basis of Western plotting and the methods of filmmaking which caused a very rapid sort of fluidity from scene to scene; all of these methods are among the earliest and most primitive staples in screen narrative treatments.

It was also the first screen appearance of G. M. Anderson, who not only was to become one of the first Hollywood studio moguls (forming Essanay studios in Chicago with George Spoor some years later), but was also the first movie cowboy. Anderson's cowboy characterization manifested itself after he established his own studio, a studio that at one time boasted names as legendary as Charles Chaplin, Gloria Swanson, and Francis X. Bushman. As "Bronco Billy," Anderson appeared in hundreds of short subjects as well as some feature-length films which he also directed and collaborated on the screenplays. The films were simple at first, but their narrative structure matured very rapidly. Bronco Billy was a good badman whose cowboy savvy and muscular frame allowed for action heroics which flavored a narrative borne out of dime novels (Anderson's not being a Westerner himself caused him to rely on such sources for his films' plots).

Anderson created what was the first cowboy hero, beginning a tradition that was followed by dozens of major stars whose very presence elicited a special thrill from movie audiences. While the Anderson films were often trite in the narrative department (lacking the depth and substance of later, more polished works), they are certainly quite impressive from the perspective that they were the first films of their kind. By the time his works achieved the narrative maturity to separate them from simple actioners, and Anderson graduated to feature films, both William S. Hart and Tom Mix had achieved notoriety for their own respective depictions of the West on film and the cowboy hero images they created. Yet the Bronco Billy character is the harbinger for every cowboy hero from Tom Mix to Hopalong Cassidy to the dozens of television counterparts who popped up during the fifties.

The films of William S. Hart could easily have been inspired by Anderson's works far more than simply that they were using the cowboy hero formula that Bronco Billy had established. Hart also played a tough guy with a fair amount of sentiment in his soul; a character not far from the real-life Hart, whose sympathy for the Indian and fascination with Indian lore gave American film some of the most honest depictions of Western civilization in its history.

Born in 1870, Hart was older than the youthful, athletic cowboy heroes Anderson or Tom Mix depicted, but his screen persona exhibited the

William S. Hart in a publicity still for *The Two Gun Man* (Paramount, 1922).

strong, silent qualities that presented another extension of the cowboy hero. His cold, icy stare and stoic demeanor were to be found as late as the 1970s in Clint Eastwood's man-with-no-name character from the Sergio Leone spaghetti Westerns that first established Eastwood as a major screen star.

Hart made an impact on the Western film as both an actor and a director. His performance, as noted above, projected a commanding stoic resolve. Through this characterization came strong defiance in the face of a criminal adversary. The narrative flowed through his characterization to present what ultimate manhood in a Western setting was according to Hart's boyhood recollections. These early character traits were milestones in that they continued to be used as examples of accepted masculinity in the American film for years to come. Yet through this characterization, Hart displayed none of the omnipotence found in later incarnations. He used this persona to depict man as an imperfect being who is still at the mercy of his environment and circumstances. The character adhered religiously to a strong moral code of ethics, establishing another Western movie tradition, and was basically an extension of Hart's love for the authentic Western "types" he actually knew as a child.

As a director, Hart has been accused of being a bit too sentimental. In some ways this is true, his deep affection for the era he was presenting being sometimes too evident in his portrayals. He did have the basic elements of camera placement down quite well and used close-ups very effectively to establish the various characters in the then strictly visual medium. Like his character, Hart the filmmaker had his own code of ethics regarding the making of his Westerns and did not necessarily create them for mass consumption, refusing to sacrifice art for artifice, or his strong beliefs in the world he was recreating on film for wagging heads among the city-bred critical circles (of course criticism had not been perfected for film study yet).

Hart's work is important in the realm of American film for a variety of complex reasons, but from the perspective of the Hollywood tough guy, it is his screen character and execution of screen characterization among all of his players in a Western setting that most closely lends itself to the development of movie toughness. In his last film, *Tumbleweeds* (1925), his career culminates with a Western feature that is not only a classic, but carefully utilized every acting and filmmaking trait of the Hart Westerns to their absolute fullest. Hart's deep feeling for the art of filmmaking and for an accurate depiction of the West sets *Tumbleweeds* apart from Westerns that relied on stunts and comic sidekicks (although some comedy relief is provided by Lucien Littlefield—a rarity in Hart Westerns).

Hart abhorred fakery of any kind in screen depictions of the West, and this is especially evident in *Tumbleweeds* where all of the action sequences are carefully constructed so as not to seem clumsy in their superhuman stunt effects. This may cause some to find Hart's Westerns dry and stilted, especially in retrospect, but his films were of a different nature than the amusing Saturday afternoon fodder that was initially popularized by Tom Mix.

Mix actually was making films before Hart and was still active in fine form at the time of Hart's retirement. In contrast to the Hart features, the

Tom Mix managed to combine action and substance in many of his early films for Fox studios.

Mix films were filled with exciting stunts, with Mix's horse, Tony, achieving as strong a star following as his master, setting a precedent for famous screen horses like Trigger, Champion, Tarzan, and Topper in years to come. Hart's films were poetic and realistic, while the Mix efforts were of the wild daredevil school that remained a staple of the Western throughout the thirties and forties, and then on television during the fifties. But to state that the Mix films were filled with action is not to say that they presented all style and no substance. Mix's heroics were tied to strong Western narratives in his best pictures, and his acting reached beyond mere stunt work. Like his movie cowboy brethren, Tom Mix projected his own form of undiluted masculinity in a Western setting.

In the realm of the movie tough guy, Tom Mix was not the dashing daredevil type like Douglas Fairbanks or Errol Flynn (who were exciting, but not necessarily in a "tough" sense). Mix instead developed a character who exuded as much strength and defiance as acrobatic skills. His earliest pictures often were wholesome situational comedies in a Western setting, not unlike the Will Rogers two-reelers. Mix also appeared in several mediocre Western shorts during this early period which were made to capitalize on the actor's daredevil feats, especially his trick riding skills. The first films in which Mix exhibited the character qualities that best define his work were those he made after joining the Fox studios in 1917.

The Mix films at Fox, virtually all feature-length efforts, presented the cowboy as more than just a strong, stoic presence. The Mix films added the stunts and comedy that Hart carefully eschewed, appealing to the juvenile audiences more so than the Hart films. These films included several ideas that have since become staples (even clichés) of the Western film. Mix always unwittingly stumbled into trouble while passing through town, always got into a fight by helping somebody else, always ended up with the girl. What his films lacked in the poetic narratives of the Hart efforts, they made up for in imagination and excitement. Action sequences were conducted through the Mix characterization rather than in spite of it, while the persona Mix projected was clearly evident in all of these sequences.

The Mix films often are unavailable for reappraisal today, due to a fire at Fox which destroyed much of their negatives from the teens and twenties. However, those features that have survived present a good look at one of American film's most important characters. *Riders of the Purple Sage* (1925) is one of his better known titles, although this is an offbeat item in that it utilizes little stunt work and relies more heavily on plot structure (Mix was never a pretentious artist and made few films over five reels in length). What makes this particular film important is that is most fully presents the emphasis on production values Mix put into his Westerns. The camera work is excellent, very successfully capturing the scenic beauty of the surroundings as it directly pertains to the narrative (based on a Zane Grey story) and the Mix characterization. The film also presents Mix in a much more serious vein than the whirlwind, carefree qualities of his more stunt-laden pictures.

Mix worked into the talkies, his films of the early thirties for Universal less interesting overall than his silents. The stunts were still there, but Mix, like many of the silent actors, could not develop his capabilities to the now verbal medium. While the visuals are nice, the added element of sound is not utilized properly (one notable exception is in the 1932 feature *My Pal the King,* which has Tom leaving the action of the picture to address the audience about the plot that is occurring onscreen). Mix had trouble reciting dialogue properly, his voice rarely enunciating the words with the clarity necessary when dealing with such primitive sound equipment. While the films relied little on dialogue, committing themselves more to the visual aspects, they still appeared rather stilted.

The last Tom Mix film was a 1935 serial titled *The Miracle Rider,* a simplistic and poorly produced cheapie that belies the true talents of Tom Mix. However, the influence of Tom Mix outlasted that of even William S. Hart in that it spawned a host of imitators throughout the thirties, forties, and fifties. The Hart influence can be found in the stoic sensibilities of the John Wayne and Clint Eastwood characterizations; but the latter two are a slighter variation, the Hart influence perhaps best considered to be indirect.

Many Western stars cropped up during the late-silent to early-talkie period in American motion pictures—Tim McCoy, Harry Carey, Fred Thompson, Buck Jones, Hoot Gibson and Ken Maynard to name a few—all projecting further variations on the tough-guy theme via the American Western film. But these characteristics from silent pictures should best be considered important early manifestations of screen toughness and masculinity, the elements here being utilized as foundations for virtually all future presentations of such traits.

Military Films

In the history of motion pictures, depictions of men in the military have always presented the most typical tough-guy qualities. While the methods of presenting such images have branched off into pretty bizarre territory (bloodthirsty military men in the *Rambo* vein), the basic qualities that are evident in virtually any depiction of military men on film came from the initial presentations in silent pictures as mentioned here. Just as Hemingway's war-related novels became popular during the post–World War I period, so did films depicting the guts and glory of war. However, not all of the war pictures presented tough-guy characterizations as the axis of the narrative. Two very important silent features—*The Big Parade* (1925), with John Gilbert, and *The Patent Leather Kid* (1926), which features Richard Barthelmess as a cocky prizefighter who learns humility when he goes to war—are more romantic or melodramatic in their presentations, containing fine textures but from a different direction than the tough-guy war pictures.

Raoul Walsh's *What Price Glory* (1926) is one of two genuinely essential early films depicting military toughness that could truly be considered a harbinger for later interpretations by John Wayne and others. Featuring Edmund Lowe and Victor McLaglen as two hard, lusty characters, *What Price Glory* attempts to give a more realistic portrayal of marines. Dolores Del Rio portrays the woman who attracts both men and intensifies their fierce rivalry.

The film initially features several very boisterous comedy sequences (actual swearing is evident if you can read lips). While the characters are tough and project such fierceness, they know their job and have a begrudged-yet-genuine affection for one another that is borne out in most of the early sequences. As with any military film, the horrors of war must be portrayed, the focus of the film then changing from comedy to heavy melodrama, although not with such abruptness that the viewer is left baffled (this being a military film, a battle sequence is rather likely). This battle footage allows for a variation on the rivalrous characters of Flagg and Quirt with the emphasis being dead serious rather than in a savagely comic vein. The culmination of the film returns us to the comic situations between the two soldiers.

What Price Glory is an important film for a variety of reasons, but as far as the movie tough guy is concerned, the characterizations of Flagg and Quirt as enacted by McLaglen and Lowe are the foundation for the stereotypically tough military leaders that found their way into another wave of American war pictures during World War II, John Wayne being perhaps the most notable actor who employed a characterization stemming from those in this picture. While in retrospect these characters may seem rather standard, it is important to realize that the portrayals were the first to make such full use of the character traits that shape the way film represented its military leaders. The Quirt and Flagg roles presented the rivalry between officers buoyed by humor beneath the surface conflict.

The following year saw master of makeup Lon Chaney as Sergeant O'Hara in *Tell It to the Marines*. His conflict is not with another officer, but instead with a cocky private (William Haines) who must learn the meaning of military discipline via O'Hara's strong, effective tactics. Chaney achieved legendary status for his brilliant portrayals of exceptional people like *The Hunchback of Notre Dame* (1923) with his own makeup work bringing added depth to his already complex characterization.

As O'Hara, Chaney's performance transcends the film's narrative. He does not come off as the tough sergeant with a heart of gold, but instead plays a strong, passionate character with genuine concerns regarding his men and the military. The character John Wayne played in *Sands of Iwo Jima* (1948) and the one essayed by Clint Eastwood for *Heartbreak Ridge* (1986) are both directly influenced by this Chaney portrayal. In fact, Chaney's performance is so effective he was given an honorary lifetime

Edmund Lowe (left) and Victor McLaglen vie for the affections of Dolores Del Rio in *What Price Glory* (Fox, 1926).

membership to the U.S. Marine Corps at the time of this film's initial release.

This characterization is especially interesting so many years hence due to the varying degrees of acceptance it has undergone over the years. This sort of tough military leader was effective in the twenties, thirties, and especially the forties when another war was taking place. However, by the fifties, sixties, and seventies such characters were dismissed as animalistic anachronisms. And then in the eighties, these characters again came into vogue with films like *Heartbreak Ridge* and Sylvester Stallone's *First Blood* series. Chaney's portrayal is a true portent for such later portrayals as these and others. O'Hara is truly concerned about his men, paying special attention to the self-confident wiseacre Skeet Burns (Haines), but exudes no sensitive qualities at all. His concern is a hard-edged military concern that stems from his apparent belief in the stereotypical masculine role in a military society. The film's denouement shows his beliefs to be in the right, eventually accepted by the bold, brash Skeet Burns, who sees the necessity of the traits that O'Hara is trying to infuse into his men.

The film is important for showing another dimension of Chaney the actor than that which is already well known, as well as for presenting the

Lon Chaney's portrayal of Sergeant O'Hara in *Tell It to the Marines* (MGM, 1926) paved the way for more military characterizations in the John Wayne vein. Also pictured with Chaney is Eleanor Boardman.

most clear-cut forerunner to so many military tough-guy presentations in subsequent army dramas. Whether these characters were the good guys or the bad guys, depending on the era the film was made, the character traits were always generally the same, owing a great deal to the pattern set by Chaney in *Tell It to the Marines*.

Conclusion

Silent film is important for a variety of reasons, but mostly due to its having established so many of the movie techniques that were further developed over the years. As acting is a very individualized practice, it is difficult to trace its development. Some actors are better and more innovative than others. But the traits that describe virtually any movie tough guy, the basic elements that characterize the stereotypical toughness underlying his individual characterization—all were created in the silent era. These traits did not stem from any one actor or any one film, but from the three aforementioned screen genres (or subgenres) that were led by major characters whose personalities exuded such brands of toughness as were to be used to help define later, more personal methods.

As we now observe the men who most creatively and effectively put an indelible stamp on a series of presentations utilizing one tough-guy character which they carefully honed to perfection over subsequent performances, we will see the way these basic traits that were first established in silent pictures manifested themselves. What we have at this point is a skeleton pattern of what the American movie tough guy is in the various contexts of film narrative. The following actors put flesh on these bones through their own ideas about how to exhibit a special brand of screen toughness.

Edward G. Robinson

For all the individual quirks and traits George Bancroft bestowed upon the movie gangster in *Underworld*, the absolute definition of screen gangleaders was manifested by Edward G. Robinson in Mervyn LeRoy's classic *Little Caesar* (1930). It was more than the first film in Robinson's career to display all of the stage-trained actor's abilities. In various interviews, LeRoy stated that Robinson's portrayal of Rico Bandello in this film was enhanced by the actor's adding so much depth to the part through facial expressions, the precise recitation of the dialogue, and especially the little audiovisual reactions that Robinson created totally on his own. While accounts state that Robinson's real-life persona sharply contrasted that of Rico, it is this character to whom his screen persona would always relate. Even in his occasional escapes from the Rico-oriented roles (e.g., *The Amazing Doctor Clitterhouse*), Robinson's tough-guy status was difficult to completely shield. As a result of his characterization in *Little Caesar*, Edward G. Robinson became one of *the* tough guys of American motion pictures.

Robinson had appeared in a handful of films prior to his role in *Little Caesar*, but none of these films is particularly memorable. What is worth noting is a role he played on stage in *The Racket* (1927), which closely relates to his Rico character. It, along with a few other similar roles he essayed during the 1929–30 play seasons, allowed for him to achieve a handle on some of the basic characteristics of playing a tough gangster type. Stage work helped him to enhance his Rico characterization with the extra little quirks he added to the role. This aided Robinson in putting an indelible stamp on his performance and allowed for him to extend from these traits to other, often broader peculiarities added to roles he played in a variety of different tough-guy–oriented films—from the screen adaptation of Jack London's *The Sea Wolf* (1941) to amusing parodies of the gangster he made famous in films as diverse as *Little Giant* (1933) and Disney's *Never a Dull Moment* (1967).

The film *Little Caesar* opens with Robinson as Rico Bandello and Douglas Fairbanks, Jr., as Joe Massara sitting in a seedy diner. Immediately

Rico comes off as tough, with a facial expression that looks like a permanent grimace and a voice that sounds like a perpetual snarl. This character contrasts perfectly with Massara, who appears dapper, refined, almost above his small-time hood profession. What subsequently develops in the *Little Caesar* narrative is rather complex, centering around Rico's relationship with Joe as well as his aspirations to make it to the top of the criminal heap. Joe loses interest in being a criminal when the two of them become more involved in crimes of greater notoriety and heinousness as they become part of an established gang of racketeers. Rico, however, not only works his way to the top of this gang very rapidly, easing out leader Sam Vettori (Stanley Fields), but retains his attachment to Joe, who is now moving up in the "respectable" world as a professional dancer. Yet is is not merely Joe's dancing that Rico objects to, but also his dancing partner Olga Stassoff (Glenda Farrell), whom Rico sees as alienating Joe's affections. Homosexuality is very gingerly intimated as Rico admonishes Joe for his new-found profession:

> RICO: Should a young guy like you be wasting his time? I took pride in you Joe, I brought you into the gang. But now you're getting to be a sissy.

This point is taken further when the discussion comes to Olga:

> RICO: That skirt can go hang, it's *her* that's made a softy out of you.
> JOE: You lay off Olga, Rico!
> RICO: I ain't layin' off her, I'm after her. She and me can't both have you, one of us has got to lose. Well it ain't gonna be me! There's ways of stoppin' that dame!
> JOE: I love her, we're in love! Doesn't that mean anything to you?
> RICO: Nothing! Less than nothing! Love — soft stuff!

In masking his affections for Joe to the gang, or, perhaps, explaining them in masculine terms, Rico states that Joe is needed for his ability to look ungangster-like to the outside public:

> RICO: He can go into a hotel and order a *suite*, and it's all right!

The Rico Bandello character, then, is a tough guy whose masculinity is so perverse it shields him from all aspects of femininity, including a relationship with a woman. Rico's maleness places him into buddy situations that develop, from his perspective, into asexual relationships that go deeper than the superficiality of mere workmates. It basically represents, especially in his relationship with Joe and feelings toward him, the latent homosexuality that Freudian psychologists believe exists between all close friends of the same sex. It also is a presentation of Rico's indefatigable ego that insists on having full control over all of the lives that surround him, especially the person to whom he feels closest.

Finally, Rico's toughness could also be attributed to his sensitivity that he tries desperately to shield at all times. Rico never had the pleasure of genuine friendship and is further pressured by the constant hounding of police sergeant Flaherty (Thomas Jackson), causing him to feel the need to cling to the one person he feels a kindred spirit with, as well as some form of affection. This is most clearly presented when, during the climax of the film, Rico holds a gun on Joe, ready to shoot, but cannot, despite the fact that Joe has gone to the police, and they are now after Rico.

The final scene in *Little Caesar* is movie legend, with Rico shot down by police just behind a billboard advertising Joe and Olga's Broadway debut; a brilliant visual study in character contrasts. Robinson croaks out the final line, "Mother of mercy, is this the end of Rico?" with the awe that one would expect from a dying hoodlum whose ego was so gigantic that he often referred to himself in the third person. The look in his eyes as he lay dying is one of shock and bewilderment, seemingly stating that his ego was so enormous, he actually believed himself to be invulnerable to the copper's bullet.

Little Caesar is important due to its presenting so many of the staples that haunted gangster pictures for years afterward. While *Underworld* may have made use of some of the most basic elements in showing the tough guy as a gangster, *Little Caesar* made use of the dialogue that *Underworld* did not have. Lines like, "It's curtains for you"; "Take him for a ride"; "You can dish it out, but can't take it"; and "big shot" soon became staples of subsequent gangster melodramas.

Robinson's portrayal of Rico was more visionary even than George Bancroft's Bull Weed character in *Underworld*. Bull Weed did at least have some comrades to look to, despite his tragic presence. Rico, on the other hand, is an absolute loner whose rise to the top is done in spite of his gang and not because of them. His tragic state is enhanced by his alienation from even the other gangsters, whom he disregards as "soft" in comparison to his own exploits. While the narrative makes great use of Rico's ego, it is Robinson who plays it for all it's worth. This is best shown in the scene where Rico is down and out, hiding from the cops after Joe has blown the whistle on him. Rico is sitting on a rented cot in a decrepit flophouse listening to two men discuss a recent newspaper account regarding Rico (they are mercifully unaware of their bunkmate's status). They then read out loud a newspaper story in that morning's issue which quotes Sergeant Flaherty as saying Rico was hiding out due to cowardice, the interview closing with the line, "Meteoric was Rico's rise from the gutter, in that it was inevitable his career should end there." Throughout the discussion and the subsequent

Edward G. Robinson as Rico Bandello in *Little Caesar* (Warner Bros., 1930).

reading of the interview Robinson really allows the viewer to see into Rico's tremendous ego. Rico sits up in his cot, reacts big to the accusations, both physically and vocally, via snarls and grunts that exhibit his disbelief that he is actually hearing himself bad-mouthed so terribly. In fact, his ego is so damaged he immediately leaves his hiding place, goes to the nearest phone, and calls Flaherty up to chew him out about the article. "I knew he'd come out of hiding if I kept giving it to him in the papers," says a pleased Flaherty. The call is traced, thus leading up to the classic "mother of mercy" climax.

Robinson brilliantly characterized all of the established tough-guy qualities in gangster Rico and then added greater scope. He used tiny bits of physical and verbal business to accentuate various traits of Rico's personality, defining the character within the context of the narrative so expertly it was to typecast the versatile actor for the remainder of his career. While he rarely played anyone as complex as Rico in his subsequent gangster roles, Robinson had already developed and firmly established a firm and lofty position in the annals of movie tough guys with this chilling portrayal.

Robinson's best tough-guy work following *Little Caesar* occurred in roles that allowed him to play off of the tragic elements within the character as well as the quirks within the character's personality. Edward Ludwig's *The Last Gangster* (1937) does this nicely. As gangster Joe Krozac, Robinson exhibits not only the nasty qualities of a killer, bootlegger, and terribly sexist criminal, but also has an opportunity to display warmth and pain stemming from love for his son. The story features Robinson, as Krozac, being sent to prison just as his naive European wife is about to give birth. His wife is kept in the dark about his ugly lifestyle until newspaper reporters reveal the heartbreaking truth about her beloved spouse. She decides to run away with their son and create a new life for herself. When Krozac is discharged from prison, the boy is grown and is unaware of his existence. Krozac's former gang kidnaps the boy and threatens to beat him if Krozac doesn't reveal where a certain cache of loot is hidden. Eventually, Krozac and the boy escape and try to find their way to the boy's home.

This performance allows Robinson to extend even further beyond the tragic circumstances of Rico, as Krozac exudes warmth and pride toward the boy, whose wholesomeness he finds unattractive but whose youthful vitality he finds irresistible. Scenes which feature the two of them on the road alone, camping under the pouring rain at night, are deeply moving, especially when Krozac tries passionately to tell the lad that he is his real father, the boy dismissing these ravings as fantasies. While Krozac does not exactly do pathos during these scenes, he does present the warmth that Rico lacked so completely. This gangster does not dismiss love as being "soft stuff." Instead he very openly hungers for love from the lad. Yet this is also due to the ego that Robinson's gangster characters always seemed to thrive on. Krozac is simply more open about his egotism than Rico, even to the point of championing Napoleon on more than one occasion. What Robinson does with the Krozac character is to present the tough guy as a gangster with a soul, something that had not been done up to that point. Before this, gangsters were of the Rico school (e.g., Cagney's Tom Powers in *Public Enemy* or Bogart's Duke Mantee in *The Petrified Forest*) where they survived without exhibiting whatever compassion they had, except only in very brief instances (Rico's inability to shoot Joe Massara, Duke Mantee's having to be coaxed to kill the pedantic Alan Squier).

Krozac's love for his son and pride in him stems a great deal from his wanting another Joe Krozac in the world. Yet this display of ego is somewhat more acceptable than Rico's fantasized belief in his own invulnerability. Krozac's ego is the mainspring that brings about his most human qualities. Even though this boy does not know him, and believes another man to be his father, and despite the fact that the exploits that most impress Krozac are those the boy learned from his surrogate father, Krozac still sees the boy as his own and is proud of even the feats accomplished with the other man he calls Dad.

The Last Gangster is a generally lesser known Robinson film (it was made at MGM rather than the actor's home studio—Warner Bros.), yet Krozac remains among his best and most emotional gangster roles, allowing him to exhibit passions other than hatred, rebelliousness, or love only for his character's own exploits.

Kid Galahad (1937) was another film that allowed Robinson to display warmth above and beyond his gangster role. However, in this film Robinson plays a wealthy gangster, or, a big-time underworld figure, who does not rely on the shoot-'em-up tactics of the Ricos or the Krozacs. His warmth shows in scenes with his family, namely his grey-haired Italian-born Mama and his overprotected kid sister.

The plot of this film is a standard one (involving corruption in the boxing racket as Robinson's Nick Donati character tries to make a bellhop with a good left hook into a champion, much to the chagrin of rival gangster Turkey Morgan, played by Humphrey Bogart), but it is all that is needed for Robinson to exhibit the qualities that help define the Donati character with the same grace and style the actor gave to any of his performances. What *Kid Galahad* best represents is how Robinson gave so much individual substance to each character even in a film that was fraught with hackneyed dialogue and a thin plot. It is due almost totally to his performance that this otherwise trite picture emerges as a perfectly effective entertainment of its period.

Robinson exhibited versatility as an actor within his tough-guy persona in a variety of films, the first of which was probably the *Little Caesar* satire *The Little Giant* (1933). However, it is the 1938 film *A Slight Case of Murder* that best presents the comic extension of Robinson's screen gangster. Groucho Marx has written that had Robinson not been typed as the tough guy early on, he could very well have developed his skills along the comedy line. His fresh, natural comic abilities are evident in several films, but *A Slight Case of Murder* is the effort in which Robinson is best allowed to display such talents. All of the ruthless, egocentric qualities of the Ricos and Krozacs Robinson had played manifest themselves in the comic character of bootlegger Remy Marco, who decides to be a straight-laced brewer once prohibition is repealed. The only problem is that he has never tasted his own beer, which is dreadful. An amusing subplot features Bobby Jordan of the Dead End Kids as a nasty reform school inmate whom Remy is giving a temporary home, remembering his own troubled youth.

Marco's egocentric behavior has all of the Napoleonesque quirks that shaped Robinson's earlier, more dramatic portrayals. The only difference is that these qualities are exaggerated further in order to enter a comic realm. Robinson very broadly burlesques his established screen persona with wild reactions to the dubious exploits of his henchmen, and a verbal delivery that is even faster and less eloquent than the straight gangster roles allowed.

What this film best presents is Robinson's total control over the tough-guy persona he created and subsequently honed to perfection since *Little Caesar* a few short years before. He knows this character so well that he has no trouble shaping it into whatever context he wishes, even the offbeat context of broad farce. Remy Marco is very easily recognizable as a comic Rico Bandello through Robinson's own indelible characterization. He still snarls and sneers, but this time in a comic vein.

An ordinarily dramatic scene, where three recently murdered foes of Remy are found dead in his upstairs guest room, is played for laughs as Remy and henchmen Mike, Innocence, and Lefty (played by classic comic gangster types Allen Jenkins, Joseph Downing, and Edward Brophy) hurry to get the bodies disposed of, placing them on the front porches of people they don't like. When they find there is a huge reward for the corpses, dead or alive, they hurriedly retrieve them. This wild comic variation on gangland slayings is enhanced by the noted gangster player enacting the leading role of a comic gangleader.

A Slight Case of Murder led into a charming, offbeat performance in *The Amazing Dr. Clitterhouse.* In this item Robinson is cast in the offbeat role of a sophisticated, albeit eccentric, doctor of psychology who becomes involved in a gang to study the gangster for a thesis. This hilarious film allows Robinson to leave his standard tough-guy persona completely to play an entirely different character within the premise of his usual gangster sagas. This takes the parody of *A Slight Case of Murder* and goes it one better in allowing Robinson to play comedy through a different characterization than usual, but within the same narrative framework as his usual gangster pictures.

It is interesting to note that period reviews for *The Amazing Dr. Clitterhouse* were unimpressed with Robinson's enacting the title role, although they did give him an "A" for effort. They compared him unfavorably to sophisticated Sir Cedric Hardwicke's portrayal in the original stage version. However when approaching this film in retrospect, one can see how Robinson's being chosen to play this character enhanced the narrative further in that he is still basically remembered as the tough-guy actor who played gangsters like *Little Caesar.*

It not only testifies to Robinson's acting versatility, but also presents him in such a different role within the very same plot that usually presented him as a gangster. So when Clitterhouse pays close attention to the hoodlumesque exploits of badman Rocks Valentine (Humphrey Bogart), we see him examining a character he usually plays from within a characterization that is strange to him and to us, but he is playing the new role so beautifully it is utterly believable.

In 1940 Robinson was a gangster again, this time using the standard character in a totally different framework. *Brother Orchid* features Robinson as Little John Sarto, a gangleader who leaves his thugs and decides to tour Europe and increase his cultural perspicacity. He returns to find that there is no longer a place for him in the gang, so he forms his own outfit to rival his old mob. A fracas results in Sarto's being found lying unconscious by a group of harmless, gentle souls from a nearby monastery. He is taken care of and soon must adapt to this very different environment.

In direct contrast to the character he portrayed in *The Amazing Dr. Clitterhouse*, Robinson was now another typical gangster (similar to Remy Marco in that his inadequacies were overplayed for humorous effect), only in the offbeat setting of a quiet, honest monastery. The body of this film is a study of Robinson's by now much imitated tough-guy persona in a setting that will create laughter simply by manifesting itself within the context of the narrative. Putting this character in with a group of gentlemen who are the antithesis of his tough-guy role, and then have them emerge as so attractive to Sarto that he actually lends himself to their ways and attempts to become one of them, is what makes *Brother Orchid* so fascinating. It not only further displays Robinson's acting versatility, but also exhibits the resilience of his wonderful and important tough-guy characterization.

The next notable variation on the *Little Caesar* theme was Robinson's lending his characterization to that of Jack London's evil Wolf Larsen in the screen adaptation of *The Sea Wolf* (1941). One of the literary characters that is in many ways even more evil than Rico Bandello, Wolf Larsen gave Robinson an opportunity to return to a pure form of snarling meanness that had no comic effect whatsoever, other than an outrageous reaction to the character's brutality and utter lack of humanity. Robinson so carefully paints his ugly picture of Larsen that the very appearance of this character in each scene is at once intimidating and frightening in a vile, demonic way. Larsen lives by the passage "Better to reign in hell than to serve in heaven" from Milton's *Paradise Lost*; a demented approach to leadership from the perspective of a warped, twisted, heinous mind.

The film treats Wolf Larsen in a very complex manner, explaining his ruthlessness as a series of deep psychoses. It is Robinson's job, then, to take his established persona and present it not only through an established literary figure, but in a manner that allows the audience to see the psychological problems that torment Larsen, not the least of which is his occasional lapses into total blindness; a secret he keeps from his crew, who were virtually all shanghaied and hate him passionately. John Garfield appears in the film as an example of the virility that signified a new tough guy that was emerging in American film, as Robinson exhibited the old tough-guy quirks through a character that finally had to be studied in greater depth so that it could be utilized in the new, different medium that showed tough guys as younger, more sexy examples of stereotypical masculinity.

Key Largo (1948) may be the film that presents the culmination of the

Robinson (left) as maniacal Wolf Larsen in the filmization of Jack London's *The Sea Wolf* (Warner Bros., 1941) with John Garfield.

Robinson tough-guy characterization (Robinson remained active for 25 more years, but in roles that were merely repeats of greater performances, some good and others not as good). As the gangster Johnny Rocco, an aging Rico Bandello was shown in the new world of postwar toughness. Robinson had been playing a few "mature" roles as of late (*Double Indemnity*, from 1944, is the best example), so *Key Largo* is a fitting final look at Rico via an older, more complex badman who is studied with even greater depth than was Wolf Larsen a few films before. But this time Robinson is not playing a literary character, he is Rico Bandello had Rico survived *Little Caesar* and lived to see this advanced age. Johnny Rocco has no scruples, no feeling for the paraplegic elderly man or young woman he is holding hostage. He is, however, somewhat fascinated by the assessment given by the educated and relaxed hostage Frank McCloud (Humphrey Bogart), who describes Rocco's ego by stating people like him don't want anything specific, they just want "more." Rocco excitedly agrees, "Yes, yes that's right! I want 'more'!" Rocco has weathered more than Rico, and thus his evil tendencies are better controlled and not nearly as manic. Robinson astutely presents this character as a maturation of his earlier established persona, allowing us to see it as Robinson honing his tough-guy type into the evil, mature, and seasoned Johnny Rocco. He isn't as quick to kill as Rico and, although he enjoys his ego fed constantly, also isn't easily duped by his own egocentric tendencies as was Rico (this ultimately causing Rico's downfall). This was the last role that showed Robinson's indelible tough-guy characterization for all it was worth.

Robinson's subsequent films featured the actor in a variety of roles. While his adept acting ability always surfaced, none of these roles accurately exhibited his tough-guy persona (and any attempts were mere reworkings of already established methods of presentation, e.g., Disney's *Never a Dull Moment* showing similar comic elements as found in *Brother Orchid*, with Robinson relegated to character role status); no longer did he genuinely exhibit the extension of the Rico Bandello character that remains to this day an important example of prime movie toughness. The scene that stands out at the end of Robinson's career turns out to be his final one in films.

In the posthumously released *Soylent Green* (1973), Robinson plays one of the best death scenes in American film. The future, as depicted in this science-fiction melodrama, allows persons to simply expire when they feel they have lived enough. They then are permitted to lay back and watch films presenting various forms of their favorite color via landscapes and such that no longer exist in this unfeeling society. Robinson represents the old man who recalls the beauty of natural things that were expended during his lifetime, things he did not appreciate while they did exist. Thus this scene shows his character recalling the wonderful images that were once actual parts of his life but are now gone.

Robinson the actor has gone, but the importance of his tough-guy characterization is almost impossible to accurately gauge in that it has influenced virtually every movie badman in American film from *Little Caesar* to the present.

Edward G. Robinson Filmography

The Bright Shawl (First National, 1923) 80 minutes
Directed by John S. Robertson, Screenplay by Edmund Goulding (based on the novel by Joseph Hergesheimer), Photographed by George Folsey.
With Richard Barthelmess, Dorothy Gish, Jetta Goudal, William Powell, Mary Astor, Andre de Beranger, *E.G.R.*, Margaret Seddon, Anders Randolf, Luis Alberni, George Humbert.

The Hole in the Wall (Paramount, 1929) 73 minutes
Directed by Robert Florey, Screenplay by Pierre Collings (based on the play by Fred Jackson), Photographed by George Folsey, Edited by Morton Blumenstock.
With Claudette Colbert, *E.G.R.*, David Newell, Nelly Savage, Donald Meek, Alan Brooks, Louise Closser Hale, Katherine Emmet, Marcia Kagno, Barry Macollum, George McQuarrie, Helen Crane.

Night Ride (Universal, 1929) 80 minutes
Directed by John Robertson, Screenplay by Edward Lowe (based on a story by Henry la Cossit), Edited by A. Ross and Milton Carruth.
With Joseph Schildkraut, Barbara Kent, *E.G.R.*, Harry Stubbs, DeWitt Jennings, Ralph Welles, Hal Price, George Ovey.
"Edward G. Robinson is excellent as Tony Carotta"—*New York Times*, January 20, 1930.

A Lady to Love (MGM, 1930) 92 minutes
Directed by Victor Seastrom, Screenplay by Sidney Howard (based on his play *They Knew What They Wanted*), Photographed by Merrit Gerstad, Edited by Conrad Nervig and Leslie Wilder.
With Vilma Banky, *E.G.R.*, Robert Ames, Richard Carle, Lloyd Ingraham, Anderson Lawler, Gum Chin, Henry Armetta, George Davis.

Outside the Law (Universal, 1930) 67 minutes
Directed by Tod Browning, Screenplay by Browning and Garret Fort, Photographed by Roy Overbaugh, Edited by Milton Carruth.
With *E.G.R.*, Mary Nolan, Owen Moore, Edwin Sturges, John George, Delmer Watson, DeWitt Jennings, Rockliffe Fellows, Fran Burke.

East Is West (Universal, 1930) 75 minutes
Directed by Monte Bell, Screenplay by Winifred Eaton (based on the play by Samuel Shipman and John Hymer), Edited by Harry Marker.
With Lupe Velez, Lew Ayers, *E.G.R.*, E. Allyn Warren, Tetsu Komai, Henry Kolker, Mary Forbes, Edgar Norton.
"Edward G. Robinson as the suey king is allowed too much footage for mugging and repetitious action"—*Variety*, November 5, 1930.

The Widow from Chicago (First National, 1930) 64 minutes
Directed by Eddie Cline, Screenplay by Earl Baldwin, Photographed by Sol Polito, Edited by Edward Schroeder.
With Alice White, Neil Hamilton, *E.G.R.*, Frank McHugh, Lee Shumway, Brooks Benedict, John Elliot, Dorothy Matthews, Ann Cornwall, E. H. Calvert, Betty Francisco, Harold Goodwin, Mike Donlin, Robert Homans, Al Hill, Mary Foy, Allan Coran.

Little Caesar (First National, 1930) 80 minutes
Directed by Mervyn LeRoy, Screenplay by Francis Faragoh (based on the

novel by William R. Burnett), Photographed by Tony Gaudio.

With *E.G.R.*, Douglas Fairbanks, Jr., Glenda Farrell, Sidney Blackmer, Thomas Jackson, Ralph Ince, Stanley Fields, George E. Stone, William Collier, Jr., Maurice Black, Noel Madison.

Smart Money (Warner Bros., 1931) 90 minutes
Directed by Alfred Green, Screenplay by Kubec Glasmon, John Bright, Lucien Hubbard, and Joseph Jackson, Photographed by Robert Kurrie, Edited by Jack Kilifer.

With *E.G.R.*, James Cagney, Evelyn Knapp, Ralf Harolde, Noel Francis, Margaret Livingstone, Maurice Black, Boris Karloff, Morgan Wallace, Billy House, Paul Porcasi, Polly Walters, Ben Taggart, Gladys Lloyd, Clark Burroughs, Edwin Argus, John Larkin, Walter Percival, Mae Madison, Allan Lane, Eulalie Jensen, Charles Lane, Edward Hearn, Eddie Kane, Clint Rosemond, Charles O'Malley, Gus Leonard.

Note: The only film in which Cagney and Robinson, the screen's two greatest gangster actors, appeared together.

Five Star Final (First National, 1931) 89 minutes
Directed by Mervyn LeRoy, Screenplay by Bryon Morgan (based on the play by Louis Weitzenkorn), Photographed by Sol Polito, Edited by Frank Ware.

With *E.G.R.*, H. B. Warner, Marion Marsh, Anthony Bushell, Frances Starr, Ona Munson, George E. Stone, Oscar Apfel, Purnell Platt, Alice MacMahon, Boris Karloff, Robert Elliot, Gladys Lloyd, Harold Waldridge, Evelyn Hall, David Torrence, Polly Walters, James Donlin, Frank Darien.

The Hatchet Man (First National, 1932) 74 minutes
Directed by William Wellman, Screenplay by J. Grubb Alexander (based on the play *The Honorable Mr. Wong* by Achmed Abdulla and David Belasco), Photographed by Sid Hickox, Edited by Owen Marks.

With *E.G.R.*, Loretta Young, Dudley Digges, Leslie Fenton, Edmund Breese, Tully Marshall, Noel Madison, Blanche Frederici, J. Carroll Naish, Toshia Mori, Charles Middleton, Ralph Ince, Otto Yamaoka, Evelyn Selbie, E. Allyn Warren, Eddie Piel, Willie Fung, Gladys Lloyd, Anna Chang, James Leong.

Two Seconds (First National, 1932) 68 minutes
Directed by Mervyn LeRoy, Screenplay by Harvey Thew (based on the play by Elliot Lester), Photographed by Sol Polito, Edited by Terrill Morse.

With *E.G.R.*, Preston Foster, Vivienne Osborne, J. Carroll Naish, Guy Kibbee, Adrianne Dare, Fredrick Burton, Dorothea Wolbert, Edward McWade, Berton Churchill, William Janney, Lew Brice, Franklin Parker, Frederick Howard, Helen Phillips, June Gittleson, Jill Dennett, Luana Walters, Otto Hoffman, John Kelly, Mat McHugh.

Screen toughs Robinson (left) and James Cagney battle it out in *Smart Money* (Warner Bros., 1931).

Tiger Shark (First National, 1932) 80 minutes
Directed by Howard Hawks, Screenplay by Wells Root (based on the story "Tuna" by Houston Branch), Photographed by Tony Gaudio, Edited by Thomas Pratt.

With *E.G.R.*, Zita Johann, Richard Arlen, Leila Bennett, Vince Barnett, J. Carroll Naish, William Ricciardi.

"Mr. Robinson gives a fine, finished performance as Mike, blending love and hatred in exactly the right manner." — *New York World–Telegram* September 23, 1932.

Silver Dollar (First National, 1932) 84 minutes
Directed by Alfred Green, Screenplay by Carl Erickson and Harvey Thew (based on the biography of H.A.W. Tabor by David Karsner), Photographed by James van Trees, Edited by George Marks.

With *E.G.R.*, Bebe Daniels, Alice MacMahon, Jobyna Howland, DeWitt Jennings, Robert Warwick, Russell Simpson, Harry Holman, Charles Middleton, John Matson, Marjorie Gatson, Emmet Corrigan, Wade Boteler, William LeMaire, David Durand, Lee Kohlman, Teresa Conover, Leon Ames.

The Little Giant (First National, 1933) 74 minutes
Directed by Roy Del Ruth, Screenplay by Robert Lord and Wilson Mizner (based on a story by Lord), Photographed by Sid Hickox, Edited by George Marks, Music conducted by Leo Forbstein.

With *E.G.R.*, Helen Vinson, Mary Astor, Kenneth Thomson, Russell Hopton, Shirley Grey, Donald Dillaway, Louise Mackintosh, Berton Churchill, Helen Mann, Selmer Jackson, Dewey Robinson, John Kelly, Sidney Bracey, Bob Perry, Adrianne Morris, Rolfe Sedan, Charles Colman, Bill Elliot, Nora Cecil, Lester Dorr, Guy Usher, Harry Tenbrook.

Note: The 1946 Universal feature of the same name, which starred Bud Abbott and Lou Costello, is not a remake.

"An amusing bit of fluff which allows Mr. Robinson to reveal unsuspected comedy talents" — *New York Herald–Tribune* May 26, 1933.

I Loved a Woman (First National, 1933) 90 minutes
Directed by Alfred Green, Screenplay by Charles Kenyon and Sidney Sutherland (based on the book by David Karsner), Photographed by James van Trees, Edited by Bert Levy.

With Kay Francis, *E.G.R.*, Genevieve Tobin, J. Farrell MacDonald, Henry Kolker, Robert Barrat, George Blackwood, Murray Kinnell, Robert McWade, Walter Walker, Henry O'Neill, Lorna Layson, Sam Godfrey, E. J. Radcliffe, Paul Porcasi, William Mong.

Dark Hazard (First National, 1934) 72 minutes
Directed by Alfred Green, Screenplay by Ralph Block and Browne Homes (based on the novel by William R. Burnett), Photographed by Sol Polito, Edited by Herbert Levy.

With *E.G.R.*, Genevieve Tobin, Glenda Farrell, Robert Barrat, Gordon Westcott, Hobart Cavanaugh, George Meeker, Henry B. Walthall, Sidney Toler, Emma Dunn, Willard Robertson, Barbara Rogers, William Mong.

The Man with Two Faces (First National, 1934) 72 minutes
Directed by Archie Mayo, Screenplay by Tom Reed and Niven Bush (based on the play *The Dark Tower* by George Kaufmann and Alexander Woolcott), Photographed by Tony Gaudio, Edited by William Holmes.

With *E.G.R.*, Mary Astor, Ricardo Cortez, Mae Clarke, Louis Calhern, John Eldredge, Arthur Byron, Henry O'Neill, David Landau, Emily Fitzroy, Margaret Dale, Dorothy Tree, Arthur Aylesworth, Virginia Sale, Mary Russell, Howard Hickman, Dick Winslow.

The Whole Town's Talking (Columbia, 1935) 93 minutes
Directed by John Ford, Screenplay by Jo Swerling and Robert Riskin (based on the novel by William Burnett), Photographed by Joseph August, Edited by Viola Lawrence, Produced by Lester Cowan.

With *E.G.R.*, Jean Arthur, Arthur Hohl, Wallace Ford, Arthur Byron, Donald Meek, Paul Harvey, Ed Brophy, Etienne Giardot, James Donlan, J. Farrell McDonald, Effie Ellsler, Robert Emmett O'Connor, John Wray, Joe Sawyer, Frank Sheridan, Clarence Hummel Wilson, Ralph Remley, Virginia Pine, Ferdinand Munier, Cornelius Keefe, Francis Ford, Lucille Ball, Robert Homans, Grace Halo, Walter Long, Ben Taggart, Al Hill, Gordon DeMain, Sam Flint, Emmett Vogan, Bess Flowers, Mary Gordon, Tom London, Charles King.

"Mr. Robinson, turning in a performance that goes up near the top of the comedy list for this year, plays a dual role"—*New York Sun* March 1, 1935.

Barbary Coast (United Artists, 1935) 91 minutes
Directed by Howard Hawks, Screenplay by Ben Hecht and Charles MacArthur, Photographed by Ray June, Edited by Edward Curtis, Music Directed by Alfred Newman, Produced by Samuel Goldwyn.

With *E.G.R.*, Miriam Hopkins, Joel McCrea, Walter Brennan, Frank Craven, Brian Donlevy, Otto Hoffman, Rollo Lloyd, Donald Meek, Roger Gray, Clyde Cook, Harry Carey, J. M. Kerrigan, Matt McHugh, Wong Chung, Russ Powell, Frederik Vogeding, Dave Wengren, Anders Van Haden, Jules Cowles, Cyril Thornton, Harry Semels, Otto Francis, Larry Fisher, George Simpson, David Niven, Herman Bing.

Note: A 1974 TV movie featuring William Shatner, and subsequent short-lived TV series, is not a remake despite its featuring the same title.

Bullets or Ballots (First National, 1936) 81 minutes
Directed by William Keighley, Screenplay by Seton Miller (based on a story by him and Martin Mooney), Photographed by Hal Mohr, Edited by Jack Kilifer.

With *E.G.R.*, Joan Blondell, Humphrey Bogart, Barton MacLane, Frank McHugh, Joseph King, Richard Purcell, George E. Stone, Louise Beavers, Henry O'Neill, Frank Faylen, William Pawley.

Note: Robinson's first of five films opposite Humphrey Bogart.

Kid Galahad (Warner Bros., 1937) 101 minutes
Directed by Michael Curtiz, Screenplay by Seton Miller (based on the novel by Francis Wallace), Photographed by Tony Gaudio, Edited by George Amy.

With *E.G.R.*, Bette Davis, Humphrey Bogart, Wayne Morris, Jane Bryan, Harry Carey, Soledad Jiminez, Joe Cunningham, Ben Welden, Frank Faylen, William Haade, Joseph Crehan, Veda Ann Borg, Mary Sunde.

Note: retitled *Battling Bellhop* for television in order to avoid confusion with the Elvis Presley starrer *Kid Galahad*, which is a partial remake of this film.

The Last Gangster (MGM, 1937) 81 minutes

Directed by Edward Ludwig, Screenplay by John Lee Mahin (based on a story by William Wellman and Robert Carson), Photographed by William Daniels, Edited by Ben Lewis.

With *E.G.R.*, James Stewart, Rose Stradner, Lionel Stander, Douglas Scott, John Carradine, Sidney Blackmer, Edward Brophy, Alan Baxter, Grant Mitchell, Frank Conroy, Moroni Olsen, Ivan Miller, William Robertson, Louise Beavers, Donald Barry, Ben Welden.

A Slight Case of Murder (Warner Bros., 1938) 85 minutes

Directed by Lloyd Bacon, Screenplay by Earl Baldwin and Joseph Schrank (based on the play by Damon Runyon and Howard Lindsey), Photographed by Sid Hickox, Edited by James Gibbon, Produced by Hal Wallis.

With *E.G.R.*, Jane Bryan, Willard Parker, Ruth Donnelly, Allen Jenkins, John Litel, Eric Stanley, Harold Huber, Edward Brophy, Paul Harvey, Bobby Jordan, Joseph Downing, Margaret Hamilton, George E. Stone.

The Amazing Dr. Clitterhouse (Warner Bros., 1938) 87 minutes

Directed by Anatole Litvak, Screenplay by John Huston and John Wexley (based on the play by Barre Lyndon), Photographed by Tony Gaudio, Edited by Warren Low.

With *E.G.R.*, Claire Trevor, Humphrey Bogart, Gale Page, Donald Crisp, Allen Jenkins, Thurston Hall, John Litel, Henry O'Neill, Maxie Rosenbloom, Curt Bois, Bert Hanlon, Ward Bond, Billy Wayne, Thomas Jackson, Edward Gargan, Eric Stanley, Irving Bacon, Vera Lewis.

I Am the Law (Columbia, 1938) 83 minutes

Directed by Alexander Hall, Screenplay by Jo Swerling (based on magazine articles by Fred Allhoff), Photographed by Henry Freelich, Edited by Viola Lawrence.

With *E.G.R.*, Barbara O'Neill, John Beal, Wendy Barrie, Otto Kruger, Arthur Loft, Marc Lawrence, Douglas Wood, Robert Middlemass, Ivan Miller, Charles Halton, Louis Jean Heydt, Emory Parnell, Joseph Downing, Horace McMahon, Fred Burton, Lucien Littlefield.

Confessions of a Nazi Spy (Warner Bros., 1939) 102 minutes

Directed by Anatole Litvak, Screenplay by Milton Kimms and John Wexley (based on the book *The Nazi Spy Conspiracy* by Leon Turrou), Photographed by Sol Polito, Edited by Owen Marks.

With *E.G.R.*, Francis Lederer, George Sanders, Paul Lukas, Henry O'Neill, Lya Lys, Grace Stafford, Sig Ruman, Henry Victor.

Blackmail (MGM, 1939) 81 minutes
Directed by H.C. Potter, Screenplay by David Hertz and William Ludwig, based on the story by Endre Bohem and Dorothy Yost, Photographed by Clyde De Vinna, Edited by Howard O'Neill.
With *E.G.R.*, Gene Lockhart, Ruth Hussey, Bobs Watson, Guinn "Big Boy" Williams, John Wray, Arthur Hohl, Esther Dale, Joe Whitehead, Joseph Crehan, Victor Kilian, Gil Perkins, Mitchell Lewis, Ted Oliver, Willie Best, Art Miles.

Dr. Erlich's Magic Bullet (Warner Bros., 1940) 103 minutes
Directed by William Dieterle, Screenplay by John Huston, Heinz Herald, and Norman Burnside (based on a story by Burnside), Photographed by James Wong Howe, Edited by Robert Burks.
With *E.G.R.*, Ruth Gordon, Otto Kruger, Donald Crisp, Sig Ruman, Maria Ouspenskaya, Henry O'Neill, Edward Morris, Harry Davenport, Montague Love, Albert Basserman, Louis Jean Heydt, Donald Meek, Irving Bacon, Ann Todd, Polly Stewart, Louis Calhern, Frank Lackteen.

Brother Orchid (Warner Bros., 1940) 91 minutes
Directed by Lloyd Bacon, Screenplay by Earl Baldwin (from a story by Richard Connell), Photographed by Tony Gaudio, Edited by William Holmes.
With *E.G.R.*, Ann Sothern, Humphrey Bogart, Ralph Bellamy, Donald Crisp, Allen Jenkins, Charles D. Brown, Cecil Kellaway, Joseph Crehan, Wilfred Lucas, Morgan Conway, Richard Lane, John Ridgely, Dick Wessel, Tom Tyler, Paul Phillips, Don Rowan, Granville Bates, Nanette Vallon, Tim Ryan, Pat Gleason, Tommy Baker, John Qualen, Charles Coleman.

A Dispatch from Reuters (Warner Bros., 1940) 89 minutes
Directed by William Dieterle, Screenplay by Milton Krimms (from a story by Valentine Williams and Wolfgang Wilhelm), Photographed by James Wong Howe, Edited by Warren Lowe.
With *E.G.R.*, Edna Best, Eddie Albert, Albert Basserman, Nigel Bruce, Gene Lockhart, Montague Love, Otto Kruger, James Stephenson, Walter Kingsford, David Bruce, Alec Craig, Hugh Sothern, Paul Wiegel.

The Sea Wolf (Warner Bros., 1941) 100 minutes
Directed by Michael Curtiz, Screenplay by Robert Rossen (based on the novel by Jack London), Photographed by Sol Polito, Edited by George Amy.
With *E.G.R.*, John Garfield, Ida Lupino, Alexander Knox, Gene Lockhart, Barry Fitzgerald, Stanley Ridges, Francis MacDonald, David Bruce, Howard Da Silva, Frank Lackteen, Ralfe Harolde, Louis Mason.

Manpower (Warner Bros., 1941)
Directed by Raoul Walsh, Screenplay by Richard Macaulay and Jerry Wald, Photographed by Ernest Haller, Edited by Ralph Dawson.
With *E.G.R.*, George Raft, Marlene Dietrich, Alan Hale, Frank McHugh, Eve Arden, Barton MacLane, Walter Catlett, Joyce Compton, Lucia Carroll, Ward Bond, Egon Brecher, Cliff Clark, Joseph Crehan.

Unholy Partners (MGM, 1941) 94 minutes
Directed by Mervyn LeRoy, Screenplay by Earl Baldwin, Lester Samuels

and Bartlett Cormack, Photographed by George Barnes, Edited by Harold Kress.

With *E.G.R.*, Laraine Day, Edward Arnold, Marsha Hunt, William T. Orr, Don Beddoe, Charles Dingle, Charles Cane, Walter Kingsford, Charles Halton, Clyde Fillmore, Marcel Dalio, Frank Faylen, Joseph Downing, William Benedict, Charles B. Smith, Frank Dawson, Tom Seidel.

Larceny, Inc. (Warner Bros., 1942) 95 minutes
Directed by Lloyd Bacon, Screenplay by Everett Freeman and Ed Gilbert (based on the play *The Night Before Christmas* by Laura and S. J. Perelman), Photographed by Tony Gaudio, Edited by Ralph Dawson.

With *E.G.R.*, Jane Wyman, Broderick Crawford, Jack Carson, Anthony Quinn, Edward Brophy, Harry Davenport, John Qualen, Barbara Jo Ellen, Grant Mitchell, Jackie Gleason, Andrew Tombes, Joseph Downing.

"Mr. Robinson is a beautifully hard-boiled yegg, the principal joy is to watch him"—*New York Times*, April 25, 1942.

Destroyer (Columbia, 1943) 99 minutes
Directed by William Seiter, Screenplay by Frank Wead, Lewis Meltzer and Borden Chase (based on a story by Wead), Photographed by Franz Planer, Edited by Gene Havilick.

With *E.G.R.*, Glenn Ford, Marguerite Chapman, Edgar Buchanan, Leo Gorcey, Regis Toomey, Ed Brophy, Warren Ashe, Craig Woods, Curt Bois, Al Hill, Bobby Jordan, Roger Clark, Dean Benton.

Flesh and Fantasy (Universal, 1943) 93 minutes
Directed by Julien Duvivier, Screenplay by Ernest Pascal (based on stories by Oscar Wilde, Laslo Vadnay, and Ellis St. Joseph), Photographed by Paul Ivano and Stanley Cortez, Edited by Art Hilton.

With *E.G.R.*, Charles Boyer, Barbara Stanwyck, Betty Field, Robert Cummings, Thomas Mitchell, Charles Winninger, Anna Lee, Dame Mae Whitty, C. Aubrey Smith, Robert Benchley, Edgar Barrier, David Hoffman, Mary Forbes, Ian Wolfe, Doris Lloyd, June Lang, Lee Phelps.

Note: This feature is comprised of three separate episodes, the first one involving Robinson. The film is produced by Charles Boyer.

Tampico (20th Century–Fox, 1944) 75 minutes
Directed by Lothar Mendes, Screenplay by Kenneth Gamer (based on an original story by Ladislas Fodor), Photographed by Charles Clark, Edited by Robert Fritch.

With *E.G.R.*, Lynn Bari, Victor McLaglen, Robert Bailey, Marc Lawrence, E. J. Ballantine, Mona Maris, Tonio Salwert, Carl Ekberg, Roy Roberts, George Sorrell, Charles Lang.

Mr. Winkle Goes to War (Columbia, 1944) 80 minutes
Directed by Alfred E. Green, Screenplay by Waldo Salt, George Corey and Louis Soloman (from the novel by Theodore Pratt), Photographed by Joseph Walker, Edited by Richard Fanite.

With *E.G.R.*, Ruth Warrick, Ted Donaldson, Bob Haymes, Richard Lane,

Robert Armstrong, Richard Gaines, Walter Baldwin, Art Smith, Ann Shoemaker, Paul Stanton, Buddy Yarus, William Forrest.

Double Indemnity (Paramount, 1944) 106 minutes
Directed by Billy Wilder, Screenplay by Wilder and Raymond Chandler (based on the novel by James M. Cain which was itself based on the 1927 slaying of New Yorker Albert Snyder by his wife Ruth and her lover Judd Gray, for his insurance), Photographed by John Seitz, Edited by Doane Harrison.
With Fred MacMurray, Barbara Stanwyck, *E.G.R.*, Porter Hall, Jena Heather, Tom Powers, Byron Barr, Richard Gaines, Fortunio Bonanova, John Philiber, George Magrill, Bess Flowers, Dick Rush, Edmund Cobb.
"Robinson plays an insurance company sleuth with splendid authority"— *New York Herald–Tribune*, September 7, 1944.

Our Vines Have Tender Grapes (MGM, 1945) 105 minutes
Directed by Roy Rowland, Screenplay by Dalton Trumbo (based on the novel by George Victor Martin), Photographed by Robert Surtees, Edited by Ralph E. Winters.
With *E.G.R.*, Margaret O'Brien, James Craig, Agnes Moorehead, Jackie "Butch" Jenkins, Morris Carnovski, Francis Gifford, Sara Haden, Louis Jean Heydt, Francis Pierlot, Arthur Space, Don Kapla.
"Edward G. Robinson is solid and loveable...one of the finest performances in his long and varied career"— *New York Times*, September 7, 1945.

Scarlet Street (Universal, 1946) 103 minutes
Produced and Directed by Fritz Lang, Screenplay by Dudley Nichols (based on the novel and play *La Chienne* by Georges de la Faouchardiere), Photographed by Milton Krasner, Edited by Arthur Hilton.
With *E.G.R.*, Joan Bennett, Dan Duryea, Jess Barker, Margaret Lindsey, Rosalind Ivan, Samuel S. Hinds, Arthur Loft, Vladimir Sokoloff, Charles Kemper, Russell Hicks, Anita Bolster, Cy Kendall.

The Stranger (RKO, 1946) 94 minutes
Directed by Orson Welles, Screenplay by Anthony Veiller (based on the story by Victor Trivas and Decia Dunning), Photographed by Russell Metty, Edited by Ernest Nims.
With *E.G.R.*, Loretta Young, Orson Welles, Philip Merivale, Richard Long, Brian Keith, Billy House, Konstantin Shayne, Martha Wentworth, Isabel O'Madigan, Pietro Sasso.
"Robinson matches staccato line for staccato line with Welles as his nemesis..."— *New York Herald–Tribune*, July 11, 1946.

The Red House (United Artists, 1947) 100 minutes
Directed by Delmer Daves, Screenplay by Daves (based on the novel by George Agnew Chamberlain), Photographed by Bert Glennon, Edited by Merrill White.
With *E.G.R.*, Lon McCallister, Judith Anderson, Allene Roberts, Julie

London, Rory Calhoun, Ona Munson, Harry Shannon, Arthur Space, Walter
Sande, Pat Flaherty.

All My Sons (Universal, 1948) 94 minutes
    Directed by Irving Reis, Screenplay by Charles Erskine, who also pro-
duced (based on Arthur Miller's play), Photographed by Russell Metty, Edited
by Ralph Dawson.
    With *E.G.R.*, Burt Lancaster, Mady Christians, Louisa Horton, Howard
Duff, Frank Conroy, Lloyd Gough, Arlene Francis, Henry Morgan, Elizabeth
Fraser, Walter Soderling, Therese Lyon, Charles Meredith, William John-
stone, Herbert Vigran, Helen Wood, Joseph Kerr.

Key Largo (Warner Bros., 1948) 101 minutes
    Directed by John Huston, Screenplay by Huston and Richard Brooks
(based on the play by Maxwell Anderson), Photographed by Karl Freund,
Edited by Rudi Fehr.
    With Humphrey Bogart, *E.G.R.*, Lauren Bacall, Lionel Barrymore, Claire
Trevor, Thomas Gomez, Harry Lewis, John Rodney, Marc Lawrence, Monte
Blue, Jay Silverheels, Rodric Redwing.
    Note: This was Robinson's last film opposite Bogart.

Night Has a Thousand Eyes (Paramount, 1948) 80 minutes
    Directed by John Farrow, Screenplay by Barre Lyndon and Jonathan
Latimer (based on the novel by Cornell Woolrich), Photographed by John F.
Seitz, Edited by Eda Warren.
    With *E.G.R.*, Gail Russell, John Lund, Virginia Bruce, William Demarest,
Richard Webb, Jerome Cowan, Onslow Stevens, John Alexander, Roman
Bohnen, Luis Van Rooten, Henry Guttman, Mary Adams, Phil Van Zandt.

House of Strangers (20th Century–Fox, 1949) 101 minutes
    Directed by Joseph L. Mankiewicz, Screenplay by Philip Yordan (based on
the novel by Jerome Weidman), Photographed by Milton Kramer, Edited by
Harmon Le Maire.
    With *E.G.R.*, Susan Hayward, Richard Conte, Luther Adler, Paul Valen-
tine, Efrem Zimbalist, Jr., Debra Paget, Hope Emerson, Esther Minciotti,
Diane Douglas, Sid Tomack, Mike Stark, Mushy Callahan.

Operation X (Columbia, 1950) 79 minutes
    Produced and directed by Gregory Ratoff, Screenplay by Robert Thoeren
and William Rose (based on the novel *David Golder* by Irene Nemirowsky),
Photographed by Georges Perinal, Edited by Raymond Poulton.
    With *E.G.R.*, Nora Swinburne, Peggy Cummings, Richard Greene, Finlay
Currie, Gregory Ratoff, Ronald Adam, Walter Rilla, James Robertson Justice.
    Note: Also titled *My Daughter Joy*.

Actors and Sin (United Artists, 1952) 85 minutes
    Produced, directed, and written by Ben Hecht, Edited by Otto Ludwig.

Edward G. Robinson, late 1940s.

With *E.G.R.*, Marsha Hunt, Dan O'Herlihy, Rudolph Anders, Alice Key, Rick Roman, Eddie Albert, Alan Reed, Tracy Roberts, Paul Guilfoyle, Doug Evans, Jenny Hecht, Jody Gilbert, John Crawford.

Note: Two separate episodes were made, the first entitled *Actor's Blood* and featuring Robinson, the second entitled *Women and Sin* and starring Eddie Albert, et al.

Vice Squad (United Artists, 1953) 88 minutes

Directed by Arthur Laven, Screenplay by Lawrence Roman (based on the novel *Harness Bull* by Leslie T. White), Photographed by Joseph Biroc, Edited by Arthur Nadel.

With *E.G.R.*, Paulette Goddard, K. T. Stevens, Porter Hall, Adam Williams, Edward Binns, Lee Van Cleef, Jay Adler, Joan Vohs, Dan Riss, May Ellen Kay.

The Big Leaguer (MGM, 1953) 73 minutes

Directed by Robert Aldrich, Screenplay by Herbert Baker, Photographed by William Mellor, Edited by Ben Lewis.

With *E.G.R.*, Vera-Ellen, Jeff Richards, Richard Jaeckel, William Campbell, Carl Hubbell, Paul Langton, Lalo Rios, Bill Crandall, Frank Ferguson, John McKee, Mario Siletti, Robert Caldwell.

The Glass Web (Universal, 1953) 82 minutes

Directed by Jack Arnold, Screenplay by Robert Blees and Leonard Lee (based on the novel by Max S. Ehrlich), Photographed by Maury Gertzman, Edited by Ted J. Kent.

With *E.G.R.*, John Forsythe, Marcia Henderson, Kathleen Hughes, Richard Denning, Hugh Sanders, Jean Willes, Harry O. Tyler, Clark Howat, Paul Dubov, John Hiestand, Bob Nelson, Dick Stewart, Jeri Lon James.

Note: Filmed in 3-D.

Black Tuesday (United Artists, 1954) 80 minutes

Directed by Hugo Fregonese, Story and Screenplay by Sydney Boehm, Photographed by Stanley Cortez, Edited by Robert Golden.

With *E.G.R.*, Peter Graves, Jean Parker, Milburn Stone, Warren Stevens, Jack Kelly, Sylvia Findley, James Bell, Victor Perrin.

The Violent Men (Columbia, 1955) 95 minutes

Directed by Rudolph Mate, Screenplay by Harry Kleiner (based on the novel by Donald Hamilton), Photographed by Burnett Guffey and W. Howard Greene, Edited by Jerome Thoms.

With *E.G.R.*, Barbara Stanwyck, Glenn Ford, Dianne Foster, Brian Keith, May Wynn, Warner Anderson, Basil Ruysdael, Lita Malan, Richard Jaeckel, James Westerfield, Jack Kelly.

"Robinson plays *Little Caesar* in buckskin"—*New York Herald–Tribune*, January 27, 1955.

Tight Spot (Columbia, 1955) 97 minutes

Directed by Phil Karlson, Screenplay by William Bowers (based on the novel *Dead Pigeon* by Leonard Kantner), Photographed by Burnett Guffey, Edited by Vila Lawrence.

With Ginger Rogers, *E.G.R.*, Brian Keith, Lucy Marlowe, Lorne Green, Katherine Anderson, Allen Nourse, Peter Leeds, Doye O'Dell, Even McVeagh, Helen Wallace, Frank Gerstle, Skipper McNally.

A Bullet for Joey (United Artists, 1955) 84 minutes

Directed by Lewis Allen, Screenplay by Geoffrey Holmes and A. J. Bezzerides, Photographed by Harry Neumann, Edited by Leon Barsha.

With *E.G.R.*, George Raft, Audrey Totter, George Dolenz, Peter Hansen, Peter Van Eyck, Karen Verne, Ralph Smiley, Henri Letondal, John Cliff, Joseph Vitale, Bill Bryant, Stan Malotte, Toni Gerry.

Illegal (Warner Bros., 1955) 90 minutes

Directed by Lewis Allen, Screenplay by W. R. Burnett and James Webb (based on the play *The Mouthpiece* by Frank J. Collins), Photographed by Peverell Marley, Edited by Thomas Reilly.

With *E.G.R.*, Nina Foch, Hugh Marlowe, Robert Ellenstein, DeForrest Kelley, Jay Adler, James McCallion, Edward Platt, Albert Dekker, Jan Merlin, Ellen Corby, Jayne Mansfield, Clark Howatt, Henry Kulky, Addison Richards, Howard St. John.

Hell on Frisco Bay (Warner Bros., 1956) 100 minutes

Directed by Frank Tuttle, Screenplay by Sidney Boehm and Martin Rackin (based on a novel by William P. McGivern), Photographed by John Seitz, Edited by Folmar Blangsted.

With Alan Ladd, *E.G.R.*, Joanne Dru, William Demarest, Paul Stewart, Fay Wray, Perry Lopez, Renata Vanni, Nestor Paiva, Stanley Adams, Willis Bouchey, Peter Hanson, Tina Carver, Rodney Taylor.

"Robinson is tops as a ruthless gangster"—*New York Post*, January 7, 1956.

Nightmare (United Artists, 1956) 88 minutes

Directed by Maxwell Shane, Screenplay by Shane (based on a novel by Cornell Woolrich), Photographed by Joseph Biroc, Edited by George Gittens.

With *E.G.R.*, Kevin McCarthy, Connie Russell, Virginia Christine, Rhys Williams, Gage Clark, Barry Atwater, Marian Carr, Billy May.

The Ten Commandments (Paramount, 1956) 221 minutes

Produced and Directed by Cecil B. DeMille, Screenplay by Aemeas MacKenzie, Jessie Lasky, Jr., Jack Garriss, and Frederic M. Frank (based on the Holy Scripture), Photographed by Loyal Griggs, Edited by Anne Bauchens.

With Charleton Heston, Yul Brynner, Anne Baxter, *E.G.R.*, Yvonne De Carlo, Debra Paget, John Derek, Sir Cedric Hardwicke, Nina Foch, Martha Scott, Judith Anderson, Vincent Price, John Carradine, Eduard Franz, Olive Deering, Don Curtis, Douglass Dumbrille, H. B. Warner, Henry Brandon, Kenneth MacDonald, Addison Richards, Onslow Stevens, Clint Walker, Frank Wilcox, Frankie Darro, Kathy Garver, Walter Woolf King, Frank Lackteen, Carl "Alfalfa" Switzer, Robert Vaughn.

A Hole in the Head (United Artists, 1959) 123 minutes

Produced and Directed by Frank Capra, Co-produced by Frank Sinatra, Screenplay by Max Shulman (based on his play), Photographed by William Daniels, Edited by William Hornbeck.

With Frank Sinatra, *E.G.R.*, Eddie Hodges, Eleanor Parker, Carolyn

Jones, Thelma Ritter, Keenan Wynn, Joi Lansing, George De Witt, James Komack, Dub Taylor, Connie Sawyer, Benny Rubin, Ruby Dandridge, B. S. Pully.

Seven Thieves (20th Century–Fox, 1960) 104 minutes
Directed by Henry Hathaway, Screenplay by Sidney Boehm (based on the novel *Lions at the Kill* by Max Catto), Photographed by Sam Leavett, Edited by Dorothy Spencer.
With Rod Steiger, *E.G.R.*, Joan Collins, Eli Wallach, Michael Dante, Alexander Scourby, Barry Kroeger, Sebastian Cabot, Jonathan Kidd.

My Geisha (Paramount 1961) 118 minutes
Directed by Jack Cardiff, Screenplay by Norman Krasna, Photographed by Stanley Sayer, Edited by Archie Marshek.
With Shirley MacLaine, Yves Montand, *E.G.R.*, Bob Cummings, Yoko Tani, Tatsuo Saito, Tamae Kyokawa, Ichi Hayakawa.

Two Weeks in Another Town (MGM, 1962) 105 minutes
Directed by Vincente Minnelli, Screenplay by Charles Schree (based on the novel by Irwin Shaw), Photographed by Milt Krasner, Edited by Adrienne Fazan and Robert Kern, Jr.
With Kirk Douglas, Cyd Charrisse, *E.G.R.*, George Hamilton, Dahlia Lavi, Claire Trevor, James Gregory, Rosanna Schiaffino, Joanna Roos, George MacReady, Leslie Uggams, Tony Randall.

The Prize (MGM, 1964) 136 minutes
Directed by Mark Robson, Screenplay by Ernest Lehman (based on the novel by Irving Wallace), Photographed by William Daniels, Edited by Adrienne Fazan.
With Paul Newman, *E.G.R.*, Elke Sommer, Diane Baker, Micheline Presle, Gerard Oury, Sergio Fantoni, Kevin McCarthy, Leo G. Carroll, Sacha Pietoeff, Jacqueline Beer, Karl Swenson, Peter Coe.

Good Neighbor Sam (Columbia, 1964) 128 minutes
Produced and Directed by David Swift, Screenplay by James Fitzell, Photographed by Burnett Guffey, Edited by Charles Nelson.
With Jack Lemmon, Romy Schneider, Dorothy Provine, *E.G.R.*, Mike Connors, Edward Andrews, Louis Nye, Joyce Jameson, Charles Lane.

The Outrage (MGM, 1964) 97 minutes
Directed by Martin Ritt, Screenplay by Michael Kanin (based on the 1951 Akira Kurosawa film *Rashomon*), Photographed by James Wong Howe, Edited by Frank Santillo.
With Paul Newman, Lawrence Harvey, *E.G.R.*, Claire Bloom, William Shatner, Howard Da Silva, Albert Salmi, Thomas Chalmers, Paul Fix.
"Robinson's portrayal . . . is earthy and direct"—*New York Times*, October 8, 1964.

Cheyenne Autumn (Warner Bros., 1964) 148 minutes
Directed by John Ford, Screenplay by James R. Webb (suggested by Mari Sandoz's novel), Photographed by William Clothier, Edited by Otho Levering.
With Richard Widmark, Carroll Baker, Karl Malden, James Stewart, *E.G.R.*, Sal Mineo, Dolores Del Rio, Ricardo Montalban, Gilbert Roland, Arthur Kennedy, Patrick Wayne, Elizabeth Allen, John Carradine, Victor Jory, Mike Mazurki, Ken Curtis, George O'Brien.

A Boy Ten Feet Tall (Paramount, 1965) 88 minutes
Directed by Alexander Mackendrick, Screenplay by Dennis Cannan (based on the novel *Sammy Going South* by W. H. Canaway), Photographed by Erwin Hillier, Edited by Jack Harris.
With *E.G.R.*, Fergus McCelland, Constance Cummings, Harry Corbett, Paula Stassino, Zia Mohyeddin, Orlando Martins, John Turner, Zina Walker, Jack Gwillim, Patricia Donahue, Jared Allen.

The Cincinnati Kid (MGM, 1965) 114 minutes
Directed by Norman Jewison, Screenplay by Ring Lardner, Jr., and Terry Southern (based on the novel by Richard Jessup), Photographed by Phillip Lathrop, Edited by Hal Ashby.
With Steve McQueen, *E.G.R.*, Ann Margret, Karl Malden, Tuesday Weld, Joan Blondell, Rip Torn, Jack Weston, Cab Calloway, Jeff Corey, Karl Swenson, Dub Taylor, Claude Hall, John Hart, Hal Taggart.
"The elderly card shark is played consummately by Robinson"—*Saturday Review*, November 6, 1965.

The Blonde from Peking (Paramount, 1968) 80 minutes (AKA La Blonde de Pekin)
Directed by Nicolas Gessner, Screenplay by Mark Behm, Photographed by Claude Lecomte, Edited by Jean-Michel Gauthier.
With Mirielle Darc, Claudio Brook, *E.G.R.*, Pascale Roberts, Francoise Brionne, Joe Warfield.

The Biggest Bundle of Them All (MGM, 1968) 105 minutes
Directed by Ken Annakin, Screenplay by Sy Salkowitz, Photographed by Pierco Portalupi, Edited by Ralph Sheldon.
With Robert Wagner, Raquel Welch, Godfrey Cambridge, Vittorio DeSica, *E.G.R.*, Davy Kaye, Victor Spinetti, Yvonne Snason, Mickey Knox.

Grand Slam (Paramount, 1968) 120 minutes
Directed by Giuliano Montaldo, Screenplay by Mino Roli, Caminito, Marcello Fondato, Anotonio De La Loma, and Marcello Coscia, Photographed by Antonio Moscasoli, Edited by Nino Baragli.
With *E.G.R.*, Janet Leigh, Adolph Celi, Klaus Kinski, George Rigaud, Robert Hoffman, Riccardo Cucciolla, Jussara, Miguel Del Castillo.
Note: aka *Ad Ogni Costo*.

It's Your Move (Kinesis Films, 1968) 91 minutes
Directed by Robert Fiz, Screenplay by Fiz, Photographed by Antonio Mascasoli, Edited by Mario Morra.
With *E.G.R.*, Terry Thomas, Maria Grazia Buccella, Jorge Rigaud.
Note: never released theatrically in the U.S. Originally titled *Uno Scacco Tutto Matto* or *Mad Checkmate*.

Operation St. Peter's (Paramount, 1968) 88 minutes
Directed by Lucio Fulci, Screenplay by Ennio De Concini, Photographed by Erico Menczer.
With Lanod Buzzanca, *E.G.R.*, Heinz Ruhmann, Jean-Claude Brialy, Dante Maggio, Ugo Fancareggi, Uta Levka, Antonella Delle Porta.

Never a Dull Moment (Buena Vista, 1968)
Directed by Jerry Paris, Screenplay by A. J. Carothers, Photographed by William Snyder, Edited by Marsh Hendry.
With Dick Van Dyke, *E.G.R.*, Dorothy Provine, Henry Silva, Joanna Moore, Tony Bill, Slim Pickens, Jack Elam, Ned Glass, Mickey Shaughnessy, Phillip Coolidge, James Milhollin, Dick Winslow, Jerry Paris, Tony Caruso.
"Robinson gives an effortless interpretation of a top criminal"—*New York Daily News*, August 15, 1968.

MacKenna's Gold (Columbia, 1969) 136 minutes
Directed by J. Lee Thompson, Screenplay by Carl Foreman, Photographed by Harold Wellman, Edited by Bill Lenny.
With Gregory Peck, Omar Sharif, Telly Savalas, Keenan Wynn, Julie Newmar, Ted Cassidy, Raymond Massey, Burgess Meredith, *E.G.R.*, Eli Wallach, Eduardo Ciannelli, John Garfield, Jr., Victor Jory.

U.M.C. (CBS TV, 1969) 100 minutes
Directed by Boris Sagal, Teleplay by A. C. Ward.
With Richard Bradford, *E.G.R.*, James Daly, Kim Stanley, Maurice Evans, Kevin McCarthy, J. D. Cannon, William Windom, Shelley Fabares.

The Old Man Who Cried Wolf (ABC TV, 1969) 73 minutes
Directed by Walter Grauman, Teleplay by Luther Davis.
With *E.G.R.*, Martin Balsam, Diane Baker, Percy Rodrigues, Ruth Roman, Ed Asner, Martin Brooks, Sam Jaffe, Bill Elliot.

Song of Norway (Cinerama, 1970) 142 minutes
Directed by Andrew Stone, Screenplay by Stone, Photographed by Davis Boulton, Edited by Virginia Stone.
With Toralv Maurstad, Florence Henderson, *E.G.R.*, Oscar Homolka, Christina Schollin, Frank Poretta, Robert Morley, Harry Secombe.

Soylent Green (MGM, 1973) 102 minutes
Directed by Richard Fleischer, Screenplay by Stanley R. Greenburg

(Based on Harry Harrison's *Make Room, Make Room*), Photographed by Richard H. Kline, Edited by Samuel E. Beetley.

With Charleton Heston, Leigh Taylor-Young, Chuck Connors, Joseph Cotten, *E.G.R.*, Brock Peters, Paula Kelly, Mike Henry, Leonard Stone, Whit Bissell, Dick Van Patten.

Note: Released posthumously.

James Cagney

Up until his death in 1986, James Cagney considered himself not a tough guy, but a song and dance man. He continually would dismiss the many screen classics he helped shape with his image and would consider it all "just a job. A way of putting groceries on the table." Of all the actors listed in this book, however, Cagney may very well be the greatest technical craftsman in his field. His tough guy allowed not only versatility—and was more then merely an influence on several acting styles—but presented, more than any other similar persona, the widest range of emotions. Always maintaining the same basic screen image, Cagney would run the gamut from the slapstick of *The Bride Came C.O.D.* to the heavy dramatics of something like *White Heat* and play two totally different roles, allowing for every conceivable emotion within the characterization. Two things that made this even more impressive are that he could extend so far beyond his screen image while still retaining its basic stylistic rudiments and that his acting was borne out of a natural ability rather than years of practice with Stanislavsky, Lee Strasberg, Uta Hagen, or any of the other great acting specialists.

Cagney was indeed a song and dance man once he entered films, playing in a variety of minor roles until landing a supporting part in William Wellman's *Public Enemy* (1931). Originally Cagney was slated to portray the passive Matt Doyle, follower to the leadership of the film's leading character, Tom Powers, a ruthless young punk. Shortly after production began Wellman saw his casting error and had Cagney switch roles with Edward Woods, who was essaying the Tom Powers role.

Made after *Little Caesar*, *Public Enemy* was allowed by the Warner boys only because Wellman promised an even tougher gangster picture than its predecessor. Wellman indeed delivered the goods, but *Public Enemy* really isn't very similar to *Little Caesar* other than the fact that both are crime dramas presenting the rise and fall of a ruthless hood. Tom Powers is different than Rico Bandello mostly because Tom is a younger man and dealing with a much different form of alienation. Rico is alone;

Tom is enveloped by a family and friends who love him. Rico's mother, shown in one brief sequence, is quite capable of selling her boy down the river if she can profit by it. Tom's mother is one of those sweet, grey-haired naive sorts who found their way into many gangster sagas of the early thirties. Tom has a girl, a big brother, and some genuine ambitions. But like most adolescents, he does not have the patience to achieve his big ideas and see his dreams come into fruition by going through the procedures, step-by-step, that will see him achieve this success legally. Tom is too ambitious, and wants instead to beat the system. This is a form of ego, but not as blatant as Rico's.

Through his brother we get a sibling rivalry in a setting that befits the narrative (unlike Rico, the viewers get to see Tom grow from childhood and understand the foundation of his later nastiness). Tom's brother Mike is an all–American do-no-wrong sort who does things by the numbers and succeeds. This pressures Tom and makes what little patience he has difficult to deal with from the perspective that he needs to succeed above and beyond his brother sooner than the elder Powers succeeds beyond Tom's projected ambitions. Tom is shown as a tough street kid who isn't truly bad (albeit rather mischievous), but is made bad via classical conditioning as his righteous older brother and neighborhood goody-goody girls continually call him bad. He soon becomes mixed up with the wrong crowd and starts out his life of crime by running illegal errands for an adult fence known simply as "putty-nose" who has quite a business getting young boys to do his dirty work (and sometimes getting gunned down). By the time Tom has reached the heights of gangsterdom (during Prohibition), the viewers have already come to know and understand him even for his most evil ways, much more so than we understood Rico (here we just had to guess, basing our assumptions on Rico's present stratum of life).

In his autobiography, Cagney recalls his childhood as actually taking place on similar streets to those presented in *Public Enemy*, something that allows the actor to enhance his characterization by making it more realistic via background knowledge (something that assisted most of Cagney's best roles in subsequent pictures). And Tom Powers is the perfect example of an alienated young man, a harbinger for James Dean's portrayals some twenty years later. As we try to understand Tom Powers in accordance with his upbringing, we try to understand the typical adolescent who enters adulthood feeling alienated by a society that is too structured for his or her liberal ideas. In the thirties, crime was the outlet (substances like narcotics could not be alluded to in films of this era). Tom becomes a criminal as an attack on the society he feels so suppressed by (his brother being perhaps its closest human representation).

Perhaps the best way to understand Tom Powers is by examining the most famous scenes in *Public Enemy* (which are among the most famous in

American film history), the first being the "grapefruit sequence." In this scene, we see Tom as a young criminal who is hampered by the bland, lifeless girl he is living with (played by Mae Clarke). Tom has been seeing another, more vivacious young lady (played by Jean Harlow) who fits in better with the wild, fast life that young Powers has chosen for himself. At the breakfast table one morning Kitty (Mae Clarke), looking plain and neatly coiffed, confronts the frazzled Tom Powers:

> TOM: I didn't ask ya for any lip, I asked ya for a drink!
> KITTY: I know dear, but I wish. . .
> TOM: There ya go with that wishin' stuff again. I wish you was a wishin' well. So I could tie a bucket to ya and *sink* ya!
> KITTY: Maybe you found somebody you'd like better.

Kitty's last line is what prompts Tom to reach across the table, grab a grapefruit half and push it into the unsuspecting woman's face. It is a shocking moment that usually causes bemused laughter as a response from an audience. It has since been used to point out screen toughness, nastiness, masculinity, and sexism. What it remains is a staple of Cagney's character that had such an impact that it has become movie legend. Yet the scene is done in such a way that we are on his side, and not hers. In our understanding of Tom Powers we also know how much he hates to be pressured.

Kitty, whom he is already becoming quite bored with, pressures him by verbally backing him into a corner and asking (in the form of a statement, no less) just where she stands in their relationship. Powers, pushing the grapefruit into her face, is more or less stating he has no time for such triviality. Now, since this scene has become an object of study, it is often shown out of context. Thus many people have seen only this brief sequence where an embittered, frazzled punk pushes a grapefruit in a seemingly innocent, nice young lady's face. Without knowing the background of either character via the preceding portion of the film's narrative, it is impossible to understand the motivation for Tom's actions. While undeniably vicious and sexist, it is also understandable from the perspective that we are watching a hoodlum here, not a priest, and he is a hoodlum as a result of too many people like Kitty who constantly put him down as being a bad seed.

The other scene parallels the final moments in *Little Caesar*. Powers, riding high on his ego, tries to avenge his partner's murder by engaging the rival gang in a shoot-out. Tom, filled with the same big dreams and ambitions (albeit now mixed with an ego as a result of his successes), takes them on

The famous "grapefruit scene." Cagney and Mae Clarke in *Public Enemy* (Warner Bros., 1931).

alone. He then staggers out onto the street, his body riddled with bullet holes, under a late-night sky that's pouring rain down upon him. He staggers for a few blocks, then falls to the pavement and gasps, "I ain't so tough!" So ends one of society's classic victims. He does exhibit the same sort of ego Rico does, but his dying line is not spoken from the same awed perspective. Where Rico was flabbergasted by his own mortality, Tom merely comes to grips with reality.

What *Public Enemy* does is present the character of Tom Powers as an embittered lad whose life of crime is a result of society not allowing him better outlets for his energies. His big ideas and strong ambitions are hindered by his older brother and others insisting that he enter the conventional work force and who dismiss his ambitions as pipe dreams. This lack of encouragement stimulates his rebellious spirit and he gradually stumbles into a life of crime. Cagney's portrayal of Tom is fierce without the tenderness that characterized his subsequent tough-guy roles. In fact, in Richard Schickel's book *James Cagney; A Celebration*, he calls the film an anomaly in the actor's career due to its lack of tenderness as an underlying current to his characterization. This is true, but what *Public Enemy* best represents is the basic toughness that Cagney would continue to utilize to shape his characterizations, the tenderness being one of the many added textures he would incorporate into his initial screen image of hardened badness.

A case in point is *Angels with Dirty Faces* (1938), arguably Cagney's finest work and best film. It gives us the most typical Cagney characterization, including all of the little nuances and mannerisms that impressionists love to capitalize on as Cagney attributes. As William "Rocky" Sullivan, Cagney is allowed to exhibit the full gamut of emotions that befit a tough guy, including the tenderness that Schickel referred to in his assessment of *Public Enemy*. It is also a film that carefully blames society as the culprit in regard to the making of hoodlums who go from petty theft to the highest form of organized crime. There have been so many references and imitations centering on the classic scenes in *Angels with Dirty Faces* that the film has, by now, become overanalyzed from a variety of different perspectives. In the context of time in which the film was made, however, it presented several very important aspects of societal manipulation and the crime problem in Depression America, as well as a honing of the Cagney character in a setting that most befits him.

Pat O'Brien appears as Jerry Connolly, a boyhood pal of Rocky's who, at the outset of the film, escapes the police while Rocky is captured and sent to reform school. Jerry becomes a priest; Rocky, a hardened criminal—the film making the statement that reformatories in their present state are not a deterrent to crime but instead are institutions that breed a more sophisticated criminal than what went in. When Rocky returns to his old neighborhood he immediately regains contact with Father Jerry, who acts as a surrogate big brother/guardian angel for the remainder of the film, culminating in Jerry's own one-man rampage against the organized crime that is ruining his city.

At the core of this screen study are the Dead End Kids, whose appearances in Warner films extended their presentation of troubled adolescence that they had performed in their film debut, Samuel Goldwyn's *Dead End* (1937). They are juveniles who worship Rocky and his rebellious ways, recognizing that these same ways stem from their own adolescent yearnings. Father Jerry, then, acts as big brother to all of them, the adolescent gang and the arrested adolescent Rocky. What Jerry and Rocky represent are adult models of the two paths that the juveniles may choose, the righteous path that is steeped in godly things and the evil ways that are more attractive even if only because they challenge society's conventions.

Rocky is the antithesis of Tom Powers in that Rocky is, as Andrew Bergeman once pointed out, the most lovable gangster of them all. Thus it is very easy to understand the Dead End Kids' idolization of this gangster. He is a sort of harbinger to the unconventional rock and roll stars who decades later would captivate the adolescent population much to the chagrin of their parents. Father Jerry is the parent figure here, trying desperately to cut through the gang's adolescent rebelliousness and reach their hearts. By the end of the film he realizes he needs Rocky in order to accomplish such a feat, and this leads up to one of the most famous and most emotional endings of all gangster sagas.

In leading up to this ending we see Rocky involved in the inevitable shoot-out that leaves him battling the opposing forces alone. Eventually he is trapped in a deserted warehouse that is surrounded by the police, who fire tear gas at him and wait for him to appear in one of the window openings so that they can gun him down. We see Rocky trapped by the suppressive elements of society that he had always battled. And we sympathize with this killer because he is presented to us in such an attractive manner. He is witty, aloof, self-centered, poised, and extremely secure. The priest, who represents good, is drab, dark, generally unexciting. Thus the priest's idolization of Rocky from the perspective that he could be "straightened out" stems from Father Jerry's own childhood idolization of his pal, who always possessed "cool" qualities.

Rocky is eventually captured by police, sent to prison, and sentenced to the electric chair—something we learn via newspaper headlines in a quick montage that consists of several shots of the Dead End Kids closely following Rocky's arrest, trial, and eventual sentencing. When they read the headline "Rocky guilty; To Die," they exclaim proudly, "He'll show 'em how to die in a big way!"

When Father Jerry arrives to see Rocky, it is only minutes before he is to be executed. Their discussion finds Rocky without loss of aplomb as

was typical of this particular characterization, despite the circumstances.

JERRY: Rocky, the boys saw me off when I took the train here, and you can imagine what they said. "Tell Rocky to show them what he's made of...."

ROCKY: Well I'm not going to let them down if that's what's worrying you.

Jerry goes on to ask Rocky for a favor, one that will require a great deal of courage. "Not the courage of heroics or bravado, but the type that's born in Heaven. That you and I and God know about." Rocky is confused, knowing only one kind of courage, that being to refuse to accept one's own fear.

ROCKY: Walking in there isn't going to take much. They'll strap me in and ask, "Any last words?" And I'll say, "Yeah, give me a haircut, a shave, and a massage. One of those nice new electric massages. Heh-heh!"

JERRY: But you're not afraid?

ROCKY: No, but they'd like me to be wouldn't they? I'm afraid I can't oblige them, kid. You know, Jerry, in order to be afraid you . . . you gotta have a heart. I don't think I got one. I had that cut out of me a long time ago.

JERRY: Suppose I ask you to have the heart?

This leads into Jerry's asking Rocky to go to the chair a coward so that the boys, and others like them throughout the world, will be ashamed of this antihero. "They've got to despise your memory!"

This entire sequence is played still amidst the noir lighting that was typical of the film's director, Michael Curtiz. It nicely contrasts the frenzied action sequences that immediately precede it and allows for a culmination in the Rocky-Jerry relationship as well as the Rocky character, which may very well be the most complex and fascinating tough guy in American cinema. Rocky leaves the cell and starts down his last mile to the chair hitching his shoulders and slowly swaggering along with a tough, almost expressionless face. Curtiz paces the sequence very slowly in order to achieve heightened suspense. Jerry is allowed to accompany Rocky.

ROCKY: Promise me one thing. Promise me I won't hear you pray.

JERRY: I promise you won't hear me.

Of course Rocky does turn coward after the long, suspenseful walk to the electric chair. Although this final sequence, with Rocky struggling and

Cagney (center) flanked by the Dead End Kids (from left, Bernard Punsley, Bobby Jordan, Billy Halop, Leo Gorcey, Huntz Hall, and Gabe Dell) in *Angels with Dirty Faces* (Warner Bros., 1938).

crying "Oh God don't let me die! I don't wanna burn!" is done in silhouette, its emotional power is not diminished. This is the epitome of the Cagney tough-but-tender characterization. Rocky is a punk whose hard, rebellious attitudes were formed as a result of his environment. When he doles out certain portions of affection to select people, it is outside of his crime world and streetwise peers. Rocky's tenderness is attached to a world he is unable to cope with on its own terms. The underworld that he does manage to achieve success in contrasts the world of the priest, whom Rocky secretly admires (shown in his attempts to give Father Jerry money to build a recreation center and to assist him in coaching church basketball functions). Rocky's relationship with the Dead End Kids stems from the freedom of his own adolescence, his memories of a time when crime was petty and reformatories were a part of his future. Now that they are part of his past, the shenanigans of these juveniles are as melancholy as they are nostalgic for him. Thus, when he decides to play coward at the very end, it is to save those kids and others like them from ending up in the same place, as Father Jerry said. He owes nothing to the bad guys who became his rivals and will make him a laughingstock in death as a result of this action. Rocky's affection for the priest was so strong that it eventually allowed him to realize that the priest's actions were for Rocky's good as well as the good of the community. And when he finally plays coward as his last act, it is the culmination of his affection for his boyhood pal, borne out further in Father Jerry's final statement to the kids, the last thing said in the film:

KID: Is it true what the papers said Father? That he died a coward?
JERRY: It's true boys. He died like they said. Come on boys, let's go say
          a prayer for a boy who couldn't run as fast as I could.

Rocky could not run as fast as the priest in a figurative sense as well as the literal one, and thus remains the perfect representation of Cagney's tough-but-tender screen personas who could have been saints had they been given ample opportunity to exhibit their hearts' full potentials rather than be alienated by their environment. Of course it could be argued that the Father Jerrys are alienated as youths in the same environment, but since Rocky is the one who is caught early in the film, it is he who learns sophisticated crime techniques in the reformatories. Hence the film makes the statement that the era's justice systems were more suppressive than even the poorest slum environments. This statement is made through the character of Rocky by presenting him as a basically good sort whose big heart has been blackened by such conditions. His act of cowardice in the end is just an act and thus can be considered his final statement of rebellion, this time rebelling against the environment that made him a criminal by doing right in spite of the life he unwittingly chose for himself.

In the final analysis, *Angels with Dirty Faces* presents Rocky's rebelliousness as a study in asceticism. His finally going to the chair a coward, presumably for the priest and the young delinquents who idolize him, culminates his earlier nihilism with an act that shows him to be in pursuit of subcultural purification. He chooses to do this act at the request of a friend who went from surrogate anchorite to crusading moralizer within the course of the film's narrative. Thus the denouement of *Angels with Dirty Faces* shows the "right" way (pure, moral religiosity) emerging as triumphant. But rather than presenting this triumph as solely from the priest, it is shown through the character of Rocky, making its impact far more emotionally stimulating for the viewer. It also shows a dimension of screen toughness that had rarely been presented, mostly because such qualities are generally considered the antithesis of being tough (tenderness rarely enters into a tough screen character unless it is simply a cliché—i.e., the Wallace Beery bad guy with a heart of gold who is turned to mush by Margaret O'Brien).

The clever manipulation of the narrative by director Curtiz assists Cagney's portrayal, but the many little nuances Cagney bestows upon the character of Rocky are the key to this offbeat presentation of screen toughness. Rocky is a rough leader in a maelstrom of sophisticated crime, yet his mannerisms make him attractive, interesting. And his passion for a perverse sort of capital and prestigious gain is also augmented by a genuine affection for his boyhood friends and sentimental attachment to his pre-crime (or perhaps petty crime) past.

In films where he was on the side of the law, Cagney's tough-guy characterization was put through its paces with the same rebellious attitudes, only against established corruption. Case in point: *Each Dawn I Die* (1939). Cagney is not a lawman, but an idealistic crusading reporter who attacks political corruption rather than street baddies. In fact, when Cagney is framed and sent to prison by a corrupt judicial system, it is a street thug who assists him in clearing his name. By today's standards the film is hackneyed in some ways, but it is important in its showing of the Cagney characterization in another context. Cagney's Frank Ross is similar to Rocky in that he battles the corruption of accepted politics. George Raft, as Stacey, is the Rocky counterpart in *Each Dawn I Die* who ultimately sees his own idealism through the righteous Frank Ross. As Frank's girlfriend says to Stacey:

> Frank hates crooked lawyers and politicians just as much as you do. You choose crime, the easy way to fight back. Frank is trying to do something about the problem.

The Cagney-Raft relationship in this film can be taken as an example of the relationship between Cagney's good-guy and bad-guy roles. Both have the same attitudes toward the same areas of corruption, using different methods in combating such corruption.

Angels with Dirty Faces presents Cagney the lovable bad guy; *Each Dawn I Die* shows him as a good guy whose futile attempts to battle corrupt justice systems is only successful with the help of a bad guy; and, finally, *The Roaring Twenties* (1939) displays Cagney the good guy who becomes a bad guy as a result of the America he fought for turning its collective back on him. Again Cagney, as Eddie Bartlett, is the naive idealist Frank Ross was and not the street-smart Rocky Sullivan.

After serving in the First World War, Eddie decides, at Armistice, that he wants to return to the quiet life of a garage mechanic ("Making money the hard way," states a bitter colleague played by Humphrey Bogart). In an interesting piece of ominous foreshadowing, the Bogart character stands holding his military weapon and states, "You know I'm beginning to like this thing; I think I'll take it with me." Of course in the end the boys have it out and nobody wins, hence the moral Warner Bros. foists upon the moviegoing public.

Eddie Bartlett is an unlikely Cagney Everyman who falls into the bootlegging racket accidentally and begins to enjoy it as a get-rich-quick occupation, especially after his frustration at being incapable of finding work in postwar America. The film makes some attempt to study the postwar American male from the disillusioned Eddie Bartlett to the civilians who are simply tired of hearing about the veterans, and finally to a shell-shocked vet whom Bartlett briefly shares a cell with, a man dealing with the madness of having seen "too much action, too much blood!"

Yet the film does not concentrate solely on this area of Cagney's characterization, instead using it as a basis for a rather obtrusive, quixotic subplot which features Eddie in a romantic triangle involving two of Warner's blandest contract players, Jeffrey Lynn and Priscilla Lane. Yet, although limited by such intrusions, Cagney's character unfolds in the Prohibition era action and culminates with him appearing excessively ragged once Prohibition is repealed and he no longer "practically runs the town." Yet the film never tells us specifically if it is Prohibition that leads him to this state of tatterdemalion or if it is simply the loss of perky Priscilla Lane. A stronger dramatic narrative would have eschewed this annoying subplot and concentrated on Eddie's rise and fall from disillusioned returning vet who makes a name in bootlegging to the seedy end of one of society's victims.

Unquestionably the turning point in Cagney's career was his legendary Oscar-winning performance in *Yankee Doodle Dandy* (1942), which saw him eschew the tough guy to play real-life showman George M. Cohan, "The Man Who Owned Broadway." It became his favorite film (and remains a favorite of many), but unfortunately is not classic Cagney as per the tough guy he created and honed so well. It is a loose narrative bolstered by wonderful musical numbers (and all the gloss of anything at MGM), and for this it has become a classic (even despite a very nasty "colorized" version that was released to television in 1986).

Through this classic musical, Cagney the actor achieved a certain self-awareness. He now wanted to present himself onscreen in a fashion that he himself found satisfactory. He had grown tired of the tough-guy image, never having had any true respect for it, and decided to use his heightened position in motion pictures to pioneer independent production.

With brother William, Cagney established independent production initially with the feature *Johnny Come Lately* (1943). This fluffy bit of inspired whimsy is very much a departure from the norm for Cagney, but the brothers were careful in selecting a strong supporting cast (Marjorie Main, George Cleveland, Margaret Hamilton, and stage actress Grace George in her first and last screen appearance) in case this offbeat property didn't work. It didn't. The film opens with the Cagney character reading Dickens, then finds him revitalizing a sagging newspaper with his wits; finally the film leads us to a fist-flying climax that is closer to Cagney but far from the gentle cleverness of the rest of the film.

The next Cagney brothers venture appears today as blatant propaganda, and so it was. *Blood on the Sun* (1945) features Cagney as a crusading reporter in Japan right around the time the Japanese are planning to bomb Pearl Harbor. This film was followed by another offbeat item, a filmization of William Saroyan's *Time of Your Life*. This affectionate production stays close to the original stage version and was reportedly enjoyed by Saroyan himself, who wrote Cagney a letter stating "I enjoyed it so much I forgot who wrote it."

While none of these independent productions are truly remarkable (none are wretched either), they are important for showing an extension of Cagney that few actors indulged in themselves. Cagney had some abilities as a filmmaker, and enough savvy to utilize his clout in the industry to make pictures that he personally felt better exhibited his talents. The tough-guy image that he is so well known for, and was so instrumental in bringing him to the legendary status he achieved even prior to his retirement, was the area of his work that he so casually dismissed as "just a job." His work in musicals and the independent productions he was active in was what he believed to be his true screen persona or, perhaps, the way he felt he should be characterized onscreen. He was desperately tired of playing the tough-but-tender thug and sorely needed a variation on this theme, despite the fact that he appeared in some terribly important American screen dramas.

It is interesting that these independent productions were made for release by United Artists—the studio that was founded years before by

Cagney performed for the last time as *Terrible Joe Moran*, a 1984 movie made for television.

Charlie Chaplin, Douglas Fairbanks, Mary Pickford, and D. W. Griffith in hopes of allowing these artists to control their works without intervention by anticreative studio moguls (something that allowed Chaplin to make some of the screen's greatest films, and kept the comedian from falling to the depths that Keaton or Laurel and Hardy hit toward the end of their careers). Unfortunately, however, the Cagney venture failed and the films did not do terribly well at the box office.

Stronger ironies came for Cagney when his next film, again for Warners, turned out to be yet another gangster saga. *White Heat* (1949), however, added further complexities to the character of Cody Jarrett that Tom Powers and Rocky Sullivan didn't have. Jarrett was a psychopath, a character that seemed to emerge often in post–World War II American filmmaking. Initially, however, Jarrett was simply depicted (in the script) as being a caustic, violent sort without motivation for his cruel actions. Since these actions went far beyond the cruelty of Rocky Sullivan, Cagney felt they should have motivation. It was the actor who decided that Jarrett be a psychopath who has periodic fits due to his heavy brain troubles. It was eventually attributed to an Oedipus complex, Jarrett caring only for his mother — another wicked gangster in the Ma Barker mode. When Jarrett is sent to prison, undercover officer Hank Fallon (Edmund O'Brien) poses as another con and attempts to take Ma's place. The result is a fascinating psychological drama that succeeds in adding the further textures to the Cagney tough-guy image and the standard crime narrative of American film.

Cagney's performance as Jarrett is often cited as the epitome of acting from this period. This is best emphasized in two key scenes from *White Heat*. The first has Cagney sitting in the jail cafeteria, finding out that his Ma is dead. Upon hearing the news, which is passed down along the table via whispers from convict to convict, Jarrett slowly comes to grips with the fact that the person he deems as most important no longer exists. "Dead?" he whimpers. "Dead?" He then very slowly erupts into fits of shrieking and blubbering accompanied by spastic gestures, the likes of which none of his headache fits had brought on. It takes dozens of security guards to restrain him as his adrenaline reaches superhuman proportions and he crawls quickly and maniacally across the tables screaming "Mama! Mama!" The scene ends as abruptly as it began, with Jarrett carried out of the eating area, the door slamming shut, and total silence prevailing once again (a fascinating contrast in sound that makes the emotional impact of the sequence even more stunning). This scene is a portent for the final moments of the film when Cagney finds that Hank Fallon, who has by now taken Ma's

Cagney in his Oscar-winning role as showman George M. Cohan in *Yankee Doodle Dandy* (MGM, 1942).

place, is an undercover officer: "A copper! And I was treating him like my kid brother! I was gonna split 50-50 with a copper!"

Again Jarrett erupts into blubbering fits, escaping from the police fire that surrounds him as he stands atop a huge oil tank giggling maniacally. In one of the most famous moments in all of motion pictures, he stands triumphantly and shouts "Made it Ma, top of the world!" as the tank explodes, bringing an end to Jarrett and allowing the maelstrom of violence to culminate with the same force as Jarrett had exhibited throughout the film.

For the ten years after *White Heat* the aging Cagney appeared in a series of mediocre films designed to capitalize on his tough-guy persona, never with any truly interesting results. Often the actor's lack of enthusiasm was quite evident. Finally, *Man of a Thousand Faces* gave him another opportunity to play a real-life person (this time silent screen legend Lon Chaney) and thus study the traits of this person in order to achieve realism within his portrayal. What emerged was an extension of Cagney's own screen persona within the framework of the Chaney characterization.

But Chaney was very much a fitting character for Cagney to portray. He was aggressive, talented, tormented, and very passionate. The tough-yet-tender Cagney character fit well within the framework of such a persona. Cagney was getting older, so portraying street punks was behind him. He had weathered many storms both onscreen and off. Chaney, who learned the art of pantomime from growing up with deaf parents, used his body and facial expressions as an actor much the same way Cagney did (Cagney's stemming from his beginnings as a dancer). Cagney is effective pulling off the Hollywood-ized melodramatics of the narrative, due only to his own acting prowess. But he makes real the character of Chaney through his expert reenactment of several Chaney roles, bringing forth the passion Chaney had for his work as an actor (and reemphasizing the same passion Cagney had for his, despite his ambivalence).

By 1961, this movie tough guy finally began feeling played out. His proposed last film, Billy Wilder's frenetic and hilarious cold war comedy *One, Two, Three* (1961), didn't give the actor a chance to breathe. He executed the fast-paced verbal bits beautifully, but upon completion of the project, slipped into retirement. Several attempts were made to bring him back into films over the next two decades; the offers for *My Fair Lady* and *Godfather II* almost managed to succeed in coaxing him out of retirement. But it wasn't until 1981 and the filmization of E. L. Doctorow's *Ragtime* that moviegoers once again saw Cagney on the silver screen. While he received top billing for his small part as Rhinelander Waldo, and critics made the most of this marginal role, it was not the Cagney of yore. He was old, tired, speaking in a small raspy voice, and for the first time in his career looked as though he was *trying* to be a tough guy rather than allowing such toughness to flow naturally from his characterization. Talk was made of him then appearing as an elderly Bat Masterson in an upcoming project which never materialized, his bow finally occurring with the television film *Terrible Joe Moran* (1984). Actually, his performance as an old prizefighter who is now confined to a wheelchair better befit him than the *Ragtime* cameo. He played a tough character who lacked physically what he'd once had, but retained his fighting spirit. Cagney was weak and ill throughout the filming, but he too retained his spirit and went ahead with the project. It was to be his last. His health continued to fail until he died in 1986.

As an actor and a tough guy, Cagney is most important. It was through this image, however, that Cagney the man managed to help establish acting guilds for the protection of screen thespians and film institutes for the preservation of his craft, and thereby receiving for his efforts a life achievement award from the American Film Institute in 1974. His aloof attitude toward his work is belied by such noble actions for the cause of motion picture preservation.

James Cagney is a legendary name in American film, not only for his contributions to such important offscreen activities as those mentioned above, but also to the timeless artistry of his portrayals. His characterization continues to define attitudes of the oppressed American male in a society that fails to understand his madness. As with Dylan Thomas's poem "Do Not Go Gentle into That Good Night," the Cagney character raged against opposition and violently refused to cater to that which he felt suppressed his true nature. In a world of silver-screen fantasy, James Cagney gave film history a character that will forever remain very real.

James Cagney Filmography

Sinner's Holiday (Warner Bros., 1930) 55 minutes
Directed by John G. Adolfi, Screenplay by Harvey Thew and George Rosener (based on the play *Penny Arcade* by Marie Baumer), Photographed by Ira Morgan, Edited by James Gibbons.
With Grant Withers, Evalyn Knapp, *J.C.*, Joan Blondell, Lucille Laverne, Noel Madison, Otto Hoffman, Warren Hymer, Purnell B. Pratt, Ray Gallagher, Hank Mann.

The Doorway to Hell (Warner Bros., 1930) 78 minutes
Directed by Archie Mayo, Screenplay by George Rosener (based on the

Cagney was the "lovable bad guy" in many of his films. He is pictured here with Loretta Young in *Taxi!* (Warner Bros., 1932).

story *A Handful of Clouds* by Rowland Brown), Photographed by Chick Magill, Edited by Bob Crandall.

    With Lew Ayers, Charlie Judells, Jackie Lamar, Robert Elliot, *J.C.*, Kenneth Thomsen, Jerry Mandy, Noel Madison, Ruth Hall.

    Alternate title: *A Handful of Clouds*

Other Men's Women (Warner Bros., 1931) 70 minutes

    Directed by William Wellman, Screenplay by William Wells (based on the story by Maude Fulton), Photographed by Chick McGill, Edited by Ed McDermott

    With Grant Withers, Mary Astor, Regis Toomey, *J.C.*, Joan Blondell, Fred Kohler, J. Farrell McDonald, Lillian Worth, Walter Long.

The Millionaire (Warner Bros., 1931) 82 minutes

    Directed by John G. Adolfi, Screenplay by Maude Powell and Julian

Josephson (based on the story *Idle Hands* by Earl Derr Biggers), Photographed by James van Trees, Edited by Owen Marks.

With Evalyn Knapp, George Arliss, *J.C.*, Bramwell Fletcher, Florence Arliss, Noah Beery, Ivan Simspon, Sam Hardy, J. Farrell McDonald.

Public Enemy (Warner Bros., 1931) 84 minutes

Directed by William Wellman, Screenplay by Kubec Glasmon and John Bright (based on the original story *Beer and Blood* by Bright), Adaption and dialogue by Harvey Thew, Photographed by Dev Jennings, Edited by Ed McCormack.

With *J.C.*, Jean Harlow, Edward Woods, Joan Blondell, Beryl Mercer, Mae Clarke, Donald Cook, Murray Kennell, Robert Emmett O'Connor, Mia Marvin, Leslie Fenton, Rita Flynn, Clark Burroughs, Frank Coughlan, Jr., Frankie Darro, Snitz Edwards, Adele Watson, Dorothy Gee.

Note: in Great Britain this film was titled *Enemies of the Public*.

Smart Money (Warner Bros., 1931) 90 minutes

Directed by Alfred E. Green, Screenplay by Kubec Glasmon, John Bright, Lucien Hubbard, and Joseph Jackson, Photographed by Robert Kurrie, Edited by Jack Killifer.

With Edward G. Robinson, *J.C.*, Evalyn Knapp, Ralf Harolde, Noel Francis, Margaret Livingstone, Maurice Black, Boris Karloff, Morgan Wallace, Billy House, Paul Porcasi, Polly Walters, Ben Taggart, Gladys Lloyd, Clark Burrows, Edwin Argus, John Larkin, Walter Percival, Mae Madison.

Note: the only film in which Robinson and Cagney appeared together.

Blonde Crazy (Warner Bros., 1931) 73 minutes

Directed by Roy Del Ruth, Screenplay by Kubec Glasmon and John Bright, Photographed by Sid Hickox, Edited by Ralph Dawson.

With *J.C.*, Joan Blondell, Louis Calhern, Noel Francis, Guy Kibbee, Ray Milland, Polly Walters, Charles Lane, William Burress, Peter Erkelenz, Maude Eburne, Walter Percival, Nat Pendelton, Russell Hopton, Dick Cramer, Ray Cooke, Edward Morgan, Phil Sieman.

Note: in Great Britain this film was titled *Larceny Lane*.

Taxi! (Warner Bros., 1932) 70 minutes

Directed by Roy Del Ruth, Screenplay by Kubec Glasmon and John Bright (based on the play *The Blind Spot* by Kenyon Nicholson), Photographed by James Van Trees, Edited by James Gibbons.

With *J.C.*, Loretta Young, George E. Stone, Guy Kibbee, David Landau.

The Crowd Roars (Warner Bros., 1932) 85 minutes

Directed by Howard Hawks, Screenplay by Kubec Glasmon and John Bright (based on a story by Hawks and Seton I. Miller), Photographed by Sid Hickox and John Stunmar, Edited by Thomas Pratt.

With *J.C.*, Joan Blondell, Frank McHugh, Eric Linden, Ann Dvorak, Guy Kibbee, William Arnold, Leo Nomas, Charlotte Merriam, Regis Toomey.

Winner Take All (Warner Bros., 1932) 68 minutes
Directed by Roy Del Ruth, Screenplay by William Mizner and Robert Lord (based on the magazine story *133 at 3* by Gerald Beaumont), Photographed by Robert Kurrle, Edited by Thomas Pratt.
With *J.C.*, Marian Nixon, Virginia Bruce, Guy Kibbee, Clarence Muse, Dickie Moore, Allan Lane, John Roche, Ralf Harolde, Alan Mowbray.

Hard to Handle (Warner Bros., 1932) 81 minutes
Directed by Mervyn LeRoy, Screenplay by William Mizner and Robert Lord (based on a story by Houston Branch), Photographed by Barney "Chick" McGill, Edited by William Holmes.
With *J.C.*, Mary Brian, Ruth Donnelly, Allan Jenkins, Claire Dodd, Gavin Gordon, Emma Dunn, Robert McWade, John Sheehan, Matt McHugh.

Picture Snatcher (Warner Bros., 1933) 77 minutes
Directed by Lloyd Bacon, Screenplay by Allen Rivkin and P. J. Wolfson, Photographed by Sol Polito, Edited by William Holmes.
With *J.C.*, Ralph Bellamy, Patricia Ellis, Alice White, Ralf Harolde, Robert Emmett O'Connor, Robert Barrat, George Pat Collins, George Chandler, Sterling Holloway, Billy West, Tom Wilson.

The Mayor of Hell (Warner Bros., 1933) 90 minutes
Directed by Archie Mayo, Screenplay by Edward Chodorov (based on a story by Islin Auster), Photographed by Chick McGill, Edited by Jack Kilifer.
With *J.C.*, Madge Evans, Dudley Digges, Frankie Darro, Allen Clayton "Farina" Hoskins, Dorothy Peterson, John Marston, Charles Wilson, Hobart Cavanaugh, Raymond Borzage.

Footlight Parade (Warner Bros., 1933) 104 minutes
Directed by Lloyd Bacon and Busby Berkely, Screenplay by Manuel Seff and James Seymour, Photographed by George Barnes, Edited by George Amy.
With *J.C.*, Joan Blondell, Ruby Keeler, Dick Powell, Guy Kibbee, Ruth Donnelly, Claire Dodd, Hugh Herbert, Frank McHugh, Arthur Hohl, Gordon Westcott, Renee Whitney, Phillip Faversham, Juliet Ware, Herman Bing, Paul Porcasi.

Lady Killer (Warner Bros., 1933) 76 minutes
Directed by Roy Del Ruth, Screenplay by Ben Markson (based on the novel *The Fighting Man* by Rosalind Keating Shaffer and adapted by Markson and Lillie Hayward), Photographed by Tony Gaudio, Edited by George Amy.
With *J.C.*, Mae Clarke, Leslie Fenton, Margaret Lindsey, Henry O'Neill, Willard Robertson, Douglas Cosgrove, Raymond Hatton, Russell Hopton.

Jimmy the Gent (Warner Bros., 1934) 67 minutes
Directed by Michael Curtiz, Screenplay by Bertram Milhauser (based on the original story by Laird Doyle and Ray Nazzarro), Photographed by Ira Morgan, Edited by Thomas Richards.

With J.C., Bette Davis, Alice White, Allen Jenkins, Arthur Hohl, Alan Dinehart, Phillip Reed, Hobart Cavanaugh, Mayo Methot, Ralf Harolde, Joseph Sawyer, Phillip Faversham, Mora Lane, Joseph Crehan, Robert Warwick.

Here Comes the Navy (Warner Bros., 1934) 86 minutes
Directed by Lloyd Bacon, Screenplay by Ben Markson and Earl Baldwin (based on the story by Markson), Photographed by Arthur Edeson, Edited by George Amy.
With J.C., Pat O'Brien, Gloria Stuart, Frank McHugh, Dorothy Tree, Bob Barratt, Willard Robertson, Guinn "Big Boy" Williams, Maude Eburne, Martha Merrill.

G-Men (Warner Bros., 1935) 85 minutes
Directed by William Keighley, Screenplay by Seton I. Miller (based on *Public Enemy No. 1* by Gregory Rogers), Photographed by Sol Polito, Edited by Jack Kilifer.
With J.C., Ann Dvorak, Margaret Lindsey, Robert Armstrong, Barton MacLane, Lloyd Nolan, William Harrigan, Ed Pawley, Russell Hopton, Noel Madison, Regis Toomey, Addison Richards, Harold Huber, Raymond Hatton.

The Irish in Us (Warner Bros., 1935) 84 minutes
Directed by Lloyd Bacon, Screenplay by Earl Baldwin, Photographed by George Barnes, Edited by James Gibbons.
With J.C., Pat O'Brien, Olivia de Havilland, Frank McHugh, Allen Jenkins, Mary Gordon, J. Farrell MacDonald, Thomas Jackson, Harvey Perry, Bess Flowers, Mabel Colcord, Edward Keane, Herb Haywood.

A Midsummer Night's Dream (Warner Bros., 1935) 132 minutes
Directed by Max Reinhardt and William Dieterle, Screenplay by Charles Kenyon and Mary McCall, Jr. (based on the play by William Shakespeare), Photographed by Hal Mohr, Edited by Ralph Dawson.
With J.C., Dick Powell, Joe E. Brown, Jean Muir, Hugh Herbert, Ian Hunter, Frank McHugh, Victor Jory, Olivia de Havilland, Ross Alexander, Grant Mitchell, Nini Theilade, Veree Teasdale, Anita Louise, Mickey Rooney.

Frisco Kid (Warner Bros., 1935) 77 minutes
Directed by Lloyd Bacon, Screenplay by Warren Duff and Seton I. Miller (based on an original story by Duff and Miller), Photographed by Sol Polito.
With J.C., Margaret Lindsey, Ricardo Cortez, Lily Damita, Donald Woods, Barton MacLane, George E. Stone, Addison Richards, Joseph King, Robert McWade.

Ceiling Zero (Warner Bros., 1935) 95 minutes
Directed by Howard Hawks, Screenplay by Frank Wead (based on the play by Wead), Photographed by Arthur Edeson, Edited by William Holmes.

With *J.C.*, Pat O'Brien, June Travis, Stuart Erwin, Henry Wadsworth, Isabel Jewell, Barton MacLane, Martha Tibbetts, Craig Reynolds.

Great Guy (Grand National, 1935)
Directed by John G. Blystone, Screenplay by Henry McCarthy, Henry Johnson, James Edward Grant, Harry Ruskin (based on *The Johnny Cave Stories* by James Edward Brant), Photographed by Jack McKenzie, Edited by Russell Schoengarth.
With *J.C.*, Mae Clarke, James Burke, Edward Brophy, Henry Kolker, Bernadene Hayes, Edward J. McNamara.

Something to Sing About (Grand National, 1936) 80 minutes
Directed by Victor Schertzinger, Screenplay by Austin Parker (based on a story by Schertzinger), Photographed by John Stumar, Edited by Gene Milford.
With *J.C.*, Evelyn Daw, William Frawley, Mona Barrie, Gene Lockhart, James Newhill, Harris Barris, Candy Candido, Cully Richards, William B. Davison, Richard Tucker, Dwight Frye.

Boy Meets Girl (Warner Bros., 1937) 80 minutes
Directed by Lloyd Bacon, Screenplay by Bella Spewack and Sam Spewack, Photographed by Sol Polito, Edited by William Holmes.
With *J.C.*, Pat O'Brien, Marie Wilson, Ralph Bellamy, Frank McHugh, Dick Foran, Bruce Lester, Ronald Reagan, Paul Clark, Penny Singleton, Dennie Moore.

Angels with Dirty Faces (Warner Bros., 1938) 97 minutes
Directed by Michael Curtiz, Screenplay by Warren Duff and John Wexley (based on an original story by Rowland Brown), Photographed by Sol Polito, Edited by Owen Marks.
With *J.C.*, Pat O'Brien, Humphrey Bogart, Ann Sheridan, Billy Halop, Leo Gorcey, Huntz Hall, Bobby Jordan, Gabe Dell, Bernard Punsley, George Bancroft, Frankie Burke, William Tracy, John Hamilton.

The Oklahoma Kid (Warner Bros., 1939) 85 minutes
Directed by Lloyd Bacon, Screenplay by Warren Duff, Robert Buckner, and Edward Paramore (based on an original story by Paramore), Photographed by James Wong Howe, Edited by Owen Marks.
With *J.C.*, Humphrey Bogart, Rosemary Lane, Donald Crisp, Harvey Stevens, Hugh Sothern, Charles Middleton, Ed Pawley, Ward Bond.

Each Dawn I Die (Warner Bros., 1939) 92 minutes
Directed by William Keighley, Screenplay by Norman Reilly Raine, Warren Duff, and Charles Perry (based on an original story by Jerome Odlum), Photographed by Arthur Edeson, Edited by Thomas Richards.
With *J.C.*, George Raft, Jane Bryan, George Bancroft, Maxie Rosenbloom, Stanley Ridges, Alan Baxter, Victory Jory, John Wray, Ed Pawley, Willard

Robertson, Emma Dunn, Paul Hurst, Louis Jean Heydt, Joe Downing, Thurston, Hall, Clay Clement, Harry Cording.

The Roaring Twenties (Warner Bros., 1939) 104 minutes
     Directed by Raoul Walsh, Screenplay by Jerry Wald, Richard Macaulay and Robert Rossen (based on an original story by Mark Hellinger), Photographed by Ernie Haller, Edited by Jack Kilifer.
     With *J.C.*, Humphrey Bogart, Priscilla Lane, Jeffery Lynn, Gladys George, Frank McHugh, Paul Kelly, Elisabeth Risdon, Ed Keane, Joe Sawyer, Abner Biberman, George Humbert, Clay Clement, Ray Cooke.

The Fighting 69th (Warner Bros., 1940) 90 minutes
     Directed by William Keighley, Screenplay by Norman Reilly Raine, Fred Niblo, Jr., and Dean Franklin, Photographed by Tony Gaudio, Edited by Owen Marks.
     With *J.C.*, Pat O'Brien, George Brent, Jeffrey Lynn, Alan Hale, Frank McHugh, Dennis Morgan, Dick Foran, William Lundigan, Guinn "Big Boy" Williams, Henry O'Neill, John Litel.

Torrid Zone (Warner Bros., 1940) 88 minutes
     Directed by William Keighley, Screenplay by Richard Macaulay and Jerry Wald, Photographed by James Wong Howe, Edited by Jack Kilifer.
     With *J.C.*, Pat O'Brien, Ann Sheridan, Andy Devine, Helen Vinson, Jerome Cowan, George Tobias, George Reeves, Victor Kilian, Jack Puglia, Grady Sutton.

City for Conquest (Warner Bros., 1941) 101 minutes
     Directed by Anatole Litvak, Screenplay by John Wexley (based on the novel by Aben Kandel), Photographed by Sol Polito and James Wong Howe, Edited by William Holmes.
     With *J.C.*, Arthur Kennedy, Ann Sheridan, Frank Craven, Donald Crisp, Frank McHugh, George Tobias, Jerome Cowan, Anthony Quinn, Lee Patrick, George Lloyd, Joyce Compton, Thurston Hall, Ben Welden, Ed Keane.

The Strawberry Blonde (Warner Bros., 1941) 97 minutes
     Directed by Raoul Walsh, Screenplay by Julius and Philip Epstein (based on the play *One Sunday Afternoon* by James Hogan), Photographed by James Wong Howe, Edited by William Holmes.
     With *J.C.*, Rita Hayworth, Jack Carson, Olivia de Havilland, Alan Hale, George Tobias, Una O'Connor, George Reeves, Lucille Fairbanks, Herbert Haywood, Helen Lind, Kim Ryan.

The Bride Came C.O.D. (Warner Bros., 1941) 92 minutes
Directed by William Keighley, Screenplay by Julius and Philip Epstein,
Photographed by Ernest Haller, Edited by Thomas Richards.
With *J.C.*, Bette Davis, Jack Carson, Eugene Pallette, Stu Erwin, Harry
Davenport, William Frawley, Harry Holman, Chick Chandler, William Hop-
per, Ed Brophy.

Captains of the Clouds (Warner Bros., 1942) 113 minutes; color
Directed by Michael Curtiz, Screenplay by Arthur T. Hornman, Richard
Macaulay, Norman Reilly Raine (based on a story by Hornman and Roland
Gillett), Photographed by Sol Polito and Wilfred M. Cline, Edited by George
Amy.
With *J.C.*, Dennis Morgan, Brenda Marshall, Alan Hale, George Tobias,
Reginald Gardner, Reginald Denny, Russell Arms, Paul Cavanagh, Clem
Bevans.

Yankee Doodle Dandy (Warner Bros., 1942) 126 minutes
Directed by Michael Curtiz, Screenplay by Robert Buckner and Edmund
Joseph (based on an original story by Buckner which itself was based on the life
of George M. Cohan), Photographed by James Wong Howe, Edited by George
Amy.
With *J.C.*, Joan Leslie, Walter Huston, Richard Whorf, Jeanne Cagney,
Rosemary DeCamp, George Tobias, Irene Manning, S. Z. Sakall, George
Barbier, Walter Catlett.
Note: colorized in 1986.

Johnny Come Lately (United Artists, 1943—a William Cagney production) 97
minutes
Directed by William K. Howard, Screenplay by Johnny Van Druten (based
on the novel *McLeod's Folly* by Louis Bromfield), Photographed by Theodore
Sparkuhl, Edited by George Arthur.
With *J.C.*, Grace George, Marjorie Main, Marjorie Lord, Hattie McDaniel,
Ed McNamara, Bill Henry, Robert Barrat, George Cleveland, Margaret
Hamilton, Norman Willis, Lucien Littlefield, Irving Bacon, Wee Willie Davis.
Alternate title: *Johnny Vagabond*

Blood on the Sun (United Artists, 1945—a William Cagney production) 98
minutes
Directed by Frank Lloyd, Screenplay by Lester Cole, Photographed by
Theodore Sparkuhl, Edited by Truman K. Wood.
With *J.C.*, Sylvia Sidney, Wallace Ford, Rosemary De Camp, Robert Arm-
strong, John Emery, Leonard Strong, Frank Puglia, Jack Holloran, Hugh Ho,
Phillip Ahn, Joe Kim, Rhys Williams, Porter Hall.

13 Rue Madeleine (20th Century–Fox, 1946) 95 minutes
Directed by Henry Hathaway, Written by John Monks and Sy Bartlett,
Photographed by Norman Brodine, Edited by Harmon Jones.

With *J.C.*, Annabella, Richard Conte, Frank Latimore, Walter Abel, Melville Cooper, Sam Jaffe, Marcel Russeau, E. G. Marshall.
Note: Cagney's role originally slated for Rex Harrison.

The Time of Your Life (United Artists, 1948 — a William Cagney production) 109 minutes
Directed by H. C. Potter, Screenplay by Nathaniel Curtis (based on William Saroyan's play), Photographed by James Wong Howe, Edited by Walter Hannenmann.
With *J.C.*, William Bendix, Wayne Morris, Jeanne Cagney, Broderick Crawford, Ward Bond, James Barton, Paul Draper, Gale Page, James Lydon, Richard Erdman, Pedro DeCordoba, Tom Powers, Natalie Schaefer, Lanny Rees.

White Heat (Warner Bros., 1949) 114 minutes
Directed by Raoul Walsh, Screenplay by Ivan Goff and Ben Roberts (based on a story by Virginia Kellog), Photographed by Sid Hickcock, Edited by Owen Marks.
With *J.C.*, Virginia Mayo, Edmund O'Brien, Margaret Wycherly, Steve Cochran, John Archer, Wally Kassell, Mickey Knox, Fred Clark.

The West Point Story (Warner Bros., 1950) 107 minutes
Directed by Roy Del Ruth, Screenplay by John Monks, Charles Hoffman, Irving Wallace (based on a story by Wallace), Photographed by Sid Hickox, Edited by Owen Marks.
With *J.C.*, Doris Day, Gordon MacRae, Virginia Mayo, Gene Nelson, Alan Hale, Jr., Roland Winters, Raymond Roe, Wilton Graff, Jerome Cowan, Jack Kelly.

Come Fill the Cup (Warner Bros., 1950) 113 minutes
Directed by Gordon Douglas, Screenplay by Ivan Goff, Ben Roberts (based on a novel by Harlan Ware), Photographed by Robert Burks, Edited by Alan Crosland, Jr.
With *J.C.*, Gig Young, Phyllis Thaxter, Raymond Massey, James Gleason, Selena Royle, Larry Keating, Charlita, Sheldon Leonard, Douglas Spencer, Don Kellogg, William Bakewell, James Flavin, Norma Jean Macias, Kathleen Freeman.

What Price Glory (20th Century–Fox, 1952) 111 minutes; color
Directed by John Ford, Screenplay by Phoebe Ephron and Henry Ephron (based on the play by Maxwell Anderson and Laurence Stallings), Photographed by Joseph MacDonald, Edited by Dorothy Spencer.
With *J.C.*, Dan Dailey, Corrine Calvet, William Demarest, Craig Hill, Robert Wagner.
Note: Based on the 1926 silent classic.

A Lion Is in the Streets (Warner Bros., 1953 — a William Cagney production) 88 minutes

Directed by Raoul Walsh, Screenplay by Luther Davis, Photographed by Harry Stradling, Edited by George Amy.

With *J.C.*, Barbara Hale, Anne Francis, Warner Anderson, John McIntyre, Jeanne Cagney.

Run for Cover (Paramount, 1953) 92 minutes; color

Directed by Nicholas Ray, Screenplay by William C. Thomas, Photographed by Daniel Fapp, Edited by Howard Smith.

With *J.C.*, Viveca Lindfors, John Derek, Jean Hersholt, Grant Withers, Jack Lambert, Ernest Borgnine, Ray Teal, Irving Bacon, Gus Schilling.

Love Me or Leave Me (MGM, 1955) 122 minutes; color

Directed by Charles Vidor, Screenplay by Daniel Fuchs and Isabel Lennart, Photographed by Arthur Arling, Edited by Ralph E. Winters.

With Doris Day, *J.C.*, Cameron Mitchell, Robert Keith, Tom Tully, Harry Bellaver, Richard Gaines, Peter Leeds, Claude Stroud, Audrey Young.

Mister Roberts (Warner Bros., 1955) 123 minutes; color

Directed by John Ford and Mervyn LeRoy, Screenplay by Frank Nugent and Joshua Logan (based on the play by Logan and Thomas Heggen which was based on the novel by Heggen), Photographed by Winton Hoch, Edited by Jack Murray.

With Henry Fonda, Jack Lemmon, *J.C.*, William Powell, Ward Bond, Betsy Palmer, Phil Carey, Nick Adams, Harry Carey, Jr.

Tribute to a Bad Man (MGM, 1956) 95 minutes; color

Directed by Robert Wise, Screenplay by Michael Blankfort (based on a short story by Jack Schaeffer), Photographed by Robert Surtees, Edited by Ralph E. Winters.

With *J.C.*, Don Dubbins, Stephen McNally, Irene Papas, Vic Morrow, James Griffith, Onslow Stephens, James Bell, Jeanette Nolan, Royal Dano.

Note: Cagney's role originally slated for Spencer Tracy.

These Wilder Years (MGM, 1956) 91 minutes

Directed by Roy Rowland, Screenplay by Frank Fenton (based on a story by Ralph Wheelright), Photographed by George Folsey, Edited by Ben Lewis.

With *J.C.*, Barbara Stanwyck, Walter Pidgeon, Betty Lou Keim, Don Dubbins, Edward Andrews, Grandon Rhodes, Will Writhe, Lewis Martin, Dean Jones.

Man of a Thousand Faces (Universal, 1957) 87 minutes

Directed by Joseph Pevney, Screenplay by R. Wright Campbell, Ivan Goff, and Ben Roberts (based on a story by Ralph Wheelright on the life of Lon Chaney), Photographed by Russell Metty, Edited by Ted J. Kent.

With *J.C.*, Dorothy Malone, Jim Backus, Jane Greer, Marjorie Rambeau, Robert J. Evans, Jeanne Cagney, Jack Albertson, Roger Smith, Clarence Kolb, Hank Mann, Snub Pollard.

Never Steal Anything Small (Universal, 1958) 94 minutes color
Directed by Charles Lederer, Screenplay by Lederer, Photographed by Harold Lipstein, Edited by Russ Schoengarth.
With *J.C.*, Shirley Jones, Roger Smith, Cara Williams, Nehemiah Persoff, Royal Dano.

Shake Hands with the Devil (United Artists, 1959) 110 minutes
Directed by Michael Anderson, Screenplay by Ivan Goff and Ben Roberts, Photographed by Erwin Hellier, Edited by George Pilkington.
With *J.C.*, Don Murray, Dana Wynter, Glynis Johns, Michael Redgrave, Sybil Thorndike, Cyril Cusack, John Breslin, Harry Brogan.

The Gallant Hours (United Artists, 1960 — a Cagney-Montgomery production) 115 minutes
Directed by Robert Montgomery, Screenplay by Bernie Lay and Frank Gilroy, Photographed by Joe MacDonald, Edited by Fredrick Y. Smith.
With *J.C.*, Dennis Weaver, Ward Costello, Richard Jaeckel, Les Tremayne, Robert Burton, Raymond Bailey, Carl Benton Reid, Walter Sande, Karl Swenson.

One, Two, Three (United Artists, 1961) 108 minutes
Directed by Billy Wilder, Screenplay by Wilder and I.A.L. Diamond, Photographed by Daniel Fapp, Edited by Daniel Mandel.
With *J.C.*, Pamela Tiffin, Horst Buchholz, Arlene Francis, Lilo Pulver, Howard St. John, Leon Askin, Tile Kiwe.
Note: Cagney retired from the screen after this film, returning two decades later.

Ragtime (Paramount, 1981) 155 minutes; color
Directed by Milos Forman, Screenplay by Michael Weller (based on E. L. Doctorow's novel), Photographed by Miroslav Ondirek, Edited by Anne Coates (U.K.), Antony Gibbs, and Stanley Warnow.
With Howard Rollins, Elizabeth McGovern, Brad Dourrif, Moses Gunn, *J.C.*, Pat O'Brien, Donald O'Connor, Debbie Allen, Robert Joy, Norman Mailer.

Terrible Joe Moran (CBS–TV, 1984) 97 minutes; color
Directed by Joe Sargent, Written by Frank Cucci.
With *J.C.*, Art Carney, Peter Gallagher, Ellen Barkin, Joseph Sirola, Ed Koch, Floyd Patterson.

Cagney made guest or cameo appearances in the following:
Features
Starlift (Paramount, 1951) Directed by Roy Del Ruth; **The Seven Little Foys** (Paramount, 1955) Directed by Melville Shavelson; **Arizona Bushwackers** (Paramount, 1968) Directed by Lesley Selander (narrated).

Shorts
Practice Shots (1931), **Hollywood on Parade** (1933), **Screen Snapshots** (1934),

Hollywood Gad-About (1934), **For Auld Lang Syne** (1938), **Show Business at War** (1943), **You John Jones** (1943), **Battle Stations** (1944, narrated), **Road to the Wall** (1962, narrated), **Ballad of Smokey the Bear** (1962, as voice of cartoon character).

Cagney also directed the feature **A Short Cut to Hell** (Paramount, 1957).

Humphrey Bogart

Of all the actors in Hollywood history, Humphrey Bogart is second only to Jimmy Stewart among performers with the largest number of classic roles. Bogart starred in such legendary screen classics as *The Maltese Falcon, Casablanca, The Treasure of the Sierra Madre,* and *The African Queen.* His best work is that which centers most on his character rather than any other elements (screenplay, direction), allowing the purity of his tough-guy persona to exude the very qualities that still represent important aspects of American screen masculinity.

It is movie-buff legend that Bogart acquired virtually all of his most important screen roles by accident. And, after a strong cult following he garnered (along with the Marx Brothers) on college campuses during the 1970s, Bogart has become a legendary figure among all Hollywood personalities, placing him with similar legends Marilyn Monroe, Clark Gable, Rudolph Valentino, and Greta Garbo. This group, however (excepting Gable and Bogart), represents the least interesting aspects of the Hollywood film. They were not actors or artists, but instead personalities whose work centered almost totally on the name value they managed to achieve through studio publicists (Monroe's enhanced by her mysterious early death, Garbo's by her reclusiveness, etc.).

Bogart, especially, is a strong figure among representations of movie maleness. Not because he was a particularly strong and virile sort, but almost totally because he was not. Like Cagney, Bogart was small in stature. Unlike Cagney, he did not have the muscular frame or fighting prowess. Like Robinson, Bogart could exude snarling meanness. Unlike Robinson, Bogart could also successfully play a sniveling coward. But the two screen "types" Bogart is best known as include the hard gangster and the cool detective (his role in *Casablanca* being basically a civilian interpretation of the latter image).

The first screen role that brought Bogart any noticeable prominence was his eleventh. In *The Petrified Forest*, Bogart recreated his stage role of gangster Duke Mantee at the insistence of the film's star, Leslie Howard

Bogart's career soared when he began playing cool detective types.

(Warners had originally planned to cast Edward G. Robinson in the role). Thus, Bogart the tough guy was born, and it was an image that would remain. Though billed fifth (behind Howard, Bette Davis, Genevieve Tobin, and Dick Foran), Bogart was most instrumental in the film's success from a critical and commercial level. As the wicked gangster who holds seven people hostage in a roadside cafeteria, Bogart's Mantee became a model for other badman roles in films from this point onward. This 1936 film came after Robinson's Rico Bandello character in *Little Caesar* (1930) and Cagney's Tom Powers in *Public Enemy* (1931); thus the influences of both of these portrayals are evident in Bogart's Duke Mantee. Mantee, however, does not have the aspirations of Rico nor the tenacity of Tom Powers. Mantee is instead an example of pure meanness, based on a past that we, the viewers, are not presented with. Mantee is secure only when he has total control, becoming openly disturbed whenever that control is even slightly challenged.

Throughout most of *The Petrified Forest*, Bogart expresses himself through the character of Mantee by portraying the gangster as pensive, melancholy. The entire film is set inside a diner, where the hostages reveal a great deal about themselves and their thoughts on what each of the others stands for. Alan Squier (Leslie Howard) analyzes Mantee. Throughout this analysis, Mantee listens thoughtfully (a scene which is paralleled in *Key Largo* when Bogart analyzes badman Edward G. Robinson). As he wildy rebels against established societal values he is also hurriedly searching for his own inner peace. Squier presents Mantee with a proposition. He has a $500 life insurance policy which he would like to leave to the alienated Gaby (Bette Davis). He asks that Mantee, who is holed up in the diner awaiting word from a woman, kill him upon leaving. Mantee, understanding Squier's idealism for a woman (Mantee himself taking a bit of a risk as he awaits a female companion), states, "Okay pal, I'll try to make it so it don't hurt much." Mantee's idealism turns out to be for naught in a scene that shows him losing control of the entire scheme, as the radio announces the capture of the very woman he's waiting for, and her subsequent ratting to the police. Mantee refuses to believe it, his quiet cool erupting into a series of frustrated shouts as his gang passionately urges him to give word to move out.

The movie gangsters as played by Robinson or Cagney were brash, talkative, wise guys. Bogart is the first to exhibit less emotion through the more blatant verbal methods. All of Mantee's emotions come from his facial expressions, especially his eyes. He has little dialogue, Bogart speaking the lines in very slow, deliberate drawls. His aloof verbal delivery downplays the qualities that were the mainstays of the Cagney or Robinson portrayals, centering instead on nonverbal communication, more so than any other actor of this sort. The Mantee character is the first in a series of similar characters that Bogart would play during the thirties and early forties, each of the subsequent portrayals honing this initial image of a quiet madman who was intimidating more from his look than his verbal threats. Despite the cool facade, something inherent told the audience that this quiet example of nastiness could explode into a violent tirade at any moment.

Throughout the film, Mantee sits in a chair on a higher level than the others, almost like a schoolteacher. He stares at them and winces every time he is verbally insulted or any attempt is made to overrule his authority (Dick Foran as the athletic Bose is an interesting character contrast as his coveted manhood is threatened by the much smaller Mantee). Where Robinson would have spent the entire film talking to the other actors, fidgeting about in his seat, getting up and pacing when delivering his lines, Bogart plays Mantee like a slow ticking time bomb that is highly sensitive: Unless it is jarred, nothing will happen.

Mantee is hardly a culmination. On the contrary, he is the first square of the Bogart gangster. This character takes on a variety of different forms, but it is the idiosyncrasies of the Mantee character that represent most of the traits Bogart is best known for. With Samuel Goldwyn's presentation of Sidney Kingsley's play *Dead End* in 1937, Bogart showed a further extension of this same character in the role of "Baby Face" Martin. While the film is generally a brilliant look at lower-class values through the eyes of one of the more liberal-minded filmmakers in American cinema at the time (William Wyler), the segments that deal with Bogart's Baby Face Martin are what we're taking into account here. Martin was Mantee going home, showing the viewers from whence he came. The human incarnation of Martin is represented by the Dead End Kids (named for this, their screen debut).

This group of juvenile delinquents can either end up like Martin or like the hardworking Dave Connell (Joel McCrea), an architect who dreams of tearing down the slums. The noticeable difference, however, between honest Dave and dishonest Martin is money, as per this exchange:

> MARTIN: An architect? No kidding! You went to school, eh?
>
> DAVE: Six years of college.
>
> MARTIN: Well you was always smarter than the other kids, Dave, maybe it's all for the better. You must be in the big money now.
>
> DAVE: Sure! I'm painting a sign for [a nearby restaurant]. It'll be the first real money I've had in a long time.
>
> MARTIN: (looks at Dave bemused, then erupts into laughter) Six years of college and all you get is handouts! I'm glad I'm not like you saps. Working and slaving for what? I got mine, I took it!
>
> DAVE: Ever get scared?
>
> MARTIN: Me? What of? You can't live forever.

This exchange reveals the key to financial success in the slums—dishonesty. The lower working class could not rise to the level of wealth through their own capabilities, due to not having the same breaks as upper-class persons. The Dead End Kids realize this as they see Dave, Baby Face Martin, and the various working stiffs of the neighborhoods (of which Dave is a representation) as role models. The rich penthouse that borders their slum area (wealthy folks find the East River picturesque) is alien to them, representing a world that they are not part of and can never be.

Bogart as Martin is an extension of Bogart as Mantee, only a much deeper one. While Mantee remained mysterious throughout *The Petrified Forest*, with only a character analysis offered by Alan Squire as any genuine description of the badman's inner self, *Dead End* shows us where the badman has come from. Martin is a victim of this slum environment just as the Dead End Kids and Dave Connell are. And Martin is just sentimental enough to want to return to his past (as Cagney's Rocky Sullivan did in *Angels with Dirty Faces*). Martin wants to see Francie, an old girlfriend, and also his mother, who still lives in this low-income environment despite her son's lofty position in the underworld. It is these two confrontations that best exhibit the inner workings of Martin, or Mantee, or any of the Bogart gangster characters. They are insecure, impulsive, indulgent characters who are tortured by their own existence. Martin's attempts to present himself to Francie and to his mother bear such accusations out.

Martin's confrontation with Francie displays Martin briefly as the romantic, his love for Francie so strong it blinds him from seeing her as she has become. Francie uses prostitution to assist her in surviving her environment. Martin chooses to remember her as pure, and is thus blind to her faults. He blissfully recalls a time when the two engaged in lovemaking atop a roof on a summer night, stating, "It seems like only yesterday." "Yesterday," states Francie, "seems more like a million years ago!" Martin wants to take Francie with him. Francie realizes the two of them are in wholly different classes. "You're looking at me the way I was," she says. Martin takes a long look and Bogart shows, through brilliant facial pantomime, the reality of Francie's present stratum of life finally coming to the attention of the idealistic Martin.

> MARTIN: Why didn't you get a job?
> FRANCIE: They don't grow on trees.
> MARTIN: Why didn't you starve first?
> FRANCIE: Why didn't you?

The hardened Martin is nearly in tears, Bogart characteristically concentrating on facial expressions to communicate Martin's inner torment of the viewer (Bogart was said to have labored for hours in front of mirrors to practice different facial reactions for each character he played). We see inside the quiet badman through events in his past that come crashing into his present.

Martin's confrontation with his mother (Marjorie Main) is an even more emotional scene, due to the filial anguish Martin must suffer for simply living the life he chose. He runs up to her after seeing her from a distance, and calls her excitedly like a child with a good report card. "Mom," he shouts running toward her, "Mom!"

MA: Ya no good tramp!
MARTIN: Ain't you glad to see me?
MA: (slaps Martin's face hard) That's how glad I am!

It is important to note that Marjorie Main played Ma as sickly and very frail, not the strong Ma Kettle character she has by now become noted for. The line "Ya no good tramp" is barely audible, coming from a very weak, beaten woman. When she abruptly slaps Martin across the face, the viewer is every bit as startled as Martin. Bogart again exhibits a wide array of facial expressions to show the inner torment of the gangster character, something that had its foundation in Duke Mantee, but was coming to the forefront more successfully with Baby Face Martin, as *Dead End* gave the actor a narrative with more opportunities to exhibit these diverse emotions. Bogart manages to show Martin as sad, angry, defeated and defiant. He is both aggressive and passive at the same time, fluctuating between these opposite feelings rapidly and showing all of these emotions through his face. It is something that is far better seen than described.

MARTIN: I've killed men for looking at me the way you are.
MA: Yeah you're a killer all right . . . why don't you just go and leave me forget you . . . just go away and die.

Martin is left standing alone to ponder this conversation for only a few seconds. For the remainder of the film he is a more bitter and coarse individual. He returned to his old neighborhood for more than sentimentality. He returned to show his neighbors he had achieved success. But the two persons he was most interested in sharing his success with have failed to remain as he had remembered them. As stagnant as the slum environment and its people are, Martin's mother and his girl were two individuals whose lives were altered irreversibly by time and events. That Martin contributed to those events makes him less proud of his station in life. Thus Martin is not the deep-down good guy that Rocky Sullivan was. He is instead a ruthless killer who is incapable of finding acceptance, unable to fit into society and, finally, unable to fit into the life from whence he came. Martin is the consummate Bogart gangster because he typifies the character that must detach himself altogether for lack of being able to fit into any proper niche.

An ironic turn of events occurred when Cagney did assume the Rocky Sullivan role in *Angels with Dirty Faces*. Bogart was on hand in a supporting role as one of the wily worms of corruption central to Rocky's existence — one of the reasons for Rocky to follow the priest's advice at the end of the film and play coward to save the futures of the Dead End Kids (see Cagney chapter). As crooked attorney Jim Frazier, Bogart is far more corrupt than any of the much tougher characters he'd played. Frazier lacks

Cagney and Bogey teamed up in *The Roaring Twenties* (Warner Bros., 1939).

the sentiment of either Duke Mantee or Baby Face Martin (both of whom
were somewhat at the mercy of a woman). He is instead a wholly repugnant
wimp who has his dirty work done for him by a succession of faceless
gunmen. This may assist in displaying Bogart's versatility as an actor. Where
in *Dead End* he is still cunning and defiant while being stalked by a gun-
wielding Dave Connell, his Frazier character trembles in total fear once
Rocky corners him with a gun in his hand in *Angels with Dirty Faces*.

This is paralleled by the shoot-out in another Cagney starrer, *The Roaring Twenties* (1939), where Bogart is the tough partner of Cagney, only to
end up his enemy by the film's climax and inevitable shoot-out. Only in this

film we get a composite of Mantee and Frazier as Bogart plays the defiant tough guy who is quick to kill and allegedly difficult to frighten, only to be transformed into a sniveling, pleading coward once Cagney gets the drop on him, pleading for his life through promises immediately after arranging for his gunmen to take Cagney for a ride (prior to his knowledge that Cagney was packing a gun). This is the most interesting element of the Bogart gangster portrayal. Unlike Cagney or Robinson's gangster roles, the Bogart ones can also be presented as wimps working through a tough facade, fooling all (including the audience) until the end of the film. Even as Jim Frazier, Bogart presented the character as tough in a world of tough men. But he was the brains behind a desk who could assign less educated gunmen to carry out his violent plans. When confronted by Rocky earlier in the film, he breaks into a sweat.

Bogart's supporting roles were strong and pivotal ones for the most part, but rarely were important enough to classify him much higher than supporting actors like Allen Jenkins or Lionel Stander. Opposite Cagney in the two aforementioned films or opposite Robinson in *Kid Galahad*, *Bullets or Ballots*, or *Brother Orchid*, Bogart was allowed to be the really bad bad-man, the one without any redeeming value. When George Raft turned down the lead in new director John Huston's *The Maltese Falcon* (1941), however, another, more rewarding screen persona was exhibited by the actor.

Bogart fell very neatly into the lead role of Sam Spade, a cool, shifty detective whose mind is working rapidly, but whose composure is slow to shake. Spade is a consummate detective character, one who is cool, cunning, unafraid, and, ultimately, successful in spite of all that he must do to achieve this success. Since his emerging victoriousness is for the right, it is applauded. Since it deals with his having to turn in the woman he loves, it is tragically romantic. These are elements Bogart was unable to present in the succession of Duke Mantee clones he had essayed in a wealth of fair-to-good supporting roles since *The Petrified Forest*. With *The Maltese Falcon* he gave us a composite of traits from his gangster portrayals and seasoned them with new traits more befitting a character the likes of Sam Spade. Thus *The Maltese Falcon* is the beginning of Bogart's career from the perspective that so many of the ensuing roles he played were of prime importance to all of cinema history, this role as Sam Spade perhaps the most essential of all (and a good example of film noir).

The character of Sam Spade was defined by Bogart's performance as a low-key, humorous, sexual, cunning being. While these qualities can be associated with virtually any detective role of the forties, it is Bogart's Sam Spade portrayal that utilized these qualities best to shape his performance. Sam Spade is a good guy, but a very shady sort of good guy—the narrative making allegations to sexual endeavors with his partner Miles Archer's wife as well as Spade's own secretary. But these sexual allegations are further enhanced by the sexism of the Spade and Archer detective agency. They are first interested in the case brought before them by Mary Astor's character as a result of sex (Miles calling the case as his own, "I saw her first"). Of course once Miles is murdered and Spade joins the case not only to replace Miles but also to uncover his murderer, he uses his own sexuality to gather further information from the woman (she is unable to resist Spade's passions). And, finally, Spade is the real man who turns this woman in to the police, his parting line being, "I hope they don't hang you, precious, by that sweet neck."

Such sexist qualities make it rather bemusing that Bogart (especially this film character) became so popular during the seventies when feminism awareness was at a high point in the United States (especially on college campuses where the Bogart canon was most dearly embraced). Spade exudes all of the masculine qualities that became typical in World War II–era films that featured leading men who did not have the raw power of a John Wayne. He is the epitome of the unmasculine-to-display-emotion concept. He treats women as sex objects. He is small, yet unafraid. And he is a man among other men. The men that Spade deals with in the context of the story are Joel Cairo (Peter Lorre), a slimy homosexual stereotype; the Fat Man (Sydney Greenstreet), an obese, out-of-shape nonviolent sort; and Wilmer (Elisha Cook), a hotheaded and inexperienced young gunslinger whose overzealousness causes him to be so impulsive that he stumbles into all of the wily Spade's traps.

Sam Spade is a man in total control of the situation, while brimming with all of the qualities that best characterize masculinity without violence. The character of Rick in *Casablanca*, however, has these same qualities only in the role of the altruistic male, his altruisim (as per most World War II–era Hollywood films) stemming from patriotism. Through flashbacks we see Rick's romance with Illsa (Ingrid Bergman) and its sad end. Rick, who was jilted, is bitter. This bitterness causes him to be sardonic.

NAZI: Why did you come to Casablanca?
RICK: I came to Casablanca for the waters.
NAZI: There are no waters in Casablanca.
RICK: I was misinformed.

Rick is reunited with Illsa, and their romance can rekindle. This, however, would mean she must leave her fighting patriot husband Victor Laslow (Paul Henreid) and, thus, perhaps contribute to his downfall. Rick sees his success as too important to tamper with and, during the legendary climactic airport scene, tells Illsa she must go with Laslow: "If you don't get on that plane you'll regret it. Maybe not today, maybe not tomorrow, but soon and for the rest of your life."

Bogart and Ingrid Bergman in the Oscar-winning *Casablanca* (Warner Bros., 1943).

Rick's patriotism causes him to leave Illsa, jilting her in much the same way she did him, and for much the same reason. In contrast to how Sam Spade jilted the woman he loved (sending her to prison for killing his partner, whom he didn't even like), Rick's jilting was a study in sensitivity as well as patriotism (which is why it still works today in these more enlightened times). Rick had already established the fact that Illsa loved him more than she did Laslow, and proved to himself that she would take him over Laslow (satisfying the male ego that was damaged by her jilting him years before).

As a result, he was sensitive enough to release her from his sexual domain and convince her to return to her husband for reasons that go beyond the fact that "the efforts of three little people don't amount to a hill of beans in this crazy world."

Laslow's standing for some liberal causes makes *Casablanca* a more interesting and less dated wartime film than the majority of Hollywood flag-wavers of this period. Thus Rick's releasing Illsa to Laslow is for a much bigger cause than his own. And, finally, the climax of the film culminates with Rick allegedly preferring the asexual world occupied predominantly by males. In the film's last moments he is walking off into the fog, his bruised male ego now satisfied, his friendship with officer Louis (Claude Rains) all that he needs.

So Bogart shows, through both Sam Spade and Rick, that he is a survivor in a male-dominated world of social Darwinism. Where the gangsters are rebels who chose crime to combat a society that they could not be comfortable in, these characters are good-guy representations of the Bogart rebel persona who have shrewdly devised ways to maintain status while still rebelling against established societal mores. They are masculine men in a world of less masculine male types. They are able to overcome their shortcomings in a world where others cannot. They need not choose crime to combat the establishment, because they are able to rise above the establishment and present themselves as stronger in the context of society rather than against it.

Bogart's example of postwar paranoia came through an extension of his old gangster persona in the character of Fred C. Dobbs from John Huston's *The Treasure of the Sierra Madre* (1948). It also may very well be his greatest performance. Dobbs has many layers to his personality, his existence being a group of psychoses that cause him to change into a quivering, giggling madman within the course of the film's narrative.

The story, dealing with three men and their quest for gold, could be a statement against the capitalism that was invading the American people's consciousness just after the war (suburbia going up, material gain replacing the Depression and war shortages and rationing). Gold is at the forefront of Dobbs' mind, with greed and mistrust creeping in as well. This directly relates to the commie paranoia that also invaded the minds of Americans during this time, the fear that the Russians would invade and take from them their capitalistic lifestyles that allowed them the material things they had gone without for two decades. Dobbs was a very manic, animated character, much different from Sam Spade. He did not exude quiet cool, but was very emotional and short-tempered. Above all he was insecure. These qualities testify to the resilience of the Bogart tough-guy screen persona as it adapts itself to the collective sensibilities of middle-aged Americans of this time.

Bogart as the crazed Fred C. Dobbs in John Huston's *The Treasure of the Sierra Madre* (Warner Bros., 1948).

Dobbs does not trust even his two companions, believing that they will attempt to take his share as well as their own. His greed mirrors the keeping-up-with-the-Joneses' greed that was manifesting itself in postwar America. The commie paranoia of the time caused people to mistrust even their closest companions and workmates. Lou Costello was said to have insisted that all of his underlings sign a loyalty oath denouncing communism, socialism, and all other radical political concepts that threatened American conservatism. Dobbs is exuding the very paranoia that Americans felt at the time this film was made. While his companions are trustworthy, Dobbs' own greed and paranoia drive him into fits of mania and, eventually, death due to his own impulsive actions. The role was yet another variation of tortured masculinity that Bogart played, this time with even greater emphasis on the sad paranoiac state of most alleged "real men" of the period.

Despite past nominations, it wasn't until his performance as Charlie Allnut in *The African Queen* that Bogart was honored with an Oscar at the Academy Awards ceremonies. While easily the most offbeat role Bogey essayed, as well as among the most noted, it is also one of the least interesting. The character is a drunken old sea dog at the mercy of a bitchy, sharp-tongued woman (Katharine Hepburn), whose resemblance to puritanical egotism makes her character more abrasive than endearing. Bogey's Allnut character is a cross between a heroic male type in the Charleton Heston mold, and the lovable bumbling type more akin to the talents of Wallace Beery. While Bogart's acting prowess allows him to alternate between these two diverse personalities with a certain success, it is still somewhat dubious in that the heroic aspects seem out of place in the context of the drunken bumbler character, and vice versa. And overall, Allnut's kowtowing to the Hepburn character says less for feminism than it does for puritanism.

The consummate Bogart performance of the fifties was his role as the psychopathic killer who, with his cronies, holds a conservative American family hostage in *The Desperate Hours* (1955). Above the often faraway fears of communism, the true horror for an upper-middle-class family during the conservative fifties would be to have their nuclear family unit disrupted, along with the masculinity of the father figure (always the absolute pillar of strength—both emotional and physical—at this time) to be challenged, forcing the father to back down, even crawl.

Bogart plays Duke Mantee or Baby Face Martin had they lived to see middle age. He is not only mean and bitter, but downright maniacal in his hatred for the successful businessman who he terrorizes (Fredric March), especially calling attention to the fact that his bullying is a way of getting even with all of society's successful cattle for shunning the rebellious intruder. Bogart and March both play tortured masculine types who cling to their masculine roles so as not to lose their tough-guy status to the other. Bogart feels inadequate when facing a man who was tough enough to succeed in a suppressive society. March must stand tall for his family, especially his young son who believes in his father as a hero, like the indestructible ones in movies and on television who seem to laugh at broken bones and death. He experiences filial anguish upon seeing his father back down.

With *The Desperate Hours*, Bogart's career had come full circle as far as his tough-guy roles were concerned. Once again he was the rebellious gangster, only unlike the up-and-coming Mantee, he now played an aging, even more bitter badman. But this role was not a culmination. That was left for Bogart's last film, released in 1956, *The Harder They Fall*. (The actor died in January 1957, having suffered from cancer for some time. This last film was made while in great pain from the disease.) The culmination of his career came in the role of a disillusioned sportswriter who, instead of embracing corruption, chooses to battle it. The character Bogart plays here is a combination of his badmen and his good guys. Only he's older, and with age must modify either characterization. He does not run around with a handgun pulling capers, but instead becomes involved with a corrupt prizefighting racket (raging against society again, this time the society that disrupted his sportswriting career). But this Bogart, unlike all the others, exhibits human compassion for the foreign fighter whom the gangsters have used in the ring, paying off his opponents so that he would believe himself to be a successful pugilist. The role showed the ultimate tough guy that Bogart played. The quiet cool of Sam Spade and the rebellious attitudes of Duke Mantee (rebelling this time against the corruption rather than as a part of it) were combined in this role, the compassion coming from the aging process that mellowed this tough guy into a beaten man who still retains his masculine traits. It was a fitting farewell to the screen by one of its finest performers.

Unlike, say, Clint Eastwood, who mastered a tough-guy persona from only one perspective, Humphrey Bogart presented the tough guy on several levels. He gave a certain depth to each of his performances, even offbeat roles like the priest in *The Left Hand of God* and the juvenile reform warden in *Crime School*. While always putting the indelible Bogart stamp on each of his roles, he exhibited a wide range of expressions and attitudes within the tough-guy realm, seriously influencing scores of actors in similar roles. His Sam Spade character in *The Maltese Falcon* started a trend of detective roles in "B" movies (Boston Blackie, Crime Doctor, Philo Vance, et al.). His performance as Rick in *Casablanca* began the masculinity-through-little-emotion school of acting, while still remaining, through its closing scene, a harbinger for the sensitive male roles of the seventies. His Captain Queeg in *Caine Mutiny* was the blueprint for every psychopath in Hollywood thereafter (Anthony Perkins' Norman Bates character from Alfred Hitchcock's *Psycho* owes a great deal to Bogart's performance as Queeg).

Humphrey Bogart is one of the most important actors in the history of American film for a variety of reasons, not the least of which is his ability to present so many variations on the theme of male toughness in the cinema.

Humphrey Bogart Filmography

Broadway's Like That (Vitaphone, 1930) one reel
Directed by Murray Roth, Written by Stanley Rauh.
With Humphrey Bogart, Ruth Etting, Joan Blondell.

A Devil with Women (Fox, 1930) 76 minutes
Directed by Irving Cummings, Screenplay by Dudley Nichols and Henry M. Johnson (based on the novel by Clements Ripley), Photographed by Arthur Todd, Edited by Frank Hull.
With Victor McLaglen, Mona Maris, *H.B.*, Luana Alcaniz, Michael Vavitch, Soledad Jiminez, Mona Rico, John St. Polis, Robert Edeson.

Up the River (Fox, 1930) 92 minutes
Directed by John Ford, Screenplay by Maurine Watkins, Photographed by Joseph August, Edited by Frank Hull.
With Spencer Tracy, Claire Luce, Warren Hymer, *H.B.*, William Collier, Sr., Joan Marie Lawes, George MacFarlane, Gaylord Pendelton, Sharon Lynne, Noel Francis, George Montgomery, Robert Burns, John Swor, Robert E. O'Connor, Louise MacIntosh, Richard Keane, Johnnie Walker, Pat Somerset, Morgan Wallace.

Body and Soul (Fox, 1931) 83 minutes
Directed by Alfred Santell, Screenplay by Jules Furthman (from the play *Squadrons* by A. E. Thomas which itself was based on the story *Big Eyes and Little Mouth* by Elliot White Springs), Photographed by Glen McWilliams, Edited by Paul Weatherwax.
With Charles Farrell, Elissa Landi, Myrna Loy, *H.B.*, Donald Dillaway, Crauford Kent, Pat Somerset, Ian MacLaren, Dennis D'Auburn, Douglas Dray, Harold Kinney, Bruce Warren.

Bad Sister (Universal, 1931) 71 minutes
Directed by Hobart Henley, Screenplay by Raymond Schrock and Tom Reed (based on the story *The Flirt* by Booth Tarkington), Photographed by Karl Freund, Edited by Ted Kent.

With Conrad Nagel, Sidney Fox, Bette Davis, ZaSu Pitts, Slim Summerville, Charles Winninger, Emma Dunn, *H.B.*, Bert Roach, Dave Durand.

Women of All Nations (Fox 1931) 72 minutes
Directed by Raoul Walsh, Screenplay by Barry Connors (based on characters created by Laurence Stallings and Maxwell Anderson), Photographed by Lucian Andrott, Edited by Jack Dennis.
With Victor McLaglen, Edmund Lowe, Greta Nissen, El Brendel, Fifi Dorsay, Marjorie White, T. Roy Barnes, Bela Lugosi, *H.B.*, Joyce Compton, Jesse DeVorska, Charles Judels, Marion Lessing, Ruth Warren.

A Holy Terror (Fox, 1931) 53 minutes
Directed Irving Cummings, Screenplay by Ralph Block (based on the novel by Max Brand), Photographed by George Schneiderman, Edited by Ralph Dixon.
With George O'Brien, Sally Eilers, Rita La Roy, *H.B.*, James Kirkwood, Stanley Fields, Robert Warwick, Richard Tucker, Earl Pingree.

Love Affair (Columbia, 1932) 68 minutes
Directed by Thornton Freeland, Screenplay by Jo Swerling and Dorothy Howell, Photographed by Ted Tetzlaff, Edited by Jack Dennis.
With Dorothy Mackaill, *H.B.*, Jack Kennedy, Barbara Leonard, Astrid Allwyn, Bradley Page, Halliwell Hobbes, Hale Hamilton, Harold Minjir.

Big City Blues (Warner Bros., 1932) 65 minutes
Directed by Mervyn LeRoy, Screenplay by Ward Morehouse and Lillie Hayward (based on the play *New York Town* by Morehouse), Photographed by James Van Trees, Edited by Ray Curtis.
With Joan Blondell, Eric Linden, Inez Courtney, Evalyn Knapp, Guy Kibbee, Lyle Talbot, Gloria Shea, Walter Catlett, Jobyna Howland, *H.B.*, Josephine Dunn, Grant Mitchell, Thomas Jackson, Ned Sparks, Sheila Terry, Tom Dugan.

Three on a Match (First National, 1932) 64 minutes
Directed by Mervyn LeRoy, Screenplay by Lucien Hubbard (based on a story by Kubec Glasmon and John Bright), Photographed by Sol Polito, Edited by Ray Curtis.
With Joan Blondell, Warren William, Ann Dvorak, Bette Davis, Lyle Talbot, *H.B.*, Patricia Ellis, Sheila Terry, Grant Mitchell, Glenda Farrell, Frankie Darro, Clara Blandick, Hale Hamilton, Dick Brandon, Junior Johnson, Anne Shirley.

Midnight (Universal, 1934) 80 minutes
Directed by Chester Erskine, Screenplay by Erskine (based on the play by Paul and Claire Sifton).
With Sidney Fox, O. P. Heggie, Henry Hull, Margaret Wycherly, Lynne Overman, Katherine Wilson, Richard Whorf, *H.B.*, Granville Bates, Cora Witherspoon.
Note: Retitled *Call It Murder.* Now in public domain.

The Petrified Forest (Warner Bros., 1936) 83 minutes
Directed by Archie Mayo, Screenplay by Charles Kenyon and Delmer Daves (based on the play by Robert Sherwood), Photographed by Sol Polito, Edited by Owen Marks.
With Leslie Howard, Bette Davis, Genevieve Tobin, Dick Foran, *H.B.*, Joe Sawyer, Porter Hall, Charles Grapewin, Paul Harvey, Eddie Acuff, Adrian Morris, Nina Campana, Slim Thompson, John Alexander.

Bullets or Ballots (Warner Bros., 1936) 81 minutes
Directed by William Keighley, Screenplay by Seton Miller (based on a story by him and Zartin Mooney), Photographed by Hal Mohr, Edited by Jack Kilifer.
With Edward G. Robinson, Joan Blondell, *H.B.*, Barton MacLane, Fran McHugh, Joseph King, Richard Purcell, George E. Stone, Louise Beavers, Henry O'Neill, Frank Faylen, William Pawley.

Two Against the World (Warner Bros., 1936) 64 minutes
Directed by William McGann, Screenplay by Mike Jacoby (based on the play *Five Star Final* by Louis Weitzenkorn), Photographed by Sid Hickox, Edited by Frank McGee.
With *H.B.*, Beverly Roberts, Helen MacKellar, Henry O'Neill, Linda Perry, Carlyle Moore, Virginia Brissac, Robert Middlemass, Clay Clement.
Note: Filmed earlier as *Five Star Final* with Edward G. Robinson.

China Clipper (Warner Bros., 1936) 85 minutes
Directed by Ray Enright, Screenplay by Frank Wead, Photographed by Arthur Edeson, Edited by Owen Marks.
With Pat O'Brien, Beverly Roberts, Ross Alexander, *H.B.*, Marie Wilson, Henry B. Walthall, Joseph Crehan, Joseph King, Addison Richards, Ruth Robinson, Carlyle Moore, Lyle Moraine, Dennis Moore.

Isle of Fury (Warner Bros., 1936) 60 minutes
Directed by Frank McDonald, Screenplay by Robert Andrews and William Jacobs (based on the novel *The Narrow Corner* by W. Somerset Maugham), Photographed by Frank Good, Edited by Warren Low.
With *H.B.*, Margaret Lindsay, Donald Woods, Paul Graetz, Gordon Hart, E. E. Clive, George Regas, Sidney Bracy, Tetsu Komai, Miki Morita.

Black Legion (Warner Bros., 1937) 83 minutes
Directed by Archie Mayo, Screenplay by Abem Finkel and William Wiser Haines (based on the original story by Robert Lord), Photographed by George Barnes, Edited by Owen Marks.
With *H.B.*, Dick Foran, Erin O'Brien-Moore, Ann Sheridan, Robert Barrat, Helen Flint, Joy Sawyer, Addison Richards, Eddie Acuff, Clifford Soubier, Paul Harvey.

The Great O'Malley (Warner Bros., 1937) 71 minutes
Directed by William Dieterle, Screenplay by Milton Krims and Tom Reed (based on the story *The Making of O'Malley* by Gerald Beaumont), Photographed by Ernest Haller, Edited by Warren Low.

Bogart as Duke Mantee in *Petrified Forest* (Warner Bros., 1936).

With Pat O'Brien, Sybil Jason, *H.B.*, Ann Sheridan, Frieda Inescort, Donald Crisp, Henry O'Neil, Craig Reynolds, Hobart Cavanaugh, Gordon Hart, Mary Gordon, Michael Colcord, Frank Sheridan, Lillian Harmer, Delmer Watson, Frank Reicher.

Marked Woman (Warner Bros., 1937)
Directed by Lloyd Bacon, Screenplay by Robert Rossen and Abem Finkel, Photographed by George Barnes, Edited by Jack Kilifer.
With Bette Davis, *H.B.*, Lola Lane, Isabel Jewell, Eduardo Cianelli, Rosaline Marquis, Mayo Mathot, Jayne Bryan, Allen Jenkins, John Litel, Ben Welden.

Kid Galahad (Warner Bros., 1937) 101 minutes
Directed by Michael Curtiz, Screenplay by Seton Miller (based on the novel by Francis Wallace), Photographed by Tony Gaudio, Edited by George Amy.

With Edward G. Robinson, Bette Davis, *H.B.*, Wayne Morris, Jane Bryan, Harry Carey, William Haade, Soledad Jiminez, Joe Cunningham, Ben Welden, Joseph Creehan, Veda Ann Borg, Frank Faylen, Harland Tucker, Bob Evans, Hank Hankinson, Bob Nestell, Jack Kranz, George Blake, Mary Sunde.

Note: Retitled *Battling Bellhop* for television. Remade by Elvis Presley under the same title.

San Quentin (Warner Bros., 1937) 70 minutes
Directed by Lloyd Bacon, Screenplay by Peter Milne and Humphrey Cobb (based on the original story by Robert Tasker and John Bright), Photographed by Sid Hickox, Edited by William Holmes.

With Pat O'Brien, *H.B.*, Ann Sheridan, Barton MacLane, Joe Sawyer, Veda Ann Borg, James Robbins, Joe King, Gordon Oliver, Garry Owen, Marc Lawrence, Emmett Vogan, William Pawley, Al Hill, Max Wagner, George Lloyd, Ernie Adams.

Dead End (United Artists, 1937 — a Samuel Goldwyn Production) 93 minutes
Directed by William Wyler, Screenplay by Lillian Hellman (based on the play by Sidney Kingsley), Photographed by Gregg Toland, Edited by Daniel Mandell.

With Sylvia Sydney, Joel McCrea, *H.B.*, Wendy Barrie, Claire Trevor, Allen Jenkins, Marjorie Main, Billy Halop, Leo Gorcey, Huntz Hall, Bobby Jordan, Gabe Dell, Bernard Punsley, Charles Peck, Minor Watson, James Burke, Ward Bond, Elisabeth Risdon, Esther Dale, George Humbert, Marcelle Corday, Charles Halton.

Note: The first screen appearance of Halop, Gorcey, Hall, Punsley, Jordan, and Dell, who were thereafter known as the Dead End Kids until changing studios in 1940.

Stand-In (United Artists, 1937) 90 minutes
Directed by Tay Garnett, Screenplay by Gene Towne and Graham Barker (based on the *Saturday Evening Post* serial by Clarence Budington Kelland), Photographed by Charles Clarke, Edited by Otto Lovering and Dorothy Spencer.

With Leslie Howard, Joan Blondell, *H.B.*, Alan Mowbray, Maria Shelton, Jack Carson, Tully Marshall.

Swing Your Lady (Warner Bros., 1938) 79 minutes
Directed by Ray Enright, Screenplay by Joseph Schrank and Maurice Leo (based on the play by Kenyon Nicholson and Charles Robinson), Photographed by Arthur Edeson, Edited by Jack Kilifer.

With *H.B.*, Frank McHugh, Louise Fazenda, Nat Pendelton, Penny Singleton, Allen Jenkins, Leon Weaver, Frank Weaver, Elvira Weaver, Ronald Reagan, Daniel Boone Savage, Hugh O'Connell, Tommy Bupp, Sonny Bupp, Joan Howard, Sue Moore, Olin Howard, Sammy White.

Note: The film Bogart cited as his worst.

Crime School (Warner Bros., 1938) 86 minutes
Directed by Lewis Seller, Screenplay by Crane Wilbur and Vincent Sherman (based on an original story by Crane Wilbur), Photographed by Arthur Todd, Edited by Terry Morse.
With *H.B.*, Gale Page, Billy Halop, Bobby Jordan, Leo Gorcey, Huntz Hall, Bernard Punsley, Gabe Dell, George Offerman, Jr., Weldon Heyburn, Cy Kendall, Charles Trowbridge, Spencer Charters, Donald Briggs, Frank Jacquet, Helen MacKellar, Al Bridge, Sybil Harris.

Men Are Such Fools (Warner Bros., 1938) 70 minutes
Directed by Busby Berkeley, Screenplay by Norman Reilly Raine and Horace Jackson (based on the novel by Faith Baldwin), Photographed by Sid Hickox, Edited by Jack Kilifer.
With Wayne Morris, Priscilla Lane, *H.B.*, Hugh Herbert, Johnnie Davis, Mona Barrie, Marcia Ralston, Gene Lockhart, Kathleen Lockhart, Donald Briggs, Renie Riano, Claude Allister.

The Amazing Doctor Clitterhouse (Warner Bros., 1938)
Directed by Anatole Litvak, Screenplay by John Wexley and John Huston (based on the play by Barre Lyndon), Photographed by Tony Gaudio, Edited by Warren Low.
With Edward G. Robinson, Claire Trevor, *H.B.*, Allen Jenkins, Donald Crisp, Gale Page, Henry O'Neill, John Litel, Thurston Hall, Maxie Rosenbloom, Bert Hanlon, Curt Bois, Ward Bond, Vladimir Sokoloff.

Racket Busters (Warner Bros., 1938) 71 minutes
Directed by Lloyd Bacon, Screenplay by Robert Rossen and Leonardo Bercovici, Photographed by Arthur Edeson, Edited by James Gibbons.
With *H.B.*, George Brent, Gloria Dickson, Allen Jenkins, Walter Abel, Henry O'Neill, Penny Singleton, Anthony Averill, Oscar O'Shea, Elliot Sullivan, Fay Helm, Joseph Downing, Norman Willis, Don Rowan.

Angels with Dirty Faces (Warner Bros., 1938) 97 minutes
Directed by Michael Curtiz, Screenplay by John Wexley and Warren Duff (based on a story by Rowland Browne), Photographed by Sol Polito, Edited by Owen Marks.
With James Cagney, Pat O'Brien, *H.B.*, George Bancroft, Ann Sheridan, Billy Halop, Leo Gorcey, Huntz Hall, Bobby Jordan, Gabe Dell, Bernard Punsley, Joseph Downing, John Hamilton, Frankie Burke, William Tracy.

King of the Underworld (Warner Bros., 1938) 69 minutes
Directed by Lewis Seller, Screenplay by George Bricker and Vincent Sherman (based on the *Liberty Magazine* serial *Doctor Socrates*, by W. R. Burnette), Photographed by Sid Hickox, Edited by Frank Dewar.
With *H.B.*, Kay Francis, James Stephenson, John Eldridge, Jessie Busley,

Arthur Aylesworth, Ray Brown, Harland Tucker, Ralph Remley, Charlie Foy, Murray Alper, Joe Devlin, Elliot Sullivan.

The Oklahoma Kid (Warner Bros., 1939) 80 minutes
Directed by Lloyd Bacon, Screenplay by Warren Duff, Robert Buckner and Edward E. Paramore (based on a story by Paramore and Wally Klein), Photographed by James Wong Howe, Edited by Owen Marks.
With James Cagney, *H.B.*, Rosemary Lane, Donald Crisp, Harvey Stephens, Hugh Sothern, Charles Middleton, Ed Pawley, Ward Bond, Lew Harvey, Trevor Bardette, John Miljan, Arthur Aylesworth, Irving Bacon, Joe Devlin, Wade Boteler.

Dark Victory (Warner Bros., 1939) 106 minutes
Directed by Ed Goulding, Screenplay by Casey Robinson (based on the play by George Emerson Brewer, Jr., and Bertram Bloch), Photographed by Ernest Haller, Edited by William Holmes.
With Bette Davis, George Brent, Geraldine Fitzgerald, *H.B.*, Ronald Reagan, Henry Travers, Cora Witherspoon, Dorothy Peterson, Virginia Brissac, Charles Richman, Herb Rawlinson, Leonard Mudie, Fay Helm, Lottie Williams.

You Can't Get Away with Murder (Warner Bros., 1939) 78 minutes
Directed by Lewis Seiler, Screenplay by Robert Buckner, Don Ryan and Kenneth Gamut (based on the play *Chalked Out* by Warden Lewis E. Lawes and John Finn), Photographed by Sol Polito, Edited by James Gibbon.
With *H.B.*, Billy Halop, Gale Page, John Litel, Henry Travers, Harvey Stephens, Harold Huber, Joe Sawyer, Joseph Downing, George E. Stone, Joseph King, Joseph Crehan, John Ridgely, Herb Rawlinson.

The Roaring Twenties (Warner Bros., 1939) 106 minutes
Directed by Raoul Walsh, Screenplay by Jerry Wald, Richard Macaulay, and Robert Rossen (based on a story by Mark Hellinger), Photographed by Ernest Haller, Edited by Jack Kilifer.
With James Cagney, Priscilla Lane, *H.B.*, Gladys George, Jeffrey Lynn, Frank McHugh, Paul Kelly, Elisabeth Risdon, Ed Keane, Joe Sawyer, Joseph Crehan, George Meeker, John Hamilton, Robert Elliot, Eddie Chandler, Abner Biberman, Vera Lewis, Bert Hanlon, Murray Alper, Dick Wessel, George Humbert, Ben Welden.

The Return of Doctor X (Warner Bros., 1939) 63 minutes
Directed by Vincent Sherman, Screenplay by Lee Katz (based on the story *The Doctor's Secret* by William J. Makin), Photographed by Sid Hickox, Edited by Thomas Pratt.
With Wayne Morris, Rosemary Lane, *H.B.*, Dennis Morgan, John Litel, Lya Lys, Huntz Hall, Charles Wilson, Vera Lewis, Howard Hickman, Olin Howard, Arthur Aylesworth, Jack Mower, Creighton Hale, John Ridgely, Joseph Crehan, Glenn Langan, William Hopper.

Invisible Stripes (Warner Bros., 1939) 82 minutes

Directed by Lloyd Bacon, Screenplay by Warren Duff (based on a story by Jonathan Finn which in turn was based on the book by Warden Lewis E. Lawes), Photographed by Ernest Haller, Edited by James Gibbon.

With George Raft, Jane Bryan, William Holden, H.B., Flora Robson, Paul Kelly, Lee Patrick, Henry O'Neill, Frankie Thomas, Moroni Olsen, Margot Stevenson, Marc Lawrence, Joseph Downing, Leo Gorcey, William Haade, Tully Marshall.

Virginia City (Warner Bros., 1940) 121 minutes

Directed by Michael Curtiz, Screenplay by Robert Buckner, Photographed by Sol Polito, Edited by George Amy.

With Errol Flynn, Miriam Hopkins, Randolph Scott, H.B., Frank McHugh, Alan Hale, Guinn "Big Boy" Williams, John Litel, Douglass Dumbrille, Moroni Olsen, Dick Jones, Frank Wilcox, Russell Simpson, Victor Kilian, Charles Middleton.

It All Came True (Warner Bros., 1940) 97 minutes

Directed by Lewis Seiler, Screenplay by Michael Fessier, and Lawrence Kimble (based on the story *Better Than Life* by Louis Bromfield), Photographed by Ernest Haller, Edited by Thomas Richards.

With Ann Sheridan, Jeffrey Lynn, H.B., ZaSu Pitts, Una O'Connor, Jessie Busley, John Litel, Grant Mitchell, Felix Bressart, Charles Judels.

Brother Orchid (Warner Bros., 1940) 90 minutes

Directed by Lloyd Bacon, Screenplay by Earl Baldwin (based on the *Colliers* magazine story by Richard Connell), Photographed by Tony Gaudio, Edited by William Holmes.

With Edward G. Robinson, Ann Sothern, H.B., Ralph Bellamy, Allen Jenkins, Charles D. Brown, Cecil Kellaway, Morgan Conway, Richard Lane, Paul Guilfoyle.

They Drive by Night (Warner Bros., 1940) 93 minutes

Directed by Raoul Walsh, Screenplay by Jerry Wald and Richard Macaulay (based on the novel *Long Haul* by A. I. Bezzedries), Photographed by Arthur Edeson, Edited by Thomas Richards.

With George Raft, Ann Sheridan, Ida Lupino, H.B., Gale Page, Alan Hale, Roscoe Karns, John Litel, George Tobias, Henry O'Neill, Charles Halton.

High Sierra (Warner Bros., 1941) 100 minutes

Directed by Raoul Walsh, Screenplay by John Huston and W. R. Burnett (based on the novel by Burnett), Photographed by Tony Gaudio, Edited by Jack Kilifer.

With H.B., Ida Lupino, Alan Curtis, Arthur Kennedy, Joan Leslie, Henry Hull, Henry Travers, Jerome Cowan, Minna Gombell, Barton MacLane, Elisabeth Risdon, Cornel Wilde, Donald MacBride, Willie Best, Isabel Jewell, Paul Harvey, Spencer Charters, George Meeker.

The Wagons Roll at Night (Warner Bros., 1941), 84 minutes
Directed by Ray Enright, Screenplay by Fred Niblo and Barry Trivers (based on the novel *Kid Galahad* by Francis Wallace), Photographed by Sid Hickox, Edited by Fredrick Richards.
With *H.B.*, Sylvia Sydney, Eddie Albert, Joan Leslie, Sig Ruman, Cliff Clark, Charley Foy, Frank Wilcox, John Ridgely, Clara Blandick, Aldrich Bowker, Garry Owen, Jack Mower, Frank Mayo.

The Maltese Falcon (Warner Bros., 1941) 100 minutes
Directed by John Huston, Screenplay by Huston (based on the novel by Dashiell Hammett), Photographed by Arthur Edeson, Edited by Thomas Richards.
With *H.B.*, Mary Astor, Peter Lorre, Sydney Greenstreet, Lee Patrick, Jerome Cowan, Elisha Cook, Ward Bond, Gladys George, Barton MacLane, James Burke, Murray Alper, John Hamilton, Emory Parnell, Walter Huston.
Note: A sequel, *The Black Bird*, was made in 1975, alleged to be the exploits of Sam Spade, Jr., played by George Segal. Lee Patrick and Elisha Cook recreated their roles from the original.

All Through the Night (Warner Bros., 1942) 107 minutes
Directed by Vince Sherman, Screenplay by Leonard Spigelgass and Edwin Gilbert (based on a story by Leo Rosten and Spigelgass), Photographed by Sid Hickox, Edited by Rudi Fehr.
With *H.B.*, Kaaren Verne, Conrad Veidt, Peter Lorre, William Demarest, Jane Darwell, Frank McHugh, Jackie Gleason, Phil Silvers, Judith Anderson, Wallace Ford, Barton MacLane, Ed Brophy, Martin Kosleck, Jean Ames, Ludwig Stossel.

The Big Shot (Warner Bros., 1942) 82 minutes
Directed by Lewis Seiler, Screenplay by Bertram Millhauser, Photographed by Sid Hickox, Edited by Jack Kilifer.
With *H.B.*, Irene Manning, Richard Travis, Susan Peters, Stanley Ridges, Minor Watson, Chick Chandler, Joseph Downing, Howard da Silva.

Across the Pacific (Warner Bros., 1942) 97 minutes
Directed by John Huston, Screenplay by Richard Macaulay (based on the *Saturday Evening Post* serial *Aloha Means Goodbye* by Robert Carson), Photographed by Arthur Edeson, Edited by Frank Magee.
With *H.B.*, Mary Astor, Sydney Greenstreet, Charles Halton, Victor Sen Yung, Roland Got, Lee Tung Foo, Frank Wilcox, Monte Blue.

Casablanca (Warner Bros., 1943) 102 minutes
Directed by Michael Curtiz, Screenplay by Julius and Philip Epstein and Howard Koch (based on the play *Everbody Comes to Rick's* by Murray Bennett and Joan Alison), Photographed by Arthur Edeson, Edited by Owen Marks.
With *H.B.*, Ingrid Bergman, Paul Henreid, Claude Rains, Conrad Veidt,

Sydney Greenstreet, Peter Lorre, S. Z. Sakall, Madelaine Le Beau, Dooley Wilson, Joy Page, John Qualen, Leonid Kinsky, Helmut Dantine, Curt Bois, Marcel Dalio, Corinna Mura, Ludwig Stossel, Ilka Gruning, Charles La Torre, Frank Puglia, Dan Seymour, Grant Feest.

Action in the North Atlantic (Warner Bros., 1943) 127 minutes
Directed by Lloyd Bacon, Screenplay by John Howard Lawson, Photograhed by Ted McCord, Edited by Thomas Pratt and George Amy.
With *H.B.*, Raymond Massey, Alan Hale, Julie Bishop, Ruth Gordon, Sam Levene, Dane Clark, Peter Whitney, Dick Hogan, Minor Watson, J. M. Kerrigan, Kane Richmond.

Sahara (Columbia, 1943) 97 minutes
Directed by Zoltan Korda, Screenplay by John Howard Lawson and Korda (adaption by James O'Hanlon from a story by Phillip McDonald), Photographed by Rudolph Mate, Edited by Charles Nelson.
With *H.B.*, Bruce Bennett (Herman Brix), J. Carrol Naish, Lloyd Bridges, Rex Ingram, Richard Nugent, Dan Duryea, Carl Harbord.

Passage to Marseille (Warner Bros., 1944) 109 minutes
Directed by Michael Curtiz, Screenplay by Casey Robinson and Jack Moffitt (based on the novel *Men Without Country* by Charles Nordhoff and James Norman Hall), Photographed by James Wong Howe, Edited by Owen Marks.
With *H.B.*, Claude Rains, Michele Morgan, Phillip Dorn, Sydney Greenstreet, Peter Lorre, George Tobias, Helmut Dantine, John Loder, Victor Francen, Vladimir Sokoloff, Eduardo Cianelli.

To Have and Have Not (Warner Bros., 1945) 100 minutes
Directed by Howard Hawks, Screenplay by Jules Furthman and William Faulkner (based on the novel by Ernest Hemingway), Photographed by Sid Hickox, Edited by Christian Nyby.
With *H.B.*, Walter Brennan, Lauren Bacall, Dolores Moran, Hoagy Carmichael, Walter Molnar, Sheldon Leonard, Marcel Dalio.

Conflict (Warner Bros., 1945) 86 minutes
Directed by Curtis Bernhardt, Screenplay by Arthur T. Hornman and Dwight Taylor (based on a story by Robert Siodmak and Alfred Neumann), Photographed by Merritt Gerstad, Edited by David Weisbart.
With *H.B.*, Alexis Smith, Sydney Greenstreet, Rose Hobart, Charles Drake, Grant Mitchell, Patrick O'Moore, Ann Shoemaker, Frank Wilcox.

The Big Sleep (Warner Bros., 1946) 114 minutes
Directed by Howard Hawks, Screenplay by William Faulkner (based on the novel by Raymond Chandler), Photographed by Sid Hickox, Edited by Christian Nyby.

With *H.B.*, Lauren Bacall, John Ridgely, Martha Vickers, Dorothy Malone, Peggy Knudsen, Regis Toomey, Charles Waldron.
Note: Remade in 1978.

Dead Reckoning (Columbia, 1947) 100 minutes
Directed by John Cromwell, Screenplay by Oliver H. P. Garrett and Steve Fisher (adaption by Allen Rivkin based on a story by Gerald Adams and Sidney Biddel), Photographed by Leo Tover, Edited by Charles Nelson.
With *H.B.*, Lizabeth Scott, Morris Carnovsky, Charles Cane, William Prince, Marvin Miller, Wallace Ford, James Bell, George Chandler.

The Two Mrs. Carrolls (Warner Bros., 1947) 99 minutes
Directed by Peter Godfrey, Screenplay by Thomas Job (based on the play by Martin Vale), Photographed by Peverell Marley, Edited by Fredrick Richards.
With *H.B.*, Barbara Stanwyck, Alexis Smith, Nigel Bruce, Isobel Elsom, Patrick O'Moore, Ann Carter, Anita Bolster, Barry Bernard, Colin Campbell, Peter Godfrey.

Dark Passage (Warner Bros., 1947) 106 minutes
Directed by Delmer Daves, Screenplay by Daves (based on the novel by David Goodsis), Photographed by Sid Hickox, Edited by David Weisbart.
With *H.B.*, Lauren Bacall, Bruce Bennett (Herman Brix), Agnes Moorehead, Tom D'Andrea, Clifton Young, Douglas Kennedy.

The Treasure of the Sierra Madre (Warner Bros., 1948) 126 minutes
Directed by John Huston, Screenplay by Huston (based on the novel by B. Traven), Photographed by Ted McCord, Edited by Owen Marks.
With *H.B.*, Walter Huston, Tim Holt, Bruce Bennett (Herman Brix), Barton MacLane, Alphonso Bedoya, A. Soto Rangel, Manuel Donde, Jose Torvay, Margarito Luna, Jacqueline Dalya, Robert Blake, John Huston, Jack Holt.

Key Largo (Warner Bros., 1948) 101 minutes
Directed by John Huston, Screenplay by Huston and Richard Brooks (based on the play by Maxwell Anderson), Photographed by Karl Freund, Edited by Rudi Fehr.
With *H.B.*, Edward G. Robinson, Lauren Bacall, Lionel Barrymore, Claire Trevor, Thomas Gomez, Harry Lewis, John Rodney, Marc Lawrence, Dan Seymour, Monte Blue, William Haade, Jay Silverheels, Rodric Redwing.

Knock on Any Door (Columbia, 1949) 100 minutes
Directed by Nicholas Ray, Screenplay by Daniel Taradash and John Monks, Jr. (based on the novel by Willard Motley), Photographed by Burnett Guffey, Edited by Viola Lawrence.
With *H.B.*, John Derek, George Macready, Allene Roberts, Susan Perry, Mickey Knox, Barry Kelley, Cara Williams, Jimmy Conlin, Sumner Williams, Sid Melton, Pepe Hern, Dewey Martin.

Tokyo Joe (Columbia, 1949) 88 minutes
   Directed by Stuart Heisler, Screenplay by Cyril Hume and Bertram
Milhauser (adaption by Walter Doniger, based on a story by Steve Fisher),
Photographed by Charles Lawton, Jr., Edited by Viola Lawrence.
   With *H.B.*, Alexander Knox, Florence Marly, Sessue Hayakawa, Jerome
Courtland, Gordon Jones, Teri Shumada, Hideo Mori.

Chain Lightning (Warner Bros., 1950) 94 minutes
   Directed by Stuart Heisler, Screenplay by Liam O'Brien and Vincent
Evans (based on a story by J. Redmond Prior), Photographed by Ernest Haller,
Edited by Thomas Reily.
   With *H.B.*, Eleanor Parker, Raymond Massey, Richard Whorf, James
Brown, Roy Roberts, Morris Ankrum, Fay Baker, Fred Sherman.

In a Lonely Place (Columbia, 1950) 94 minutes
   Directed by Nicholas Ray, Screenplay by Andrew Solt (adaption by Ed-
mund North based on the novel by Dorothy B. Hughes), Photographed by
Burnett Guffey, Edited by Viola Lawrence.
   With *H.B.*, Gloria Grahame, Frank Lovejoy, Carl Benton Reid, Art Smith,
Jeff Donnell, Martha Stewart, Robert Warwick, Morris Ankrum, William
Chang, Steve Geray.

The Enforcer (Warner Bros., 1951) 87 minutes
   Directed by Bretaigne Windust, Screenplay by Martin Rackin,
Photographed by Robert Burks, Edited by Fred Allen.
   With *H.B.*, Zero Mostel, Ted De Corsia, Everett Sloane, Roy Roberts,
Lawrence Tolan, King Donovan, Bob Steele, Adelaide Klein, Don Beddow,
Tito Vuolo, John Kellogg, Jack Lambert, Patricia Jonner.

The African Queen (United Artists, 1951) 105 minutes; Technicolor
   Directed by John Huston, Screenplay by Huston and James Agee (based
on the novel by C. S. Forester), Photographed by Jack Cardiff, Edited by Ralph
Kemplen.
   With *H.B.*, Katharine Hepburn, Robert Morley, Peter Bull, Theodore
Bikel, Walter Gotell, Gerald Onn, Peter Swanick, Richard Marner.

Deadline—USA (20th Century–Fox, 1951) 87 minutes
   Directed by Richard Brooks, Screenplay by Brooks, Photographed by
Milton Krasner, Edited by William B. Murphy.
   With *H.B.*, Ethel Barrymore, Kim Hunter, Ed Begley, Warren Stevens,
Paul Stewart, Martin Gabel, Joe De Santis, Joyce MacKenzie, Audrey Christie,
Fay Baker, Jim Backus, Carleton Young.

Battle Circus (MGM, 1953) 90 minutes
   Directed by Richard Brooks, Screenplay by Brooks (based on the story by
Allen Rivkin and Laura Kerr), Photographed by John Alton, Edited by George
Boemler.

With *H.B.*, June Allyson, Keenan Wynn, Robert Keith, William Campbell, Perry Sheehan, Patricia Tiernan, Jonathan Cott.

Beat the Devil (United Artists, 1954) 93 minutes
Directed by John Huston, Screenplay by Huston and Truman Capote (based on the novel by James Helvick), Photographed by Oswald Morris, Edited by Ralph Kemplen.
With *H.B.*, Jennifer Jones, Gina Lollobrigida, Robert Morley, Peter Lorre, Edward Underdown, Ivor Banard, Bernard Lee, Marco Tulli.

The Caine Mutiny (Columbia, 1954) 125 minutes; Technicolor
Directed by Edward Dmytryk, Screenplay by Stanley Roberts and Michael Blankfort (based on the novel by Herman Wouk), Photographed by Franz Planer, Edited by William Lyon and Henry Batista.
With *H.B.*, Jose Ferrer, Van Johnson, Fred MacMurray, Robert Francis, May Wynn, Tom Tully, E. G. Marshall, Arthur Franz, Lee Marvin, Warner Anderson, Claude Akins, Katherine Warren, Jerry Paris.

Sabrina (Paramount, 1954) 113 minutes
Directed by Billy Wilder, Written by Wilder, Sam Taylor and Ernie Lehman (based on the play *Sabrina Fair* by Taylor), Photographed by Charles Lang, Edited by Arthur Schmidt.
With *H.B.*, Audrey Hepburn, William Holden, Walter Hampden, John Williams, Martha Hyer, Joan Vohs, Marcel Dallo, Marcel Hilliare.

The Barefoot Contessa (United Artists, 1954) 128 minutes; Technicolor
Directed by Joseph L. Mankiewicz, Screenplay by Mankiewicz, Photographed by Jack Cardiff, Edited by William Hornbeck.
With *H.B.*, Ava Gardner, Edmund O'Brien, Marius Gording, Valentina Cortesa, Rosanno Brazzi, Elizabeth Sellers, Warren Stevens.

We're No Angels (Paramount, 1955) 103 minutes; Technicolor/Vistavision
Directed by Michael Curtiz, Screenplay by Ranald MacDougall (based on the play *La Cuisine des Anges* by Albert Husson), Photographed by Loyal Griggs, Edited by Arthur Schmidt.
With *H.B.*, Aldo Ray, Peter Ustinov, Joan Bennett, Basil Rathbone, Leo G. Carroll, John Baer, Gloria Talbott, Lea Penman.

The Left Hand of God (20th Century–Fox, 1955) 87 minutes: Color by Deluxe/Cinemascope
Directed by Edward Dmytryk, Screenplay by Alfred Hayes (based on the novel by William Barrett), Photographed by Franz Planer, Edited by Dorothy Spencer.
With *H.B.*, Gene Tierney, Lee J. Cobb, Agnes Moorehead, E. G. Marshall, Jean Porter, Carl Benton Reid, Victor Sen Young, Phillip Ahn, Benson Fong, Richard Cutting, Leon Lontoc.

The Desperate Hours (Paramount, 1955) 112 minutes

Directed by William Wyler, Screenplay by Joseph Hayes (based on his novel and play), Photographed by Lee Garmes, Edited by Robert Swink.

With *H.B.*, Fredric March, Arthur Kennedy, Martha Scott, Dewey Martin, Gig Young, Mary Murphy, Richard Eyer, Robert Middleton, Alan Reed, Bert Freed, Ray Collins, Whit Bissell, Ray Teal.

The Harder They Fall (Columbia, 1956) 109 minutes

Directed by Mark Robson, Screenplay by Phillip Yordan (based on the novel by Budd Schulberg), Photographed by Burnett Guffey, Edited by Jerome Thoms.

With *H.B.*, Rod Steiger, Jan Sterling, Mike Lane, Max Baer, Sr., Jersey Joe Wolcott, Edward Andrews, Harold J. Stone, Carlos Montalban, Nehemiah Persoff, Felice Orlandi, Herbie Faye, Rusty Lane, Jack Albertson, Val Avery, Tommy Herman, Vinnie DeCarlo.

Bogart made guest appearances in the following:
Thank Your Lucky Stars (1943), **Report from the Front** (1944), **Hollywood Victory Caravan** (1945), **Two Guys from Milwaukee** (1946), **Always Together** (1948), **U.S. Savings Bond Trailer** (1952).

George Raft

George Raft is perhaps the most genuine of all movie tough guys. The character traits in his screen roles mirror those he held as a person with actual underworld connections. Raft had the sinister qualities of Cagney, Bogart, and Robinson, but these were actors whose knowledge of gangland was by proxy. Raft, on the other hand, was friends with several alleged mobsters. Thus his gangster persona on film embodies many special qualities not found in the other actors' portrayals. Raft also lent his offscreen code of ethics to his screen roles, incorporating a personal code of honor for all of the gangsters he played. There were several stipulations in any Raft contract, including exactly how the character treated women and children, how knowledgeable of the crime system the character was, what his idea of crime was (Raft adamantly refusing to play an out-and-out rat), and the like. While this code of honor incorporated a certain authenticity in his roles (e.g., Raft refusing to have his character steal mail, realizing that an actual badman would naturally shun a potential federal rap), it also caused him to be a bit too selective, turning down several roles that increased the star status of many performers, especially Humphrey Bogart.

Raft's personal life was every bit as tumultuous as his screen life, and both spiraled downhill rather quickly. Due mainly to his refusal to play so many important roles as a result of his selective code of honor as well as his somewhat idiosyncratic reasoning, Raft's star faded just as the gangster characters soon were no longer a trend in the American cinema. There was little, if any, resilience in Raft's acting, his screen image remaining a very short extension of his gangster persona, and not fitting to changing trends as did the career of Bogart. Some critics speculate that this is due to Raft's turning down key roles in films like *The Maltese Falcon* and *Casablanca*, both of which enhanced Bogart's status. Indeed it would be fascinating to know the results had Raft accepted even one of the roles he so casually turned down.

But then Raft's code of honor would have hindered a few of these roles, most notably when speculating upon his refusal to play the Baby Face

Martin role in *Dead End*. Raft balked at Martin's becoming a hero/idol of the juvenile delinquents in the film and wanted to include a scene where he discussed the gangster's life as lonely and dismal. This, of course, is the antithesis of the Martin character as per the narrative, and such a scene would have thrown the film's entire point out of kilter. But Raft, adherent to his beliefs in how the underworld should be presented on screen, turned the role down.

It is not a surprise that Raft, who stumbled into films as a result of his dancing prowess, made his first big impact as a gangster in Howard Hawks' *Scarface: Shame of a Nation*, which featured Paul Muni in the Capone-esque title role. Raft says little in his supporting role, yet his sinister presence was so substantial that the director would often have him stand in the background during certain scenes simply to enhance the tension. Hawks developed the bit of business of flipping a coin for Raft so that in the scenes where he is not in an active role, Raft stood by looking sinister, flipping a coin as a nervous habit for his character. This device was so substantial that it became Raft's trademark. It also established Raft as an important tough guy in films, but this would cause more anguish than anything else. Raft's friendships with real-life underworld figures like Bugsy Siegel were pivotal in causing him to insist upon showing redeeming values in all of the badmen he would portray.

In the adventure *Souls at Sea* (1937), for instance, where Raft plays a generally likable character who romances beautiful Olympe Bradna, his character still has a sinister past steeped in slave trading. Gary Cooper played the stern, compassionate fellow who provided the anchor for the Raft character. Cooper was the class act while Raft was the bad guy whose goodness was brought out initially by Cooper's favorable idealism and, later, by his love for Bradna. Raft's portrayal of this romantic tough guy earned him an Oscar nomination and further enhanced his career.

Perhaps Raft's best post–*Scarface* role was as Stacey in *Each Dawn I Die* (1939). Here he is an imprisoned gangster who finds that Frank Ross (James Cagney) is the only "square guy" he ever met. It is through the Cagney character that Stacey learns there is honesty in humanity, but it exists outside of the underworld he has known for so long. He is an idealistic gangleader, intelligent enough to call the shots rather than merely to do the gunslinging. When he escapes, with Ross's help, he promises to find the men who framed the reporter, and eventually does so even at the cost of his own life. Such altruism is pure Warner Bros. crime-drama hokum, but *Each Dawn I Die* nevertheless remains a very powerful film. It deals with psychological aspects of maximum security prisoners as well as the super-ficiality of tough dialogue and shoot-out sequences. Raft's altruistic role is important in that it exemplifies the very type of gangleader he sought to por-tray, one who is not cold and heartless. His end is an ending of idealistic

George Raft and Olympe Bradna in *Souls at Sea* (Paramount, 1937).

triumph, sort of a glorification of the George Raft interpretation of the
gangster: tough, brutal, but with a big heart lurking beneath the hard
exterior. A bit difficult to believe, but on film it somehow worked.

Raft's need to show the good side of bad men was best suited to presenting them as misunderstood, not unlike some screen presentations of
adolescence. Thus the gangster is a veritable case of arrested adolescence,
still unable to deal successfully with the establishment and follow rules that
he finds suppressive. Raft, then, seemed most comfortable in roles that
made viewers sympathize with his character. This idea is best exhibited in
Invisible Stripes, in which Raft is a parolee whose attempts at becoming a
good citizen are thwarted by society's refusal to forgive his past injustices.
His prison record keeps him from finding substantial employment, Raft

now having to deal with the prejudice of those persons who do the hiring.

As with *Souls at Sea*, Raft plays a likable character with a sordid past. The viewer knows the character and realizes he is worth forgiving for past wrongs, while the employers depicted in *Invisible Stripes* have not met him and do not realize he has paid his debt to society and now genuinely wants to go straight. *Invisible Stripes* is not one of the better gangster melodramas, nor is Raft's portrayal a very convincing portrait of a period parolee. But we do have the rudiments of the Raft screen persona once again presented from the perspective that the actor himself had designed.

Raft's best work pales in comparison to those films which star Cagney, Bogart, or Robinson despite elements that make them, at the very least, entertaining. By the forties and fifties, Raft's continuous refusal of important screen roles had relegated him to "B" programmers like *Loan Shark*, *Race Street*, and *The Man from Cairo*. Friends like Harry Ritz of the Ritz Brothers comedy act complained about lonely Raft calling them at all hours of the day and night. Despite an amusing parody of the movie gangster in Billy Wilder's *Some Like It Hot*, Raft's career never improved. By the sixties he had resorted to cameos in everything from the mindless teen comedy *For Those Who Think Young* to a pair of Jerry Lewis films, *The Ladies Man* and *The Patsy*. All of these walk-on bits were rather demeaning to the actor, but he was nevertheless grateful to filmmakers like Lewis for giving him a break, although he probably realized that Lewis, a longtime fan, was just being kind due to pitying a former movie idol.

In 1965 Raft was booked on a charge of income tax evasion. Had the case gone to trial and Raft been found guilty, the movie tough guy would have done time at San Quentin. He wept openly in court upon finding that he did not have to go to prison, and was said to have wept during interviews whenever he discussed his lack of screen work. Perhaps Raft had finally realized the poor career moves he made. In 1969, New Year's Eve, he appeared on Johnny Carson's "Tonight Show" to reminisce about the old days. He was grateful for being allowed to appear, as this former dapper movie star, at 74, had nowhere to go to ring in the new decade. The seventies, however were no kinder to Raft, who spent most of his time watching television. One friend speculated that had it not been for his TV, Raft would have committed suicide.

George Raft died in 1980, after years of plummeting in this fashion. But his importance is still valid in that his contributions to formulating the tough guy he played added many new and different traits to the way such characters were presented. Raft will always remain one of the quintessential tough guys of thirties Hollywood films due to his indelible shaping of his gangster roles by giving the characters elements of compassion and understanding, showing them as victims rather than heartless beasts whose actions were due simply to an unexplained inherent evil. It is this essential contribution to the cinema for which he will be best remembered.

George Raft Filmography

Queen of the Night Clubs (Warner Bros., 1929) 70 minutes
Directed by Bryan Foy, Screenplay by Murray Roth and Addison Burkhart, Photographed by Eddie Du Par.
With Texas Guinan, John Davidson, Lila Lee, Arthur Houseman, Eddie Foy, Jr., Jack Norworth, G.R., Jimmie Phillips, William Davison.

Quick Millions (Fox, 1931) 72 minutes
Directed by Rowland Brown, Screenplay by Courtney Terrett (from a story by Brown and Terrett), Photographed by Joseph August.
With Spencer Tracy, Marguerite Churchill, Sally Eilers, Robert Burns, John Wray, G.R., Warner Richmond, John Swor.

Hush Money (Fox, 1931), 68 minutes
Directed by Sidney Lanfield, Screenplay by Phillip Klien and Courtney Terrett, Photographed by John Seitz.
With Joan Bennett, Hardie Albright, Owen Moore, Myrna Loy, C. Henry Gordon, G.R., Douglas Cosgrove, Hugh White.

Palmy Days (United Artists, 1931) 71 minutes
Directed by Eddie Sutherland, Screenplay by Eddie Cantor, Morrie Ryskind, and David Freeman, Photographed by Norbert Brodine and Gus Peterson.
With Eddie Cantor, Charlotte Greenwood, Spencer Charters, Barbara Weeks, G.R., Paul Page, Harry Woods, Charles Middleton.

Taxi (Warner Bros., 1932) 68 minutes
Directed by Roy Del Ruth, Screenplay by Kubec Glasmon and John Bright (based on the play *The Blind Spot* by Kenyon Nicholson), Photographed by James Van Trees, Edited by James Gibbons.
With James Cagney, Loretta Young, George E. Stone, Guy Kibbee, David Landau, Ray Cooke, Leila Bennett, G.R., Matt McHugh.

Scarface: Shame of a Nation (United Artists, 1932) 99 minutes
Directed by Howard Hawks, Screenplay by Ben Hecht, Seton I. Miller, John Lee Mahin, W. R. Burnett, and Fred Palsey, Photographed by Lee Garmes and L. William O'Connell, Edited by Edward D. Curtis.

With Paul Muni, Ann Dvorak, Karen Morley, Osgood Perkins, Boris Karloff, C. Henry Gordon, *G.R.*, Purnell Pratt, Vince Barnett.

Night World (Universal, 1932) 59 minutes
Directed by Hobart Henley, Screenplay by Richard Schayer (from a story by P. J. Wolfson), Photographed by Merritt Gerstad, Edited by Maurice Pavar.
With Lew Ayers, Mae Clarke, Dorothy Reiver, Boris Karloff, Russell Hopton, Bert Roach, Dorothy Peterson, *G.R.*

Love Is a Racket (Warner Bros., 1932) 72 minutes
Directed by William Wellman, Screenplay by Courtney Terrett (adapted from the novel by Rian James), Photographed by Sid Hickox, Edited by William Holmes.
Douglas Fairbanks, Jr., Ann Dvorak, Frances Dee, Lee Tracy, Lyle Talbot, Warren Hymer, *G.R.*, Andre Luguet, William Burress.

Dancers in the Dark (Paramount, 1932) 74 minutes
Directed by David Burton, Screenplay by Herman J. Mankiewicz (based on the play *Jazz King* by James Ashmore Creelman, adapted by Brian Maslow and Howard Emmett Rogers), Photographed by Karl Strauss.
With Miriam Hopkins, Jack Oakie, William Collier, Jr., Eugene Pallette, Lyda Roberti, *G.R.*, Maurice Black, Frances Moffett.

Night After Night (Paramount, 1932) 70 minutes
Directed by Archie Mayo, Screenplay by Vincent Lawrence (based on the play *Single Night* by Louis Bromfield), Photographed by Ernest Haller.
With *G.R.*, Mae West, Constance Cummings, Wynne Gibson, Alison Skipworth, Roscoe Karns, Al Hill, Louis Calhern.

If I Had a Million (Paramount, 1932) 88 minutes
Directed by Ernst Lubitsch, Norman Taurog, Stephen Roberts, Norman MacLeod, James Cruze, William Seiter, H. Bruce Humberstone, Screenplay by Claude Binyon, Whitney Bolton, Malcom Stuart Boylan, John Bright, Sidney Buchanan, Lester Cole, Isabel Dawn, Boyce DeGaw, Walter DeLeon, Oliver H.P. Garrett, Harvey Gates, Grover Jones, Ernst Lubitsch, Lawton Mackall, Joseph L. Mankiewicz, William Slavens McNutt, Seton I. Miller, and Tiffany Thayer, based on a story by Robert D. Andrews.
With Gary Cooper, *G.R.*, W. C. Fields, Charles Laughton, Charlie Ruggles, Mary Boland, Jack Oakie, Francis Dee, Alison Skipworth, ZaSu Pitts, May Robson, Gene Raymond, Lucien Littlefield, Richard Bennett.

Undercover Man (Paramount, 1932) 74 minutes
Directed by James Flood, Screenplay by Garrett Fort and Francis Faragoh (based on the story by John Wilstach, adaption by Thomson Burtis), Photographed by Victor Milner.
With *G.R.*, Nancy Carroll, Lew Cody, Roscoe Karns, Noel Francis, Gregory Ratoff, David Landau, Paul Porcasi, Leyland Hodgson.

Pick Up (Paramount, 1933) 76 minutes

Directed by Marion Gering, Screenplay by S. K. Lauren and Agnes Brand Leahy (based on the story by Vina Delmar), Photographed by David Abel.

With Sylvia Sydney, *G.R.*, William Harrigan, Lillian Bond, Clarence Wilson, George Meeker, Louise Beavers, Florence Dudley.

The Midnight Club (Paramount, 1933) 67 minutes

Directed by Alexander Hall, Screenplay by Seton I. Miller and Leslie Charteris (based on the story by E. Phillips Oppenheimer).

With *G.R.*, Clive Brook, Helen Vinson, Alison Skipworth, Sir Guy Standing, Alan Mowbray, Ferdinand Gottschalk, Ethel Griffies.

The Bowery (United Artists, 1933) 90 minutes

Directed by Raoul Walsh, Screenplay by Howard Estabrook and James Gleason (based on the novel *Chuck Connors* by Michael L. Simmons and Betsy Roth Solomon), Photographed by Barney McGill, Edited by Allen McNeil.

With Wallace Beery, *G.R.*, Fay Wray, Jackie Cooper, Pert Kelton, George Walsh, Oscar Apfel, Harry Huber, Fletcher Norton.

Bolero (Paramount, 1934) 80 minutes

Directed by Wesley Ruggles, Screenplay by Horace Jackson (based on the story by Carey Wilson, Kubec Glasmon and Ruth Ridenour), Photographed by Leo Tover, Edited by Hugh Bennett.

With *G.R.*, Carole Lombard, Sally Rand, Francis Drake, William Frawley, Ray Milland, Gloria Shea, Gertrude Michael.

All of Me (Paramount, 1934) 70 minutes

Directed by James Flood, Screenplay by Sidney Buchman and Thomas Mitchell (based on the play *Chrysalis* by Rose Porter), Photographed by Victor Milner, Edited by Otto Lovering.

With Fredric March, Miriam Hopkins, *G.R.*, Helen Mack, Nella Walker, William Collier, Jr., Gilbert Emery, Blanche Frederici.

The Trumpet Blows (Paramount, 1934) 72 minutes

Directed by Stephen Roberts, Screenplay by Bartlett Cormack, Photographed by Harry Fischbeck, Edited by Ellsworth Hoaglund.

With *G.R.*, Adolphe Menjou, Frances Drake, Sidney Toler, Edward Ellis, Nydia Westman, Douglas Wood, Lillian Elliot.

Limehouse Blues (Paramount, 1934) 66 minutes

Directed by Alexander Hall, Screenplay by Arthur Phillips and Cyril Hume, Photographed by Harry Fischbeck, Edited by Ellsworth Hoaglund.

With *G.R.*, Jean Parker, Anna Mae Wong, Kent Taylor, Montague Love, Billy Bevan, John Rogers, Robert Lorraine, E. Alyn Warren.

Rumba (Paramount, 1935) 71 minutes

Directed by Marion Gering, Screenplay by Howard J. Greene, Photographed by Ted Tetzlaff, Edited by Hugh Bennett.

With *G.R.*, Carole Lombard, Margo, Lynne Overman, Monroe Owsley, Iris Adrian, Gail Patrick, Samuel S. Hinds, Virginia Hammond.

Stolen Harmony (Paramount, 1935) 74 minutes
Directed by Alf Werker, Screenplay by Leon Gordon, Harry Ruskin, Claude Binyon, and Lewis Foster, Photographed by Harry Fischbeck, Edited by Otho Lovering.
With *G.R.*, Ben Bernie, Grace Bradley, Goodee Montgomery, Lloyd Nolan, Ralfe Harolde, William Cagney, William Pawley.

The Glass Key (Paramount, 1935) 80 minutes
Directed by Frank Tuttle, Screenplay by Kathryn Scola, Kubec Glasmon, Harry Ruskin (based on the story by Dashiell Hammett), Photographed by Henry Sharp, Edited by Hugh Bennett.
With *G.R.*, Edward Arnold, Claire Dodd, Rosalind Keith, Charles Richmond, Robert Gleckler, Guinn Williams, Ray Milland.
Note: Remade in 1944 with Alan Ladd, Brian Donlevy, and Veronica Lake.

Every Night at Eight (Paramount, 1935) 80 minutes
Directed by Raoul Walsh, Screenplay by Gene Towne and Graham Baker (based on the story *Three on a Mike* by Stanley Garvey), Photographed by James Van Trees, Edited by W. Donn Hayes.
With *G.R.*, Alice Faye, Patsy Kelly, Frances Langford, Harry Barris, Walter Catlett, Jimmie Hollywood, Henry Taylor, Eddie Bartel.

She Couldn't Take It (Columbia, 1935) 89 minutes
Directed by Tay Garnett, Screenplay by Oliver H.P. Garrett, Photographed by Leon Shamroy, Edited by Gene Havlick.
With *G.R.*, Joan Bennett, Walter Connolly, Billie Burke, Lloyd Nolan, Wallace Ford, James Blakely, Alan Mowbray, Bill Tannen.

It Had to Happen (20th Century–Fox, 1936) 79 minutes
Directed by Roy Del Ruth, Screenplay by Howard Ellis Smith and Kathryn Scola, Photographed by Peverell Marley.
With *G.R.*, Leo Carrillo, Rosalind Russell, Alan Dinehart, Arthur Hohl, Arline Judge, Pierre Watkin, Paul Stanton, Jim Burke.

Yours for the Asking (Paramount, 1936) 68 minutes
Directed by Alexander Hall, Screenplay by Evan Green, Harlan Ware, Phillip MacDonald, Photographed by Theodor Sparkuhl.
With *G.R.*, Dolores Costello Barrymore, Ida Lupino, Reginald Owen, James Gleason, Edgar Kennedy, Lynne Overman, Skeets Gallagher.

Souls at Sea (Paramount, 1937) 92 minutes
Directed by Henry Hathaway, Screenplay by Grover Jones and Dale Van Every (based on a story by Ted Lesser), Photographed by Charles Lang, Jr., Edited by Ellsworth Hoaglund.

With *G.R.*, Gary Cooper, Frances Dee, Henry Wilcoxon, Olympe Bradna, Harry Carey, Robert Cummings, Porter Hall, George Zucco, Joseph Schildkraut, Virginia Weidler, Lucien Littlefield, Tully Marshall.

Spawn of the North (Paramount, 1938) 110 minutes
Directed by Henry Hathaway, Screenplay by Jules Furthman and Talbot Jennings, Photographed by Charles Lang, Jr., Edited by Ellsworth Hoaglund.
With *G.R.*, Henry Fonda, Dorothy Lamour, Akim Tamiroff, John Barrymore, Louise Platt, Lynne Overman, Fuzzy Knight.

You and Me (Paramount, 1938) 90 minutes
Directed by Fritz Lang, Screenplay by Virginia Van Upp (based on a story by Norman Krasna), Photographed by Charles Lang, Jr., Edited by Paul Weatherwax.
With *G.R.*, Sylvia Sydney, Harry Carey, Barton MacLane, Warren Hymer, Roscoe Karns, Robert Cummings, George E. Stone.

The Lady's from Kentucky (Paramount, 1939) 67 minutes
Directed by Alexander Hall, Screenplay by Malcom Stuart Boylan, Photographed by Theodor Sparkuhl, Edited by Harvey Johnson.
With *G.R.*, Ellen Drew, Hugh Herbert, ZaSu Pitts, Louise Beavers, Lou Payton, Forrester Harvey, Edward Pawley, Gilbert Emery.

Each Dawn I Die (Warner Bros., 1939) 92 minutes
Directed by William Keighley, Screenplay by Norman Reilly Raine, Charles Perry, and Warren Duff (based on the novel by Jerome Odlum), Photographed by Arthur Edeson, Edited by Thomas Richards.
With James Cagney, *G.R.*, Jane Bryan, George Bancroft, Maxie Rosenbloom, Stanley Ridges, Alan Baxter, Victor Jory.

I Stole a Million (Universal, 1939) 80 minutes
Directed by Frank Tuttle, Screenplay by Nathaniel West, Photographed by Milt Krasner, Edited by Ed Curtiss.
With *G.R.*, Claire Trevor, Dick Foran, Henry Armetta, Victor Jory, Joe Sawyer, Robert Elliot, Stanley Ridges, Irving Bacon.

Invisible Stripes (Warner Bros., 1939) 82 minutes
Directed by Lloyd Bacon, Screenplay by Warren Duff (based on a story by Jonathan Finn which in turn was based on the book by Warden Lewis E. Lawes), Photographed by Ernest Haller, Edited by James Gibbon.
With *G.R.*, Jane Bryan, William Holden, Humphrey Bogart, Flora Robson, Paul Kelly, Lee Patrick, Henry O'Neill, Frankie Thomas, Moroni Olsen, Margot Stevenson, Marc Lawrence, Joseph Downing, Leo Gorcey, William Haade, Tully Marshall.

They Drive by Night (Warner Bros., 1940) 93 minutes
Directed by Raoul Walsh, Screenplay by Jerry Wald and Richard

Raft (center) flanked by William Holden (left) and Humphrey Bogart in *Invisible Stripes* (Warner Bros., 1939).

Macaulay (based on the novel *Long Haul* by A. I. Bezzedries), Photographed by Arthur Edeson, Edited by Thomas Richards.

    With *G.R.*, Ann Sheridan, Ida Lupino, Humphrey Bogart, Gale Page, Alan Hale, Roscoe Karns, John Litel, George Tobias, Henry O'Neill, Charles Halton.

Manpower (Warner Bros., 1941)

    Directed by Raoul Walsh, Screenplay by Richard Macaulay and Jerry Wald, Photographed by Ernest Haller, Edited by Ralph Dawson.

    With *E.G.*, George Raft, Marlene Dietrich, Alan Hale, Frank McHugh, Eve Arden, Barton MacLane, Walter Catlett, Joyce Compton, Lucia Carroll, Ward Bond, Egon Brecher, Cliff Clark, Joseph Crehan.

The House Across the Bay (United Artists, 1940) 88 minutes

    Directed by Archie Mayo, Screenplay by Kathryn Scola, Photographed by Merritt Gerstad, Edited by Dorothy Spencer.

    With *G.R.*, Joan Bennett, Lloyd Nolan, Gladys George, Walter Pidgeon, June Knight, Billy Wayne, Peggy Shannon, Cy Kendall.

Broadway (Universal, 1942) 91 minutes

    Directed by William Seiter, Screenplay by Felix Jackson and John Bright, Photographed by George Barnes.

With *G.R.*, Pat O'Brien, Janet Blair, Broderick Crawford, Marjorie Rambeau, Ann Gwynne, S. Z. Sakall, Ed Brophy, Gus Schilling.

Background to Danger (Warner Bros., 1943) 80 minutes
Directed by Raoul Walsh, Screenplay by W. R. Burnett (based on the novel *Uncommon Danger* by Eric Ambler), Photographed by Tony Gaudio, Edited by Jack Kilifer.
With *G.R.*, Brenda Marshall, Sydney Greenstreet, Peter Lorre, Ona Massen, Turhan Bey, Willard Robertson, Kurt Katch, Daniel Ocko.

Follow the Boys (Universal, 1944) 122 minutes
Directed by Eddie Sutherland, Screenplay by Lou Breslow and Gertrude Purcell, Photographed by David Abel and John Fulton, Edited by Fred Feishans, Jr.
With *G.R.*, Vera Zorina, Charles Grapewin, Grace MacDonald, Charles Butterworth, George MacReady, Elizabeth Patterson, Regis Toomey, several guest stars including Orson Welles, W. C. Fields, Donald O'Connor, and the Andrews Sisters.

Nob Hill (20th Century–Fox, 1945) 95 minutes; Color
Directed by Henry Hathaway, Screenplay by Wanda Tuchock and Norman Reilly Raine, Photographed by Edward Cronjager, Edited by Harmon Jones.
With *G.R.*, Joan Bennett, Vivian Blaine, Peggy Ann Garner, Alan Reed, Emil Coleman, Edgar Barrie, Joseph Greene, Don Costello.

Johnny Angel (RKO, 1945) 79 minutes
Directed By Edwin L. Marin, Screenplay by Steve Fisher (based on the novel *Mr. Angel Comes Aboard* by Charles Gordin Booth, Adapted by Frank Gruber), Photographed by Harry Wild, Edited by Les Millibrook.
With *G.R.*, Claire Trevor, Signe Hasso, Lowell Gilmore, Hoagy Carmichael, Marvin Miller, Margaret Wycherly, J. Farrell MacDonald.

Whistle Stop (United Artists, 1946) 85 minutes
Directed by Leonide Moguy, Screenplay by Philip Yordan, Photographed by Russell Metty, Edited by Gregg Tallas.
With *G.R.*, Ava Gardner, Victor MacLaglen, Tom Conway, Jorja Cutright, Florence Bates, Charles Judels, Jimmy Ames.

Nocturne (RKO, 1946) 88 minutes
Directed by Edwin L. Martin, Screenplay by Jonathan Lattimer, Photographed by Harry Wild, Edited by Elmo Williams.
With *G.R.*, Lynn Bari, Virginia Huston, Joseph Pevney, Myrna Dell, Edward Ashley, Walter Sande, Mabel Page, Bernard Hoffman.

Christmas Eve (United Artists, 1947) 90 minutes
Directed by Edwin L. Martin, Screenplay by Laurence Stallings, Photographed by Gordon Avil, Edited by James Smith.

With *G.R.*, George Brent, Randolph Scott, Joan Blondell, Virginia Field, Dolores Moran, Ann Harding, Reginald Denny.

Intrigue (United Artists, 1947) 90 minutes
Directed by Edwin L. Martin, Screenplay by Barry Trivers and George Slavin, Photographed by Lucien Andriot, Edited by George Arthur.
With *G.R.*, June Havoc, Helena Carter, Tom Tully, Marvin Miller, Dan Seymour, Phillip Ahn, Marc Krah, Jay C. Flippen.

Race Street (RKO, 1948) 79 minutes
Directed by Edwin L. Marin, Screenplay by Martin Rackin (based on the story *The Twisted Road* by Maurice Davis), Photographed by J. Roy Hunt, Edited by Sam Beetley.
With *G.R.*, William Bendix, Marilyn Maxwell, Harry Morgan, Frank Faylen, Gale Robbins, Cully Richards, Mack Gray.

Johnny Allegro (Columbia, 1949) 81 minutes
Directed by Ted Tetzlaff, Screenplay by Karen DeWolf, Photographed by Joe Biroc, Edited by Jerome Thoms.
With *G.R.*, Nina Foch, George MacReady, Will Geer, Gloria Henry.

A Dangerous Profession (RKO, 1949) 79 minutes
Directed by Ted Tatzlaff, Screenplay by Martin Rackin and Warren Duff, Photographed by Robert de Grasse, Edited by Fred Knutson.
With *G.R.*, Ella Raines, Pat O'Brien, Bill Williams, Jim Backus, Roland Winters, Betty Underwood, Robert Gist.

Outpost in Morocco (United Artists, 1949) 92 minutes
Directed by Robert Florey, Screenplay by Charles Grayson and Paul de Sante-Columbe, Photographed by Lucien Andriot, Edited by George Arthur.
With *G.R.*, Marie Windsor, Akim Tamiroff, John Litel, Eduard Franz, Erno Verebes, Crane Whitley.

Red Light (United Artists, 1949) 83 minutes
Directed by Roy Del Ruth, Screenplay by George Callahan, Photographed by Bert Glennon, Edited by Richard Heermance.
With *G.R.*, Raymond Burr, Virginia Mayo, Gene Lockhart, Barton MacLane, Harry Morgan, Arthur Franz, Arthur Shields.

Lucky Nick Cain (20th Century–Fox) 87 minutes
Directed by Joseph M. Newman, Screenplay by George Callahan (based on the novel *I'll Get You for This* by James Hadley Chase, Photographed by Otto Heller, Edited by Russ Lloyd.
With *G.R.*, Colleen Gray, Enzio Staiola, Charles Goldner, Walter Rilla, Martin Benson.

Loan Shark (Lippert, 1952) 79 minutes
Directed by Seymour Friedman, Screenplay by Martin Rackin, Photographed by Joe Biroc, Edited by A. Joseph.
With *G.R.*, Dorothy Hart, Paul Stewart, John Hoyt.

I'll Get You (Lippert, 1953) 78 minutes
Directed by Seymour Friedman, Screenplay by John V. Baines, Photographed by Eric Cross, Edited by Tom Simpson.
With *G.R.*, Sally Grey, Clifford Evans, Reginald Tate.

The Man from Cairo (Lippert, 1953) 83 minutes
Directed by Ray Enright, Screenplay by Eugene Ling, Photographed by Mario Abutelli, Edited by Mario Berandrei.
With *G.R.*, Gianna Maria Canale, Massiamo Serato, Guido Celano, Irene Papas, Alfredo Varelli, Leon Leonoir, Mino Doro.

Rogue Cop (MGM, 1954) 92 minutes
Directed by Roy Rowland, Screenplay by Sydney Boehm (based on the novel by William McGivern), Photographed by John Seitz.
With Robert Taylor, Janet Leigh, *G.R.*, Steve Forrest, Anne Francis.

Black Widow (20th Century–Fox, 1954) 95 minutes; Color
Directed by Nunnally Johnson, Screenplay by Johnson (from a story by Patrick Quentin), Photographed by Charles Clark, Edited by Dorothy Spencer.
With Ginger Rogers, Van Heflin, Gene Tierney, *G.R.*, Peggy Ann Garner, Reginald Gardiner, Otto Kruger, Skip Homeier.

A Bullet for Joey (United Artists, 1955) 84 minutes
Directed by Lewis Allen, Screenplay by Geoffrey Holmes and A. J. Bezzerides, Photographed by Harry Neumann, Edited by Leon Barsha.
With Edward G. Robinson, *G.R.*, Audrey Totter, George Dolenz, Peter Hansen, Peter Van Eyck, Karen Verne, Ralph Smiley, Henri Letondal, John Cliff, Joseph Vitale, Bill Bryant, Stan Malotte, Toni Gerry.

Jet Over the Atlantic (Inter Continent, 1959) 95 minutes
Directed by Byron Haskin, Screenplay by Irving Cooper, Photographed by George Stahl, Edited by James Leicester.
With Guy Madison, Virginia Mayo, *G.R.*, Illona Massey, George MacReady, Anna Lee, Margaret Lindsay, Venetia Stevenson.

Some Like It Hot (United Artists, 1959) 120 minutes
Directed by Billy Wilder, Screenplay by Wilder and I.A.L. Diamond (based on an unpublished story by R. Thoeren and M. Logan), Photographed by Charles Lang, Jr., Edited by Arthur Schmidt.
With Jack Lemmon, Tony Curtis, Marilyn Monroe, Joe E. Brown, *G.R.*, Pat O'Brien, Nehemiah Persoff, Joan Shawlee, Billy Gray, George E. Stone, Dave Barry, Mike Mazurki, Tom Kennedy.

Rififi in Panama (Comacico, 1966) 100 minutes; Color
Directed by Denys de la Paterlliere, Screenplay by August Boudard, Photographed by Walter Wolitz, Edited by Clive Durand.
With Jean Gabin, *G.R.*, Gert Frobe, Nadja Tiller, Mirielle Darc.
Note: Also titled *Du Rififi Paname*

Skidoo (Paramount, 1968) 98 minutes; Color
Directed by Otto Preminger, Screenplay by Dorman William Cannon, Photographed by Leon Shamroy, Edited by George Rohrs.
With Jackie Gleason, Carol Channing, Frankie Avalon, Groucho Marx, *G.R.*, Frank Gorshin, Peter Lawford, Burgess Meredith.
Note: An infamous fiasco for all involved.

Five Golden Dragons (Warner–Pathé–Anglo Amalgamated, 1968) 70 minutes; Color
Directed by Jeremy Summers, Screenplay by Peter Welbeck, Photographed by John von Kotzke, Edited by Donald J. Cohen.
With Bob Cummings, Rupert Davies, Margaret Lee, Brian Donlevy, Christopher Lee, Dan Duryea, *G.R.*, Klaus Kinski.

Hammersmith Is Out (Cinerama, 1972) 114 minutes, Color
Directed by Peter Ustinov, Screenplay by Stanford Whitmore, Photographed by Richard Kline, Edited by David Blewitt.
With Elizabeth Taylor, Richard Burton, Peter Ustinov, Beau Bridges, Leon Ames, Leon Askin, *G.R.*, John Schuck, Marjorie Eaton.

Raft also made guest and cameo appearances in the following:
Stage Door Canteen (1943), **Nous Irons a Paris** (1949), **Around the World in Eighty Days** (1956), **Oceans Eleven** (1960), **The Ladies Man** (1961), **For Those Who Think Young** (1964), **The Patsy** (1964), **Casino Royale** (1967), **Sextette** (1978), **The Man with Bogart's Face** (1980).

Clark Gable

During the thirties, pollsters asked American moviegoers who they believed to be the king and queen of Hollywood. The winners were Clark Gable and Myrna Loy. Gable's name stuck due mostly to the fact that he created a legend with his screen presence, exhibiting tough-guy qualities through a character that exuded strong animal sexuality. His unabashed virility and unsubtle, straightforward approach to any and every situation epitomized the very man that women of the period found irresistible. For along with these gruff qualities was the dashing hero, the compassionate romantic, the playful fool. Gable blended these qualities within the framework of an instinctive man of action and played them in a variety of contexts, mostly dealing with pretty, passive girls and less aggressive, sexless buddies. Joan Crawford was once quoted as saying that she defied any woman playing opposite Gable to keep from feeling strong sexual urges. Women in the audience experienced the same thing, making Gable a perverse sort of harbinger to Frank Sinatra or Elvis Presley from the perspective of male sexuality.

Gable presented what was the predominant image of masculinity in American film at that time. Bogart was the portent for the neurotic male whose lack of control bled into crime and aggressiveness; Cagney was the rebellious punk; Edward G. Robinson was the manic criminal bordering on the psychotic; George Raft, the silent gangster. But Gable was the heroic, aloof he-man who could not be dragged into the modern world. He is the type that came only from dreams of envious males or romantic females. His roles accentuated the many qualities that combined to present his screen persona, and even the literary figures he portrayed (from Rhett Butler to Fletcher Christian) had the indelible Gable stamp. Now, over a quarter-century after his death, Gable is still a name that conjures up nostalgic images of Hollywood past. His characterization is one which lived joyously in a world unencumbered by the angst that male characters suffered in later films. His lack of awareness did not border at all on naiveté, instead simply detaching him from the real world and keeping him in the dream world, thus making his screen work so much of a pleasurable escape even this many years later.

One of Gable's best-remembered films is Frank Capra's multi–award winner *It Happened One Night* (Columbia, 1934). In it Gable was able to exhibit all of the qualities that made his screen image so essential: sexuality, courage, wit, passion, boldness, strength, and romanticism. His first appearance in the film presents him in a drunken stupor, telephoning his boss from a public booth and chewing him out about his thankless job. As a group gathers around him and laughs to cheer him on Gable boldly chastises his employer and then sets out to utilize his journalism expertise to find and report his own news stories for the newspaper he represents. Gable is masculinity within the thirties' middle class, soon getting mixed up with a runaway princess (Claudette Colbert) who represents female upper class. His no-nonsense manner overrules the pampered treatment this young lady of royalty is used to, and she eventually falls in love with him. Throughout the film there are many priceless sequences, the movie itself remaining one of the staples of American screwball comedy (or romantic comedy as it is now known).

It Happened One Night also allows Gable's character to spout about in a manner that especially befits macho in thirties' American film. He shows us that the poor working-class louts are far more interesting and joyous than the money-hungry capitalists. Capra's Depression-era antirich messages were always rather blatant, but through Gable he shows how a "real" man is one who can survive and celebrate life without material means. He can live by his wits, his distinctive male prowess, and his incredible idealism (when he discovers there is indeed a reward for the runaway Colbert's return, he refuses the money and only wishes that what he has invested in her be repaid).

By contrast, the man Colbert is running from is a money-hungry playboy whose passion for the arts is depicted as unmanly, marrying this aspect of his personality with his capitalistic urges. Gable, in retrospect, is the artless sort whose success as a newspaperman stems from his being in an occupation where a man must necessarily be aggressive in order to achieve. Even his harried editor begrudgingly admits that this ideal he-man is "the best newspaperman, for my money!" Gable's characteristic idealism accentuates his daring bravado and, hence, his sexuality. He epitomizes thirties macho by exhibiting all of the qualities that make up the real man. This appeals to women for reasons of sexuality, and to males due to Gable's total control over his life: job, women, social situations, and the like. The thirties male responded favorably due to Gable's presenting a fantasy surrogate who was not troubled by poverty, but instead rose above his meager financial situation, even to the point of giving a young boy his last ten bucks while commenting, "It's all right, I've got millions!"

Another method of presenting Gable's manliness in *It Happened One Night* was through the Claudette Colbert character. In order for the male to emerge as stereotypically agressive, his female companion must then be stereotypically passive. Capra carefully presented his concept of the wealthy needing the working class to survive by using thinly veiled sexism to get the point across. Colbert, the wealthy one, is hopelessly incapable of taking care of herself in any rugged or outdoor situation (typifying the feminine qualities often given to wealthy males in thirties films). Gable, the working-class hero, is able to handle himself in any situation.

We see these characters as male and female before we see them as rich and poor. Thus, upward mobility is deemed possible through associating with the rich, especially since the working class is so superior in areas outside of the world of stuffy bureaucracy. And a male can only be a man if the woman is helpless, passive, and unintelligent; for if the Colbert character was at all self-sufficient, Capra could not present upward mobility as being successful through the all-knowing ordinary man Gable represents, nor could Gable exhibit such complete masculinity by acting as bold guardian to this companion. Depression-era films in America needed to present males as omnipotent, as toughness was a prerequisite for survival in those debilitating times.

The MGM romanticization of Jack London's *Call of the Wild* (20th Century–Fox, 1935) best presented Gable in his own element, his masculinity conquering the outdoors as well as a wild beast in the form of a mongrel dog that Gable tames into a companion. His principal adversary is an unmasculine and unscrupulous sort played by Reginald Owen. His companions are chubby little Jack Oakie, whose role in the film is no more than a glorified sidekick, and beautiful Loretta Young, whose steadfastness and stubbornness are also tamed by Gable's indefatigable charm.

This is the most typical of all Gable's screen roles as it allows him to exude the manly qualities that moviegoers by this time had come to expect from him. He is a very easy figure to cling to in that he seems able to conquer any problem, be it man, beast, or nature. Such omnipotence further enhanced his legend in an era where male dominance continued to falter due to a supreme lack of prosperity. Gable continually presented the traditional view of masculinity through screen roles such as this one, allowing moviegoers to use film as more than mere escapism. Gable epitomized the type of screen character whom audiences dreamed through.

David O. Selznick's *Gone with the Wind* (MGM, 1939) has been perhaps the most ballyhooed American film, especially of the thirties, and it remains a fine example of storytelling through cinema, maintaining viewer interest for nearly four hours. Gable's Rhett Butler is the one role that everyone knows him for, despite it being one in a succession of good performances. Again it embodies the qualities that are expected of Gable.

Gable and Vivien Leigh in *Gone with the Wind* (MGM, 1939).

He is still rugged, still self-centered, and still critical of males who exhibit unmanly qualities (Gable incidentally refused to speak in a Southern accent for this film, feeling it to be too effeminate). Rhett is presented as a man's man in a world dominated by men. He is surrounded by Southern-boy stereotypes whose overzealous attitudes about "licking the yankees" make them appear impulsive and foolish, while Rhett emerges as being in total control of his passions. But in her book *Big Bad Wolves; Masculinity in the American Film* (Pantheon, 1977), Joan Mellen points out another important aspect of Margaret Mitchell's Rhett Butler, "a contribution to the male image in film which perhaps only a woman author would provide." Gable is shown as a family man, transcending the traditional masculinity he is noted for by presenting a charming portrait of a doting father to little Bonnie Blue Butler. He reportedly did not want to cry onscreen during scenes where Scarlet miscarries or when little Bonnie Blue is killed, but director Victor Fleming, whom Gable greatly admired, talked him into it. The results were among the most powerful and emotional scenes Gable did in his entire career (an interesting parallel is found in his last film, *The Misfits*). Mellen wrote, "The actor schooled in Hollywood's definition of masculinity yielded to a woman's conception of what it means to be a man and thus added a nuance to his screen persona which had hitherto been beyond him."

During the forties, Gable took somewhat of a hiatus due to a variety of reasons. First, his wife, actress Carole Lombard, was killed in a plane crash in 1942. Their marriage was said to be the one coupling that would survive the plastic Hollywood romances and last forever. Gable was said to be in such deep grief that he lost his spirit completely. In an effort to forget, he enlisted in the armed forces and served as lieutenant in the Army Air Corps. True to his screen image, Gable steadfastly refused all special treatment from the military and insisted on making his way according to the same methods as any of the enlisted men. He returned to films in 1945 and, although he made some good films, he was older and the industry had changed enough so that his brand of tough guy was now replaced by the rugged, sexless John Wayne and Randolph Scott types.

Throughout the decade of the forties, Gable was plagued by a variety of personal problems from his grief over the death of his father, continued grief over Carole Lombard, the lingering shock of war, and other troubles that beset him. He no longer cared about his appearance and gradually lost both his rascally handsome tough-guy looks and his vitality. By the fifties, he was shuttled into mature roles and, although his professionalism allowed him to do reasonably well in mediocre programmers for various studios, films like *Teacher's Pet* and *Mogambo* were only pale imitations of his past work.

Gable's last film, the posthumously released *The Misfits* (United Artists, 1961) was a fitting culmination to his career. As an aging cowboy who is haunted by dreams of a once glorious past, Gable turns in a performance that adds greater depth to the image he had perpetuated so masterfully in his pre–1942 classics. Playing romantically opposite Marilyn Monroe (in what was to be her last film as well), Gable still manages to exude at least a modicum of the sexuality he had exhibited in his early films. But the image had mellowed as had the times. No longer was it necessary to have the script calculated to present the woman as passive in order for the man to look more aggressive and, hence, more masculine. Gable was now a tough guy as a result of his own resources, but was more real in that he had old age to contend with and no longer could be the absolute example of traditional screen macho. This minor frailty added an essential human quality to the noted Gable persona and enhanced a characterization that reached such legendary proportions, it is still influencing actors over a quarter-century after the actor's death.

Clark Gable Filmography

The Painted Desert (Pathé, 1931) 80 minutes
Directed by Howard Higgin, Screenplay by Higgin and Tom Buckingham, Photographed by Ed Snyder, Edited by Clarence Kolster.
With William Boyd, Helen Twelvetrees, William Farnum, J. Farrell Mac-Donald, *C.G.*, Charles Selton, Will Walling, Wade Boteler.

The Easiest Way (MGM, 1931) 86 minutes
Directed by Jack Conway, Screenplay by Edith Ellis (based on the play by Eugene Walter), Photographed by John Mescall, Edited by Frank Sullivan.
With Constance Bennett, Adolphe Menjou, Robert Montgomery, Anita Page, *C.G.*, Marjorie Rambeau, J. Farrell MacDonald, Clara Blandick.

Dance, Fools, Dance! (MGM, 1931) 82 minutes
Directed by Harry Beaumont, Screenplay by Richard Schayer (from a story by Aurania Rouverel), Photographed by Charles Rosher, Edited by George Hively.
With Joan Crawford, Lester Vail, Cliff Edwards, William Bakewell, *C.G.*, Earl Fox, Pernell Pratt, Hale Hamilton, Natalie Moorehead.

The Secret Six (MGM, 1931) 83 minutes
Directed by George Hill, Screenplay by Frances Marion, Photographed by Harold Wenstrom, Edited by Blanche Sewell.
With Wallace Beery, Lewis Stone, Johnny Mack Brown, Jean Harlow, Marjorie Rambeau, Paul Hurst, *C.G.*, Ralph Bellamy, John Miljan.

The Finger Points (First National, 1931) 90 minutes
Directed by John Francis Dillon, Screenplay by Robert Lord, Photographed by Ernest Haller, Edited by Leroy Stone.
With Richard Barthelmess, Fay Wray, Regis Toomey, *C.G.*..

Laughing Sinners (MGM, 1931) 71 minutes
Directed by Harry Beaumont, Screenplay by Bess Meredyth (from the play *Torch Song* by Kenyon Nicholson), Photographed by Charles Rosher, Edited by George Hively.
With Joan Crawford, Neil Hamilton, *C.G.*, Marjorie Rambeau, Guy Kibbee, Cliff Edwards, Roscoe Karns, Gertrude Short.

A Free Soul (MGM, 1931) 91 minutes
Directed by Clarence Brown, Screenplay by John Meehan, Photographed by William Daniels, Edited by Hugh Wynn.
With Norma Shearer, Leslie Howard, Lionel Barrymore, *C.G.*, James Gleason, Lucy Beaumont.

Night Nurse (Warner Bros., 1931) 72 minutes

Directed by William Wellman, Screenplay by Oliver H.P. Garrett, Photographed by Chick McGill, Edited by Ed McDermott.

With Barbara Stanwyck, Ben Lyon, Joan Blondell, C.G., Charles Winninger, Vera Lewis, Blanche Frederici, Charlotte Miriam.

Sporting Blood (MGM, 1931) 82 minutes

Directed by Charles Brabin, Screenplay by Willard Mack and Wanda Tuchock (from the novel *Horseflesh* by Frederick Hazlett), Photographed by Harold Rossen, Edited by William Gray.

With C.G., Ernest Torrence, Madge Evans, Lew Cody, Marie Prevost, Harry Holman, Halam Cooley, J. Farrell MacDonald, John Larkin, Eugene "Pineapple" Jackson.

Susan Lennox — Her Rise and Fall (MGM,1931) 84 minutes

Directed by Robert Z. Leonard, Screenplay by Wanda Tuchock (from the novel by David Graham Phillips), Photographed by William Daniels, Edited by Margaret Booth.

With Greta Garbo, C.G., Jean Hersholt, John Miljan, Alan Hale, Hilda Vaughn, Russell Simpson, Cecil Cunningham.

Possessed (MGM, 1931) 76 minutes

Directed by Clarence Brown, Screenplay adaption by Lenore Coffee (from the play *The Mirage* by Edgar Selwyn), Photographed by Oliver T. Marsh, Edited by Margaret Booth.

With Joan Crawford, C.G., Wallace Ford, Skeets Gallagher, Frank Conroy, Marjorie White, John Miljan, Clara Blandick.

Hell Divers (MGM, 1931) 100 minutes

Directed by George Hill, Screenplay by Harvey Gates and Malcom Stuart Boylan, Photographed by Harold Wenstrom, Edited by Blanche Sewell.

With Wallace Beery, C.G., Conrad Nagel, Dorothy Jordan, Marjorie Rambeau, Marie Prevost, Cliff Edwards, John Miljan.

Polly of the Circus (MGM, 1932) 72 minutes

Directed by Alfred Santell, Screenplay by Carey Wilson, Photographed by George Barnes, Edited by George Hively.

With Marion Davies, C.G., C. Aubrey Smith, Raymond Hatton, David Landau, Ruth Selwyn, Maude Eburne, Little Billy Rhodes, Guinn Williams, Clark Marshall, Ray Milland, Lillian Elliot.

Red Dust (MGM, 1932) 83 minutes

Directed by Victor Fleming, Screenplay by John Lee Mahin (based on the play by Wilson Collson), Photographed by Harold Rossen, Edited by Blanche Sewell.

With C.G., Jean Harlow, Gene Raymond, Mary Astor, Donald Crisp.

Strange Interlude (MGM, 1932) 110 minutes
Directed by Robert Z. Leonard, Screenplay by Bess Meredyth and C. Gardner Sullivan (based on the play by Eugene O'Neill), Photographed by Lee Garmes, Edited by Margaret Booth.
With Norma Shearer, *C.G.*, Alexander Kirkland, Ralph Morgan, Robert Young, May Robson, Maureen O'Sullivan.

No Man of Her Own (MGM, 1932) 85 minutes
Directed by Wesley Ruggles, Screenplay by Maurine Watkins and Milton Gropper (based on a story by Edmund Goulding and Benjamin Glaser), Photographed by Leo Tover, Edited by Margaret Booth.
With *C.G.*, Carole Lombard, Dorothy Mackail, Grant Richmond, George Barbier, Elizabeth Patterson, J. Farrell MacDonald.

The White Sister (MGM, 1933) 110 minutes
Directed by Victor Fleming, Adapted for the screen by Donald Ogden Stewart (from the novel by F. Marion Crawford and Walter Hackett), Photographed by William Daniels, Edited by Margaret Booth.
With Helen Hayes, *C.G.*, Lewis Stone, Louise Closser Hale, May Robson, Edward Arnold, Alan Edwards.

Hold Your Man (MGM, 1933) 89 minutes
Directed by Sam Wood, Screenplay by Anita Loos and Howard Emmett Rogers (from a story by Loos), Photographed by Harold Rossen, Edited by Frank Sullivan.
With Jean Harlow, *C.G.*, Stuart Erwin, Dorothy Burgess, Muriel Kirkland, Gary Owen, Paul Hurst, Elizabeth Patterson.

Night Flight (MGM, 1933) 84 minutes
Directed by Clarence Brown, Screenplay by Oliver H.P. Stone, Photographed by Oliver T. Marsh, Elmer Dyer, and Charles Marshall.
With John Barrymore, Helen Hayes, *C.G.*, Lionel Barrymore, Robert Montgomery, Myrna Loy, William Gargan, C. Henry Gordon.

Dancing Lady (MGM, 1933) 94 minutes
Directed by Robert Z. Leonard, Screenplay by Allen Rivkin and P. J. Wolfson, Photographed by Oliver T. Marsh, Edited by Margaret Booth.
With Joan Crawford, *C.G.*, Franchot Tone, Fred Astaire, May Robson, Ted Healy and the Three Stooges: Moe Howard, Larry Fine, and Jerry "Curly" Howard.

It Happened One Night (Columbia, 1934) 105 minutes
Directed by Frank Capra, Screenplay by Robert Riskin (based on a story by Samuel Hopkins Adams), Photographed by Joe Walker, Edited by Gene Havlick.
With *C.G.*, Claudette Colbert, Walter Connolly, Roscoe Karns, Jameson Thomas, Alan Hale, Ward Bond, Eddie Chandler.

Note: Winner of all 5 major Academy Awards (Picture, Director, Actor, Actress, Screenplay). The first film to do so, matched only by *One Flew Over the Cuckoo's Nest* in 1975.

Men in White (MGM, 1934) 80 minutes
Directed by Richard Boleslavsky, Screenplay by Waldemar Young (based on the play by Sidney Kingsley), Photographed by George Folsey, Edited by Frank Sullivan.

With *C.G.*, Myrna Loy, Jean Hersholt, Elizabeth Allen, Otto Kruger, C. Henry Gordon, Russell Hardie, Wallace Ford.

Manhattan Melodrama (MGM, 1934) 93 minutes
Directed by W. S. Van Dyke, Screenplay by Oliver T. Marsh, H. P. Garrett, and Joseph L. Mankiewicz, Photographed by James Wong Howe, Edited by Ben Lewis.

With *C.G.*, Myrna Loy, William Powell, Leo Carrillo, Nat Pendleton, George Sidney, Isabell Jewell, Muriel Evans, Mickey Rooney.

Chained (MGM, 1934) 74 minutes
Directed by Clarence Brown, Screenplay by John Lee Mahin, Photographed by George Folsey, Edited by Robert Kern.

With Joan Crawford, *C.G.*, Otto Kruger, Stuart Erwin, Una O'Connor, Marjorie Gateson, Akim Tamiroff.

Forsaking All Others (MGM, 1934) 82 minutes
Directed by W. S. Van Dyke, Screenplay by Joseph L. Mankiewicz, Photographed by Gregg Toland and George Folsey, Edited by Tom Held.

With *C.G.*, Joan Crawford, Robert Montgomery, Charles Butterworth, Billie Burke, Frances Drake, Rosalind Russell, Arthur Treacher.

After Office Hours (MGM, 1935) 75 minutes
Directed by Robert Z. Leonard, Screenplay by Herman J. Mankiewicz, Photographed by Charles Rosher, Edited by Tom Held.

With Constance Bennett, *C.G.*, Stuart Erwin, Billie Burke, Harvey Stephens, Katherine Alexander, Hale Hamilton, Henry Travers.

Call of the Wild (20th Century–Fox, 1935) 95 minutes
Directed by William Wellman, Screenplay by Gene Fowler and Leonard Praskins (based on the book by Jack London), Photographed by Charles Rosher, Edited by Hanson Fritch.

With *C.G.*, Loretta Young, Jack Oakie, Reginald Owen, Frank Conroy, Katherine DeMille, Sidney Toler.

China Seas (MGM, 1935) 90 minutes
Directed by Tay Garnett, Screenplay by Jules Furthman and James Kevin McGuinness, Photographed by Ray June, Edited by William Levanway.

With *C.G.*, Jean Harlow, Wallace Beery, Lewis Stone, Rosalind Russell, Dudley Digges, C. Aubrey Smith, Robert Benchley.

Mutiny on the Bounty (MGM, 1935) 132 minutes
Directed by Frank Lloyds, Screenplay by Talbott Jennings, Jules Furthman and Carey Wilson (based on the book by Charles Nordhoff and James Norman Hall), Photographed by Arthur Edeson, Edited by Margaret Booth.
With *C.G.*, Charles Laughton, Franchot Tone, Herbert Mundin, Eddie Quillan, Dudley Digges, Donald Crisp, Henry Stephenson.

Wife Vs. Secretary (MGM, 1936) 88 minutes
Directed by Clarence Brown, Screenplay by Norman Krasna, Photograhed by Ray June, Edited by Frank Hull.
With *C.G.*, Jean Harlow, Myrna Loy, James Stewart, May Robson, George Barbier, Hobart Cavanaugh, Gilbert Emery.

San Francisco (MGM, 1936) 115 minutes
Directed by W. S. Van Dyke, Screenplay by Anita Loos, Photographed by Oliver T. Marsh, Edited by Tom Held.
With *C.G.*, Jeanette MacDonald, Spencer Tracy, Jack Holt, Jessie Ralph, Ted Healy, Shirley Ross, Margaret Irving.

Cain and Mabel (Warner Bros., 1936) 90 minutes
Directed by Lloyd Bacon, Screenplay by Laird Doyle, Photographed by George Barnes, Edited by William Holmes.
With Marion Davies, *C.G.*, Allen Jenkins, Roscoe Karns, Walter Catlett, David Carlyle, Hobart Cavanaugh, Ruth Donnelly.

Love on the Run (MGM, 1936) 81 minutes
Directed by W. S. Van Dyke, Screenplay by John Lee Mahin, Manuel Seff and Gladys Hurlburt (from the story by Alan Green and Julien Brodie), Photographed by Oliver T. P. Marsh, Edited by Frank Sullivan.
With *C.G.*, Joan Crawford, Franchot Tone, Reginald Owen, Mona Barrie, Ivan Lebedeff.

Parnell (MGM, 1937) 96 minutes
Directed by John M. Stall, Screenplay by John Van Druten and S. N. Behrman (based on the play by Elsie T. Schauffler), Photographed by Karl Freund, Edited by Fredrick Y. Smith.
With *C.G.*, Myrna Loy, Edna Mae Oliver, Edmund Gwenn, Alan Marshal, Donald Crisp.

Saratoga (MGM, 1937) 102 minutes
Directed by Jack Conway, Screenplay by Anita Loos and Robert Hopkins, Photographed by Ray June, Edited by Ed Ward.
With *C.G.*, Jean Harlow, Lionel Barrymore, Frank Morgan, Walter Pidgeon, Una Merkel.
Note: Jean Harlow's last film.

Test Pilot (MGM, 1938) 118 minutes
Directed by Victor Fleming, Screenplay by Vincent Lawrence and
Waldemar Young, Photographed by Ray June, Edited by Tom Held.
With C.G., Myrna Loy, Spencer Tracy, Lionel Barrymore, Samuel S.
Hinds, Marjorie Main.

Too Hot to Handle (MGM, 1938) 105 minutes
Directed by Jack Conway, Screenplay by Lawrence Stallings and John Lee
Mahin, Photographed by Harold Rossen, Edited by Frank Sullivan.
With C.G., Myrna Loy Walter Connolly, Walter Pidgeon, Leo Carrillo,
Johnny Hines.

Idiot's Delight (MGM, 1939)
Directed by Clarence Brown, Screenplay by Robert Sherwood (based on
his play), Photographed by William Daniels, Edited by Robert J. Kern.
With C.G., Norma Shearer, Edward Arnold, Charles Coburn, Joseph
Schildkraut, Burgess Meredith.

Gone with the Wind (MGM, 1939) 225 minutes; Color
Directed by Victor Fleming and George Cukor, Screenplay by Sidney
Howard (based on the novel by Margaret Mitchell), Photographed by Ernest
Haller, Edited by Hal C. Kern and James Newcomb.
With C.G., Vivien Leigh, Leslie Howard, Olivia de Havilland, Thomas
Mitchell, Hattie McDaniel, Butterfly McQueen, George Reeves, Evelyn Keyes,
Ann Rutherford, Jane Darwell, Caroll Nye, Laura Hope Crews, Victor Jory,
Oscar Polk, Everett Brown, Barbara O'Neill.

Strange Cargo (MGM, 1940) 105 minutes
Directed by Frank Borzage, Screenplay by Laurence Hazard, Photo-
graphed by Robert Planck, Edited by Robert J. Kern.
With C.G., Joan Crawford, Ian Hunter, Peter Lorre, Albert Dekker, J.
Edward Bromberg.

Boom Town (MGM, 1940) 116 minutes
Directed by Jack Conway, Screenplay by John Lee Mahin, Photographed
by Harold Rossen, Edited by Blanche Sewell.
With C.G., Spencer Tracy, Claudette Colbert, Hedy Lamarr, Frank
Morgan, Lionel Atwill.

Comrade X (MGM, 1940) 90 minutes
Directed by King Vidor, Screenplay by Ben Hecht and Charles Lederer,
Photographed by Joseph Ruttenberg, Edited by Harold F. Kress.
With C.G., Hedy Lamarr, Oscar Homolka, Felix Bressart, Eve Arden, Sig
Ruman.

They Met in Bombay (MGM, 1941) 86 minutes
Directed by Clarence Brown, Screenplay by Edwin Justus Mayer, Anita

Loos and Leon Gordon (based on the story by John Kafka), Photographed by William Daniels, Edited by Blanche Sewell.

With *C.G.*, Rosalind Russell, Peter Lorre, Jessie Ralph, Reginald Owen, Matthew Boulton.

Honky Tonk (MGM, 1941) 105 minutes
Directed by Jack Conway, Screenplay by Marguerite Roberts and John Sanford, Photographed by Harold Rossen, Edited by Blanche Sewell.

With *C.G.*, Lana Turner, Frank Morgan, Claire Trevor, Marjorie Main, Albert Dekker, Henry O'Neill, Chill Wills, Veda Ann Borg.

Somewhere I'll Find You (MGM, 1942) 108 minutes
Directed by Wesley Ruggles, Screenplay by Marguerite Roberts, Photographed by Harold Rossen, Edited by Blanche Sewell.

With *C.G.*, Lana Turner, Robert Sterling, Patricia Dane, Reginald Owen, Lee Patrick, Charles Dingle, Rags Ragland, William Henry.

Adventure (MGM, 1945) 125 minutes
Directed by Victor Fleming, Screenplay by Frank Hazlitt, Photographed by Joseph Ruttenberg, Edited by Frank Sullivan.

With *C.G.*, Greer Garson, Joan Blondell, Thomas Mitchell, Tom Tully.

Note: Gable's first film after a stint in the service, prompting the film ads to read, "Gable's back and Garson's got him!"

The Hucksters (MGM, 1947) 115 minutes
Directed by Jack Conway, Screenplay by Luther Davis (based on the novel by Frederic Wakeman), Photographed by Harold Rossen, Edited by Frank Sullivan.

With *C.G.*, Deborah Kerr, Sydney Greenstreet, Adolphe Menjou, Ava Gardner, Keenan Wynn, Edward Arnold, Frank Albertson, Jimmy Conlin.

Homecoming (MGM, 1948) 113 minutes
Directed by Mervyn LeRoy, Screenplay by Paul Osborn (based on the story by Sidney Kingsley), Photographed by Harold Rossen, Edited by John Dunning.

With *C.G.*, Lana Turner, Anne Baxter, John Hodiak, Ray Collins, Gladys Cooper, Cameron Mitchell, Marshall Thompson.

Command Decision (MGM, 1948) 112 minutes
Directed by Sam Wood, Screenplay by William Ladlow and George Froeschel (based on the play by William Wister Haines), Photographed by Harold Rossen, Edited by Harold Kress.

With *C.G.*, Walter Pidgeon, Van Johnson, Brian Donlevy, Charles Bickford, John Hodiak, Edward Arnold, Marshall Thompson.

Any Number Can Play (MGM, 1949) 112 minutes
Directed by Mervyn LeRoy, Screenplay by Richard Brooks, Photographed by Harold Rossen, Edited by Ralph E. Winters.

Gable in *Any Number Can Play* (MGM, 1949).

With *C.G.*, Alexis Smith, Wendell Corey, Audrey Totter, Frank Morgan, Mary Astor, Lewis Stone, Barry Sullivan, Leon Ames.

Key to the City (MGM, 1950) 99 minutes
Directed by George Sidney, Screenplay by Robert Riley Crutcher, Photographed by Harold Rossen, Edited by James Newcom.
With *C.G.*, Loretta Young, James Gleason, Frank Morgan, Marilyn Maxwell, Raymond Burr, Lewis Stone, Raymond Walburn.

To Please a Lady (MGM, 1950) 91 minutes
Directed by Clarence Brown, Screenplay by Barre Lyndon and Marge Dekker, Photographed by Harold Rossen, Edited by Robert J. Kern.
With *C.G.*, Barbara Stanwyck, Adolphe Menjou, Will Geer, Roland Winters, William C. McGraw, Emory Parnell, Frank Jenks.

Across the Wide Missouri (MGM, 1951) 78 minutes
Directed by William Wellman, Screenplay by Talbot Jennings, Photographed by William Mellor, Edited by John Dunn.
With *C.G.*, Ricardo Montalban, John Hodiak, Maria Elena Marquis, Adolphe Menjou, J. Carroll Naish, Jack Holt, Alan Napier.

Lone Star (MGM, 1952) 94 minutes
Directed by Vince Sherman, Screenplay by Borden Chase and Howard Estabrook, Photographed by Harold Rossen, Edited by Ferris Webster.
With *C.G.*, Ava Gardner, Broderick Crawford, Lionel Barrymore, Beulah Bondi, Ed Begley, James Burke, William Farnum.

Never Let Me Go (MGM, 1953) 69 minutes
Directed by Delmer Daves, Screenplay by Roland Millar and George Froeschel, Photographed by Robert Krasker, Edited by Frank Clarke.
With *C.G.*, Gene Tierney, Richard Hayden, Bernard Miles, Belita.

Mogambo (MGM, 1953) 115 minutes
Directed by John Ford, Screenplay by John Lee Mahin, Photographed by Robert Surtees, Edited by Frank Clarke.
With *C.G.*, Ava Gardner, Grace Kelly, Donald Sindon, Phillip Stanton.

Betrayed (MGM, 1954) 108 minutes
Directed by Gottfried Reinhardt, Screenplay by Roland Millar and George Frischel, Edited by John Dunning and Ray Poulton.
With *C.G.*, Lana Turner, Victor Mature, Louis Calhern, O. E. Hasse.

Soldier of Fortune (20th Century–Fox, 1955) 96 minutes
Directed by Edward Dmytryk, Screenplay by Ernest Gann (from his novel), Photographed by Leo Tover, Edited by Dorothy Spencer.
With *C.G.*, Susan Hayward, Michael Rennie, Gene Barry, Alex D'Arcy.

The Tall Men (20th Century–Fox, 1955) 122 minutes
Directed by Raoul Walsh, Screenplay by Sydney Boehm and Frank Nugent, Photographed by Leo Tover, Edited by Louis Loeffler.
With *C.G.*, Jane Russell, Robert Ryan, Cameron Mitchell, Juan Garcia.

The King and Four Queens (United Artists, 1956) 86 minutes
Directed by Raoul Walsh, Screenplay by Marguerite Firrs and Richard Alan Simmons, Photographed by Lucien Ballard, Edited by David Brotherton.
With *C.G.*, Eleanor Parker, Jo Van Fleet, Jean Willes, Roy Roberts.

Band of Angels (Warner Bros., 1957) 127 minutes
Directed by Raoul Walsh, Screenplay by John Twist, Ivan Goff, and Ben Roberts (based on the novel by Robert Penn Warren), Photographed by Lucien Ballard, Edited by Folmar Blangsted.
With *C.G.*, Yvonne De Carlo, Sidney Poitier, Efrem Zimbalist, Jr.

Run Silent, Run Deep (United Artists, 1958) 93 minutes
Directed by Robert Wise, Screenplay by John Gay, Photographed by Russ Harlen, Edited by David Brotherton.
With *C.G.*, Burt Lancaster, Jack Warden, Brad Dexter, Nick Cravat.

Teacher's Pet (Paramount, 1958) 120 minutes
Directed by George Seaton, Screenplay by Fay and Michael Kanin, Photographed by Franciot Edouart, Edited by Alma Macrorie.
With *C.G.*, Doris Day, Gig Young, Mamie Van Doren, Nick Adams.

But Not for Me (Paramount, 1959) 105 minutes
Directed by Walter Lang, Screenplay by John Michael Hayes, Photographed by Robert Burks, Edited by Alma Macrorie.
With *C.G.*, Carroll Baker, Lilli Palmer, Lee J. Cobb, Barry Coe.

It Started in Naples (Paramount, 1960) 100 minutes
Directed by Melville Shavelson, Screenplay by Shavelson and Jack Rose, Photographed by Robert Surtees, Edited by Alma Macrorie.
With *C.G.*, Sophia Loren, Vittorio DeSica, Marietto Paolo.

The Misfits (United Artists, 1961) 124 minutes
Directed by John Huston, Screenplay by Arthur Miller, Photographed by Russell Metty, Edited by George Tomasini.
With *C.G.*, Marilyn Monroe, Montgomery Clift, Thelma Ritter, Eli Wallach, James Barton, Estelle Winwood, Kevin McCarthy.
Note: Monroe's as well as Gable's last film.

Gable also made a guest appearance in Norman Panama's feature **Callaway Went Thataway** (MGM, 1951) which starred Fred MacMurray.

John Wayne

John Wayne is perhaps the most well-known American motion picture star next to Charlie Chaplin. He is also one of the most complex screen performers in terms of analysis. Ironically, since his roles are so similar, his career branches off into several areas of study. And although he is best known for his Westerns and military pictures, he is more often studied for a total image that is said to define masculinity in American life, stemming from the hard frontier life that pioneers handed down.

Wayne's work has been approached from a variety of different perspectives. Some admonish him for his lack of versatility, others for ugly right-wing sensibilities and prowar attitudes that they believe creep into all of his films. Others applaud his sense of patriotism, or perhaps Americanism, that is the nature of many a Wayne character, or for his strong, stoic, take-no-guff attitude. What it all results in is the fact that Wayne projected an image on film that has long been the essence of what Americans believed to be the preferred qualities for male toughness or genuine masculinity.

The John Wayne screen persona seems to be an extension of the real-life image the actor projected, especially during the sixties and seventies when the types he had played for years were being challenged by a new type of male that was emerging in American life. While his films do exude patriotism, heroism, honesty and decency (a strong moral and ethical code), courage, and defiance, they also exhibit qualities of sexism, racism, and an attitude applauding contention over pacifism. As these latter qualities came under fire during the liberal sixties and seventies, so then was it necessary for Wayne to exert his strengths and emphasize these very qualities as being "true," "pure," and "right." This caused his legend to suffer. The turning point in Wayne's popularity with the new breed of liberal thinkers was his wholly repugnant film *The Green Berets* (Warner Bros., 1968) in which the Vietnam War is approached as yet another necessary confrontation that we must engage in as we did World War II, with the same vigor and enthusiasm as had been presented in films detailing that struggle. *The Green Berets* was panned by critics of the period, but garnered a following during the

John Wayne started out as a cowboy in low-budget Westerns.

mid–1980s via video rentals as a result of Wayne's prowar popularity coming into vogue during the post–Vietnam return to conservatism, as liberal idealism again was dismissed as a lame attempt at hiding cowardice. This also caused films like Sylvester Stallone's *Rambo* and Clint Eastwood's *Heartbreak Ridge* to achieve a very high box-office status.

In order to fully understand Wayne's impact on film and the American culture his work must be approached chronologically and with careful detail. The starting point would be his 1930 feature *The Big Trail*, the first in a long series of "B" Westerns for low-budget studios that would soon evolve into a series of "A" programmers. The Wayne screen persona develops very gradually (Wayne's best performances came in his last films, where his persona was etched so deeply he could use it as he wished in whatever context, and still come off as overpowering without being arrogant). The initial Wayne appearances had the actor looking boyish, vibrant and tough, but in a more dashing Fairbanks-esque sense than we would see during World War II. His was a world of heroics and bravado, usually performed in an effort to win a girl. Wayne's method of subduing the villain was really no different than any competent star of "B" action Westerns from that period, from Gene Autry to Whip Wilson.

Wayne worked in hour-long action Westerns at Columbia, Monogram, and Warner Bros., appeared in serials at Mascot studios, and finally, in the mid-thirties, landed work at Republic studios where his onscreen image noticeably began to take shape. While his early Western quickies were forgettable, they were still valuable training for the work he was to do in later years. The turning point came with Wayne's appearance as the Ringo Kid in John Ford's 1939 Western classic *Stagecoach*, a film that was not limited to audiences who enjoyed simply action quickies. The screen persona he was slowly developing was finally put in a context that allowed the actor to expand through a richer, more colorful narrative. At the time he appeared in this film, Wayne was playing with Ray Corrigan and Max Terhune in the Three Mesquiteers cowboy series at Republic. The image he was developing in this series was the one he used in *Stagecoach*, only with the greater character depth allowed by a more detailed script.

The Ringo Kid is a bandit who has escaped from prison to kill the men who framed him. Once he has accomplished this task, the honorable Ringo will then return to prison and serve out his sentence. Such idealism and purpose were later to be etched into the Wayne screen image, but this early usage seems a bit more wistful and naive. The Ringo Kid was following a code of honor that he believed in, where later Wayne characters were far more experienced Westerners whose codes of honor had been honed from many long, hard years on the trail. Thus the idealism and naiveté were both missing, as the ethics stemmed from often bitter experiences in this manly sort of life-style. The Ringo Kid is said to have been incarcerated since the age of seventeen, and is now much older (Wayne was in his thirties when he played the role, but perhaps the Ringo Kid is supposed to be in his twenties).

Wayne plays the Kid as an adolescent: gangly, gawky, and idealistic. Thus the incarceration did not allow the Kid to reach any greater intellectual or emotional maturity since seventeen, but he does have the very special ethical qualities that seem to be lost by the end of adolescence. As Wayne made more films, his image slowly grew and became more weathered, less idealistic, harder. He became an American hero due to the fact that his screen image embodied the very qualities of the great male "forefathers" who paved the way for the freedom and prosperity that Americans are said to have enjoyed all these years. None of the Wayne films address American cultural issues that pertain in the more liberal sense, including the fostering of freethinking, an accent on youthful vitality, women as more than passive whiners, minorities as something other than the enemy.

Even a film as early as *Dark Command* (1940) lauds the strong, virile "real man" of Wayne who plays an uneducated, illiterate Texan, while the educated and cultured Walter Pidgeon character is presented as an evil vigilante whose intelligence can't outwit Wayne's easygoing "regular guy" heroics. This film still features the actor as a naive-good guy whose ethics are those he believes to be best suited for his life-style, still lacking in the experiences that will eventually shape his soon-to-be-legendary screen image.

Throughout the forties, Wayne experienced a period of growth both in his Hollywood star status and his influential screen image. With each film he is tougher, more savvy, more stoic, and, ultimately, more masculine. He made so many films during this period, and with such similarity, that the events in each seem to run into another, causing his output during this decade to be a bit of a blur, with images of cowboys and war heroes from every branch of the service growing into an inimitable tough-guy image, speaking generally the same lines and having basically the same attitudes about most controversial subjects. Some of the screen events from this period stand out, such as the fight with Randolph Scott over Marlene Dietrich in the offbeat non–Western *Pittsburgh* (1942), which parallels with a similar fight scene with the same two actors over the same actress in *The Spoilers*, a Western made the same year for the same studio.

Wayne began working on another important extension of his screen persona in war films during this period, from the programmers *Flying Tigers* (1942) and *Fighting Seabees* (1944) to the more complex *They Were Expendable* (1945). Wayne also tried his hand at light comedy opposite Claudette Colbert in the very unsuccessful *Without Reservations* (1945) and also played opposite such offbeat screen clowns as Shemp Howard in *Pittsburgh* and Oliver Hardy in *The Fighting Kentuckian* (1949). These films were basically journeyman portrayals for Wayne, who was finding his own image through the events that seemed to occur in virtually all of his films. The true turning point came with Howard Hawks' *Red River* (1948), which has become a classic (many believing it to be the greatest American Western of all), as well as the most important film Wayne made since *Stagecoach*.

Red River presented viewers with perhaps the best example of screen masculinity as per John Wayne than any of the actor's previous portrayals. Wayne's character exhibited what it was to be a man, while the role essayed

Besides being featured in nearly every branch of the service during his career, Wayne is shown here as an airline pilot in *The High and the Mighty* (Warner Bros., 1954).

by Montgomery Clift was a rebellious punk who was forced to learn how to become a better man by shaping his life-style into the image Wayne was displaying.

Red River is a film about what it means to be a man, and since Wayne is the central character in the film, it is his version of masculinity that is perceived as the ultimate truth. Wayne's character exudes the by now noted indestructible tough-guy image, while his surrogate son, played by Montgomery Clift, is a character who feels he must hide his sensitivity and emulate the toughness of his paternal counterpart. The film glorifies the Wayne character with greater passion than any of the actor's previous efforts and thus becomes the harbinger of subsequent Wayne starrers. In *Red River*, Wayne begins by starting his own herd, claiming land in spite of opposition by corrupt landgrabbers, and in true movie tough-guy spirit, he is a man who acts alone and is responsible solely to himself—an image that is applauded as the consummate image of screen masculinity.

The surrogate son, known as Matthew, is the survivor of an Indian attack (Hollywood depicted native Americans as nothing more than passive sidekicks or bloodthirsty marauders during these times) in which Wayne's girlfriend is killed. This experience toughens Matthew even prior to the formal tough-guy training Wayne employs. Matthew is first an overzealous adolescent, but under Wayne's tutelage, he mellows out.

When one closely analyzes Wayne's character in *Red River*, one cannot help but determine that this is not a good man we're seeing. Yet his unflinching assertiveness and tough-guy bravado are so captivating, they cause us to applaud even his most heinous actions. When he kills Mexicans to steal their land, it is rationalized that the Mexicans stole the land from the Indians, and thus have no genuine legal right. When he places his own brand on neighboring cattle that have gone astray, one still is forced to applaud even his unmovable toughness as the rightful owners question such ethics and yet ultimately back down to his bravado. Early in the film, such a confrontation causes one foreman to leave his boss and join up with Wayne and his group.

In *Red River* we have the Matthew character as a comparison-contrast (Montgomery Clift's boyish good looks and ability to so expertly portray brooding rebellion enhancing this role), thus allowing us to enjoy two male heroes that represent opposite tough-guy types, and yet who compliment each other as interesting counterparts. Although Clift is used as a foil—a tough guy who just isn't as tough as Wayne, who exemplifies pure movie toughness—his character at least is tough enough not to fear exuding compassion (labeled as soft or unmanly when he saves deserters Wayne is about to hang), and ultimately takes Wayne's place by the end of the film (modifying the image of leadership Wayne had projected by being tough enough to present elements of the male psyche that Wayne so carefully repressed). By the end of the film, a union is firmly established as Wayne acknowledges that Clift has finally earned his initial on the Red River brand. It is the unflinching, often callous tough guy of the past accepting the compassionate, more rational tough guy of the present (and future). In many subsequent Wayne starrers, there would be a younger man whose overzealous attitudes are soon modified by Wayne's omnipotence in the tough-guy setting, but never would the younger man modify the Wayne image except in *Red River*.

Throughout the fifties, Wayne clung to his screen image in spite of the explosion of new male tough guys that centered on youthful vitality and a brooding quality that seemed to represent a perverse sort of arrested adolescence (of which Clift could be considered a part). Yet this new breed did not dissuade filmmakers like John Ford from presenting the West's "real man" qualities.

By the time Ford made *The Man Who Shot Liberty Valance* (1962), this image was nostalgic. Such a character as Wayne's was an anachronism, despite the fact that the actor remained active throughout the fifties. The film, then, applauds the dying breed of Western tough guys whose qualities were steeped in what was (and is) considered traditionally tough. Wayne is the stoic hero who comes to the aid of Ransom Stoddard (Jimmy Stewart)—a perfect example of the male wimp in American cinema. Liberty Valance (Lee Marvin) is the brutal, repulsive male outlaw who preys upon the weakness of Stoddard (such nastiness is not applauded if directed toward settlers instead of Indians). Wayne, then, is just as tough, but stands for the "right" way. It is he who shoots the character and makes living easier for those not tough enough to take matters into their own hands and who then proceed to carry out their plans successfully.

Several analogies have been made in an attempt to analyze this film, perhaps the most interesting one being a comparison of Lee Marvin to the raucous rock and roll stars just starting to invade the youth counterculture, and comparing Jimmy Stewart to the passive father figure whose attempts to return his children to suppressive conservatism were unsuccessful. Parents of the era felt they needed a tough John Wayne type to restore such traditionalism. Thus many fathers and members of the clergy attempted to assume this role in the real world. The result was a generation gap that led to the rebellious attitudes of the sixties.

In assessing the Wayne screen image and its relationship with women, perhaps Andrew McLaglen's *McLintock!* (1963) is the best example. Maureen O'Hara (who appeared opposite Wayne in many films) does nothing at all for feminism, as her own female toughness is defeated when she attempts to challenge the stoic Wayne character. In what purports to be escapist fare, *McLintock!* enforces the most negative stereotypes regarding male-female relationships. Wayne, of course, believes in male bonding, crudity, and the woman's-place-in-the-home ideals that were just beginning to be seriously and successfully challenged when this film was made. O'Hara is the refined lady of the city with proper social breeding whose toughness stems from puritanical attitudes and her belief that Wayne and his lot are crude and uneducated (which they are). Yet her attitudes are presented in such a way that Wayne acts as her foil only from the

Wayne and frequent costar Maureen O'Hara are mudded up for *McLintock!* (United Artists, 1963).

perspective that he is merely toying with her, remaining aloof to her silly carrying on, and will ultimately enforce his tough-guy bravado and restore the proper values of ruling masculinity in this hierarchy of wild West domesticity.

The film culminates their relationship when Wayne takes O'Hara over his knee and spanks her, which inexplicably causes her to throw herself into his arms and proclaim her love for him! This enforces negative images for women by stating that they are unfailingly passive even in their attempts at being aggressive, while the Wayne image once again enforces the ridiculous stereotype that manners and education merely soften a man, while aggressive crudity is the accepted norm for toughness. By the time this film was made, Wayne's screen persona had been so firmly established that he could use this image in any context and somehow control the narrative.

True Grit (1969) is one of the best Wayne films, not only for having the popularity to prove the actor's durability even in spite of so devastating a debacle as *The Green Berets* (which would have ruined many lesser actors' careers), but also for presenting his persona as tough, but ugly—a crude, repulsive individual who nevertheless is a success because of this crudity and not in spite of it. While the success of his Rooster Cogburn character in this context once again applauds such crudity, it does so while calling attention to it as crude—that Cogburn's crude ways are successful for this man, but perhaps are not to be accepted as the norm for all men. Such an attitude is fiercely liberal in a John Wayne picture. Henry Hathaway's direction does not glorify Wayne with shots of the actor against a scenic background so as to place him on a pedestal, but instead calls attention to his rugged qualities as he lumbers about as a weathered and ornery veteran of many-a-painful battle.

This film celebrates Wayne's brand of screen toughness more than most others in that it allows his character to be presented and accepted in spite of its personal flaws by exhibiting these qualities as character flaws that do not get in the way of his success. He's crude, but effective because he's a weathered veteran with enough old-fashioned savvy to emerge victorious in any situation. The situation that he is needed for is to avenge the killing of Matty Ross's (Kim Darby) father. As the by-now-obligatory young, overzealous counterpart, we have Glen Campbell as a baby-faced Texas ranger after the same bandit for another crime. Rooster Cogburn is a perfect Wayne character in that he is allowed to emerge victorious in all battles, culminating in a display of incredible bravado as the dauntless Rooster rides toward several badmen with a pistol in one hand, a rifle in the other, and the reins in his teeth, gunning down all opposition quite handily. Whatever repugnant qualities Cogburn has, Wayne still manages to play him as a strange Western superman. It is his quintessential performance, one which earned him his only Oscar, and subsequently spawned a sequel—the predictably awful merger of *True Grit* and *The African Queen* titled *Rooster Cogburn and the Lady* (Universal, 1976), co-featuring Katharine Hepburn.

Wayne exhibits surrogate fatherhood once again in Andrew McLaglen's *Big Jake* (1974), in which his paternal instincts are stirred when his grandson and namesake is kidnapped for ransom from the wealthy wife and sons he left years before. He learns the news and arranges to rescue the youngster. Most of the familiar sequences involving overzealous

John Wayne in his last role as *The Shootist* (Paramount, 1976).

younger traveling companions, stoic confrontations with badmen, even a low-key Indian sidekick (Bruce Cabot) are all played lighter and for apparent humorous intent. This is the best example of Wayne playing solely off the image he had created and honed for so long. It is the essence of movie male toughness—the combination of Western savvy, stoic demeanor, fighting spirit, and crude rustic behavior—which makes up an image that cannot die.

By now Wayne didn't need to try to make entertaining films, as *Big Jake* is a prime example of him simply appearing in a rather standard Western narrative and milking his image for both laughs and thrills. It is a true testament to his legend that so many mediocre narratives were bolstered by his familiar character being at the forefront.

Wayne's last film was *The Shootist* (1976), in which he played an aging gunfighter dying of cancer, who is unable to escape his reputation. It was a fitting culmination to his career, as Wayne actually had terminal cancer when he filmed *The Shootist*. The entire film is a fascinating study of the Wayne character (or image) preparing to die in the same fashion as he has lived—unshakable, stoic, tough. Unlike, say, *Sands of Iwo Jima* (1948), in which Wayne is picked off quickly by a sniper's bullet, the character in *The Shootist* is aware of his imminent demise and thus prepares for it by choosing to go quietly and in seclusion. His efforts are duped and he ultimately dies in battle, but it is after an entire feature film's worth of preparation, understanding, and acceptance of all he has been in his lifetime. The character in the narrative that Wayne portrays is the character he has always played, and his exploits are those we have seen him perform in films since the late twenties. In his farewell film, Wayne is allowed to retain his image to the very end. There is a strong poignancy about the proceedings.

Throughout his career, John Wayne served as the absolute example of movie toughness as he stood for the status quo and enforced rules and responsibilities that were applauded by the conservative right. Thus the fact that his image suffered during the more liberal sixties and seventies was due to a new generation discovering suppressive elements in what his image represented. As we see his persona evolve in films, we see as much an evolution of masculine sensibilities in the American society as we do the honing of a screen characterization. In the sixties and seventies, his image had to be enforced more sternly and was sentimentally (if not victoriously) embraced by the older generation. Wayne's bold exterior never presented so much as a rebel as it presented him as the upholder of the established order. It is this that causes us to remember him as the most predominant example of the movie tough guy.

John Wayne Filmography

Salute (Fox, 1929) 86 minutes
Directed by John Ford, Screenplay by John Stone, Photographed by Joseph August, Edited by Alex Troffey.
With George O'Brien, Helen Chandler, Stepin Fetchit, William Janney, Frank Albertson, Joyce Compton, Rex Bell, *J.W.*

Rough Romance (Fox, 1930) 55 minutes
Directed by A. F. Erickson, Screenplay by Elliot Lester, Photographed by Daniel B. Clark, Edited by Paul Weatherwax.
With George O'Brien, Helen Chandler, Antonio Moreno, Noel Francis, Eddie Borden, Harry Cording, Roy Steward, *J.W.*

The Big Trail (Fox, 1930) 125 minutes
Directed by Raoul Walsh, Screenplay by Jack Peabody, Marie Boyle, Florence Postal, Photographed by Lucien Androit, Edited by Jack Dennis.
With *J.W.*, Marguerite Churchill, El Brendel, Tully Marshall.

Girls Demand Excitement (Fox, 1931) 79 minutes
Directed by Seymour Felix, Screenplay by Harlan Thompson, Photographed by Charles Clarke, Edited by Jack Murray.
With Virginia Cherrill, *J.W.*, Marguerite Churchill, Helen Jerome Eddy, William Janney, Eddie Nugent, Terrence Ray, Marion Byron.

Three Girls Lost (Fox, 1931) 80 minutes
Directed by Sidney Lanfield, Screenplay by Robert Andrews, Photographed by L. William O'Connell, Edited by Ralph Dietrich.
With Loretta Young, *J.W.*, Lew Cody, Joyce Compton, Joan Marsh.

Men Are Like That (Columbia, 1931) 67 minutes
Directed by George Seitz, Screenplay by Robert Riskin and Dorothy Howell, Photographed by Teddy Tetzlaff, Edited by Gene Milford.
With *J.W.*, Laura LaPlante, June Clyde, Forrest Stanley.

Range Feud (Columbia, 1931) 64 minutes
Directed by Ross Lederman, Screenplay by Milton Krims, Photographed by Ben Kline, Edited by Maurice Wright.
With Buck Jones, *J.W.*, Susan Fleming, Ed LeSaint, William Walling.

Maker of Men (Columbia, 1931) 71 minutes
Directed by Edward Sedgwick, Screenplay by Sedgwick and Howard J. Green, Photographed by L. William O'Connell, Edited by Gene Milford.
With Jack Holt, Richard Cromwell, Joan Marsh, Robert Allen, *J.W.*

Haunted Gold (Warner Bros., 1932) 58 minutes
Directed by Mack Wright, Screenplay by Adele Buffington, Photographed by Nick Musuraca, Edited by William Clemens.
With *J.W.*, Sheila Terry, Erville Alderson, Harry Woods, Otto Hoffman.

Shadow of the Eagle (Warner Bros., 1932) 12-chapter serial
Directed by Ford Beebe, Screenplay by Beebe, Colbert Clark and Wyndham Gittens, Photographed by Ben Kline and Victor Scheurich, Edited by Ray Snyder.
With *J.W.*, Dorothy Gulliver, Edward Hearn, Richard Tucker, Lloyd Whitlock, Yakima Canutt, Edmund Burns, Little Billy Curtis.

Hurricane Express (Mascot, 1932) 12-chapter serial
Directed by Armand Schaefer and J.P. McGowan, Screenplay by Wyndham Gittens, Colbert Clark, Barney Sarecky, Harold Tarshin, George Morgan, and J. P. McGowan, Photographed by Ernest Miller and Carl Wester, Edited by Ray Snyder.
With *J.W.*, Shirley Grey, Tully Marshall, Conway Tearle, J. Farrell MacDonald, Matthew Betz, James Burtis, Lloyd Whitlock.

Texas Cyclone (Columbia, 1932) 63 minutes
Directed by D. Ross Lederman, Screenplay by William Colt McDonald, Photographed by Benjamin Kline, Edited by Otto Meyer.
With Tim McCoy, Shirley Grey, *J.W.*, Wheeler Oakman, Walter Brennan, Vernon Dent, Harry Cording, Wallace MacDonald, Mary Gordon.

Two Fisted Law (Columbia, 1932) 64 minutes
Directed by D. Ross Lederman, Screenplay by William Colt MacDonald, Photographed by Benjamin Kline, Edited by Otto Meyer.
With Tim McCoy, Alice Day, Wheeler Oakman, Tully Marshall, Wallace MacDonald, *J.W.*, Walter Brennan, Richard Alexander.

The Big Stampede (Warner Bros., 1932) 63 minutes
Directed by Tenny Wright, Screenplay by Marion Jackson, Photographed by Ted McCord, Edited by Frank Ware.
With *J.W.*, Noah Beery, Mae Madison, Luis Alberni, Berton Churchill.

The Telegraph Trail (Warner Bros., 1933) 60 minutes
Directed by Tenny Wright, Screenplay by Kurt Kempler, Photographed by Ted McCord, Edited by William Clemens.
With *J.W.*, Marceline Day, Frank McHugh, Otis Harlan, Yakima Canutt.

Somewhere in Sonora (Warner Bros., 1933) 59 minutes
Directed by Mack V. Wright, Written by Will Levington Comfort, Photographed by Ted McCord, Edited by William Clemens.
With *J.W.*, Shirley Palmer, Henry B. Walthall, Paul Fix, Anne Faye, Billy Franey, Ralph Lewis, Frank Rice, J. P. McGowan.

The Life of Jimmy Dolan (Warner Bros., 1933) 85 minutes
Directed by Archie Mayo, Written by Bert Milhauser and Beulah Marie
Dix, Photographed by Arthur Edeson, Edited by Bert Levy.
With Douglas Fairbanks, Jr, Loretta Young, Alice MacMahon, Guy Kibbee, Fifi D'Orsay, Shirley Grey, J.W., Lyle Talbot, Farina.
Note: Remade in 1939 as *They Made Me a Criminal* with John Garfield.

The Three Musketeers (Mascot, 1933) 12-chapter serial
Directed by Armand Schaefer and Colbert Clark, Screenplay by Clark,
Wyndham Gittens, Norman S. Hall, and Barney Sarecky, Photographed by
Ernest Miller and Ed Lyons, Edited by Ray Snyder.
With J.W., Ruth Hall, Jack Mulhall, Raymond Hatton, Francis X.
Bushman, Jr., Noah Beery, Jr., Lon Chaney, Jr., Al Ferguson.
Note: Released as a feature titled *Doomed Battalion* in 1948.

Riders of Destiny (Monogram, 1933) 50 minutes
Directed and written by Robert N. Bradbury, Photographed by A. J. Stout,
Edited by Carl Pierson.
With J.W., Cecilia Parker, Gabby Hayes, Al St. John, Heinie Conklin.

Sagebrush Trail (Monogram, 1933) 58 minutes
Directed by Armand Schaefer, Written by Lindsley Parsons, Photographed by A. J. Stout, Edited by Carl Pierson.
With J.W., Nancy Shubert, Lane Chandler, Yakima Canutt, Wally Wales.

West of the Divide (Monogram, 1934) 54 minutes
Directed and written by Robert N. Bradbury, Photographed by A. J. Stout,
Edited by Carl Pierson.
With J.W., Virginia Browne Faire, Lloyd Whitlock, Gabby Hayes, Yakima
Canutt, Earl Dwire, Lafe McKee.

Lucky Texan (Monogram, 1934) 56 minutes
Directed and written by Robert N. Bradbury, Photographed by A. J. Stout,
Edited by Carl Pierson.
With J.W., Barbara Sheldon, Gabby Hayes, Yakima Canutt.

Blue Steel (Monogram, 1934) 59 minutes
Directed and written by Robert N. Bradbury, Photographed by A. J. Stout,
Edited by Carl Pierson.
With J.W., Eleanor Hunt, Gabby Hayes, Ed Peil, Yakima Canutt.

The Man from Utah (Monogram, 1934) 57 minutes
Directed by Robert N. Bradbury, Written by Lindsley Parsons,
Photographed by A. J. Stout, Edited by Carl Pierson.
With J.W., Polly Ann Young, Gabby Hayes, Yakima Canutt.

Randy Rides Alone (Monogram, 1934) 60 minutes
Directed by Harry Fraser, Written by Lindsley Parsons, Photographed by
A. J. Stout, Edited by Carl Pierson.
With *J.W.*, Alberta Vaughn, Gabby Hayes, Yakima Canutt, Earl Dwire, Tex
Phelps.

The Star Packer (Monogram, 1934) 60 minutes
Directed and written by Robert N. Bradbury, Photographed by A. J. Stout,
Edited by Carl Pierson.
With *J.W.*, Verna Hillie, Gabby Hayes, Yakima Canutt, Earl Dwire,
George Cleveland.

The Trail Beyond (Monogram, 1934) 55 minutes
Directed by Robert N. Bradbury, Written by James Oliver Curwood,
Photographed by A. J. Stout, Edited by Carl Pierson.
With *J.W.*, Verna Hillie, Noah Beery, Iris Lancaster, Noah Beery, Jr.,
Robert Fraser, Earl Dwire, Edward Parker.

'Neath Arizona Skies (Monogram, 1934) 57 minutes
Directed by Harry Fraser, Screenplay by B. R. Tuttle, Photographed by A.
J. Stout, Edited by Carl Pierson.
With *J.W.*, Sheila Terry, Jay Wilsey, Yakima Canutt, Jack Rockwell, Gabby
Hayes.

Lawless Frontier (Monogram, 1935) 59 minutes
Directed and written by Robert N. Bradbury, Photographed by A. J. Stout,
Edited by Carl Pierson.
With *J.W.*, Sheila Terry, Gabby Hayes, Earl Dwire, Yakima Canutt, Jack
Rockwell.

Rainbow Valley (Monogram, 1935) 52 minutes
Directed by Robert N. Bradbury, Screenplay by Lindsley Parsons, Photo-
graphed by William Hyer, Edited by Carl Pierson.
With *J.W.*, Lucille Browne, LeRoy Mason, Gabby Hayes, Buffalo Bill, Jr.,
Bert Dillard.

Paradise Canyon (Monogram, 1935) 59 minutes
Directed by Carl Pierson, Screenplay by Lindsley Parsons, Photographed
by A. J. Stout, Edited by Gerald Roberts.
With *J.W.*, Marion Burns, Yakima Canutt, Reed Howes, Perry Murdock,
Gino Corrado.

The Dawn Rider (Monogram, 1935) 56 minutes
Directed and written by Robert N. Bradbury, Photographed by A. J. Stout,
Edited by Carl Pierson.
With *J.W.*, Marion Burns, Yakima Canutt, Reed Howes, Denny Meadows,
Bert Dillard.

Westward Ho (Republic, 1935) 60 minutes
Directed by Robert N. Bradbury, Screenplay by Lindsley Parsons, Photographed by A. J. Stout, Edited by Carl Pierson.
With *J.W.*, Sheila Manners, Frank McGlynn, Jr., Dick Curtis, Yakima Canutt, Mary McLaren.

Desert Trail (Monogram, 1935) 54 minutes
Directed by Collin Lewis, Screenplay by Lindsley Parsons, Photographed by A. J. Stout, Edited by Carl Pierson.
With *J.W.*, Mary Kornman, Paul Fix, Eddie Chandler, Lafe McKee, Henry Hull, Al Ferguson.

New Frontier (Monogram, 1935) 59 minutes
Directed by Carl Pierson, Screenplay by Robert Emmett, Photographed by Gus Peterson, Edited by Gerald Roberts.
With *J.W.*, Muriel Evans, Mary MacLaren, Earl Dwire, Murdock MacQuarrie, Warner Richmond.

Lawless Range (Republic, 1935) 59 minutes
Directed by Robert N. Bradbury, Screenplay by Lindsley Parsons, Photographed by A. J. Stout, Edited by Carl Pierson.
With *J.W.*, Sheila Manners, Earl Dwire, Frank McGlynn, Jr., Dick Curtis, Yakima Canutt.

The Lawless Nineties (Republic, 1936) 55 minutes
Directed by Joseph Kane, Screenplay by Joseph Poland, Photographed by William Nobles.
With *J.W.*, Ann Rutherford, Lane Chandler, Harry Woods, Fred "Snowflake" Toones, Gabby Hayes.

King of the Pecos (Republic, 1936) 54 minutes
Directed by Joseph Kane, Screenplay by Bernard McConville and Dorell and Stuart McGowan, Photographed by Jack Martin, Edited by Joseph H. Lewis.
With *J.W.*, Muriel Evans, Cy Kendall, Jack Clifford, Frank Glendon, Herbert Heywood.

The Oregon Trail (Republic, 1936) 59 minutes
Directed by Scott Pembroke, Screenplay by Lindsley Parsons and Robert Emmett, Photographed by Gus Peterson, Edited by Carl Pierson.
With *J.W.*, Ann Rutherford, Yakima Canutt, E. H. Calvert, Fern Emmett, Gino Corrado.

The Sea Spoilers (Universal, 1936) 63 minutes
Directed by Frank Strayer, Screenplay by George Waggoner, Photographed by A. J. Stout, Edited by John P. Fulton.

With *J.W.*, Nan Grey, Fuzzy Knight, William Bakewell, Russell Hicks, George Irving.

Conflict (Universal, 1936) 60 minutes
Directed by David Howard, Screenplay by Charles A. Logue and Walter Weems (based on the story *The Abysmal Brute* by Jack London), Photographed by A. J. Stout, Edited by Jack Ogilvie.
With *J.W.*, Jean Rogers, Tommy Bupp, Eddie Borden, Ward Bond, Harry Woods, Frank Sheridan.

California Straight Ahead (Universal, 1937) 67 minutes
Directed by Arthur Lubin, Screenplay by Herman Boxer, Photographed by Harry Neumann, Edited by Charles Craft and E. Horsley.
With *J.W.*, Louise Latimer, Robert McWade, Tully Marshall, Theodore Von Eltz.

I Cover the War (Universal, 1937) 78 minutes
Directed by Arthur Lubin, Screenplay by George Waggoner, Photographed by Harry Neumann, Edited by Charles Craft.
With *J.W.*, Gwen Gaze, Don Barclay, James Bush, Pat Somerset, Charles Brokaw, Arthur Aylesworth.

Idol of the Crowds (Universal, 1937) 62 minutes
Directed by Arthur Lubin, Screenplay by George Waggoner and Harold Buckley, Photographed by Harry Neumann, Edited by Charles Craft.
With *J.W.*, Sheila Bromley, Billy Burrud, Russell Gordon, Charles Brokaw, Clem Bevans.

Adventure's End (Universal, 1937) 68 minutes
Directed by Arthur Lubin, Screenplay by Ben Ames Williams, Photographed by Gus Peterson and John Fulton, Edited by Charles Craft.
With *J.W.*, Diana Gibson, Moroni Olsen, Montague Love, Ben Carter, Maurice Black.

Born to the West (Paramount, 1938) 59 minutes
Directed by Charles Barton, Screenplay by Zane Grey, Photographed by J. D. Jennings, Edited by John Link.
With *J.W.*, Marsha Hunt, Johnny Mack Brown, Monte Blue, Alan Ladd, James Craig, John Patterson.

Pals of the Saddle (Republic, 1938) 60 minutes
Directed by George Sherman, Written by Stanley Roberts and Betty Burbidge, Photographed by Reggie Lanning, Edited by Tony Martinelli.
With *J.W.*, Ray "Crash" Corrigan, Max Terhune, Doreen McKay, Frank Milan, Jack Kirk.

Wayne was one of the Three Mesquiteers with Max Terhune (left) and Ray "Crash" Corrigan (right).

Overland Stage Raiders (Republic, 1938) 55 minutes
Directed by George Sherman, Screenplay by Luci Ward, Photographed by William Nobles, Edited by Tony Martinelli.
With J.W., Louise Brooks, Ray Corrigan, Max Terhune, Fern Emmett, Frank LaRue.

Santa Fe Stampede (Republic, 1938) 58 minutes
Directed by George Sherman, Screenplay by Luci Ward and Betty Burbridge, Photographed by Reggie Lanning, Edited by Tony Martinelli.
With J.W., June Martel, Ray Corrigan, Max Terhune, William Farnum, LeRoy Mason.

Red River Range (Republic, 1938) 59 minutes
Directed by George Sherman, Screenplay by Stanley Roberts, Betty Burbridge and Luci Ward (based on a story by Ward), Photographed by Jack Marta, Edited by Tony Martinelli.
With J.W., Ray Corrigan, Max Terhune, Polly Moran, Kirby Grant, William Royle.

Stagecoach (United Artists, 1939) 96 minutes
Directed by John Ford, Screenplay by Dudley Nichols (based on a story by Ernest Haycox), Photographed by Bert Glennon and Ray Binger, Edited by Dorothy Spencer and Walter Reynolds.
With *J.W.*, Claire Trevor, Thomas Mitchell, John Carradine, Andy Devine, Louise Platt, George Bancroft, Berton Churchill, Donald Meek, Tim Holt, Tom Tyler, Yakima Canutt.

The Night Riders (Republic, 1939) 58 minutes
Directed by George Sherman, Screenplay by Betty Burbridge and Stanley Roberts, Photographed by Jack Marta, Edited by Lester Orlebeck.
With *J.W.*, Ray Corrigan, Max Terhune, Doreen McKay, Ruth Rogers, Tom Tyler, Kermit Maynard.

New Frontier (Republic, 1939) 56 minutes
Directed by George Sherman, Screenplay by Luci Ward and Betty Burbridge, Photographed by Reggie Lanning, Edited by Tony Martinelli.
With *J.W.*, Phyllis Isley (Jennifer Jones), Ray Corrigan, Raymond Hatton, Dave O'Brien.

Allegheny Uprising (RKO Radio Pictures, 1939) 81 minutes
Directed by William Seiter, Screenplay by P.J. Wolfson (based on the story *The First Rebel* by Neil Swanson), Photographed by Nicholas Musuraca, Edited by George Crone.
With *J.W.*, George Sanders, Brian Donlevy, Wilford Lawson, Robert Barrat, John Hamilton, Eddie Quillan, Chill Wills, Moroni Olsen, Monte Montague, Eddie Walker, Ian Wolfe.

Dark Command (Republic, 1940) 92 minutes
Directed by Raoul Walsh, Screenplay by Grover Jones, Lionel Houser and F. Hugh Herbert (based on the novel by W. R. Burnett), Photographed by Jack Mata, Edited by William Morgan.
With *J.W.*, Claire Trevor, Walter Pidgeon, Gabby Hayes, Roy Rogers, Marjorie Main.

Three Faces West (Republic, 1940) 79 minutes
Directed by Bernard Vorhaus, Screenplay by F. Hugh Herbert and Samuel Ornitz, Photographed by John Alton, Edited by William Morgan.
With *J.W.*, Sigrid Gurie, Charles Coburn, Spencer Charters, Helen MacKellar, Sonny Bupp.

The Long Voyage Home (United Artists, 1940) 105 minutes
Directed by John Ford, Screenplay by Dudley Nichols (based on the play by Eugene O'Neill), Photographed by Greg Tolland, Edited by Walter Reynolds.
With *J.W.*, Thomas Mitchell, Ian Hunter, Barry Fitzgerald, Wilfrid

Lawson, Mildred Natwick, John Qualen, Ward Bond, Arthur Shields, Joe Sawyer, Rafaela Ottiana, Billy Bevan.

Seven Sinners (Universal, 1940) 81 minutes
Directed by Tay Garnett, Screenplay by John Meehan and Harry Tugend, Photographed by Rudolph Mate, Edited by Jack Ogilvie.
With J.W., Marlene Dietrich, Broderick Crawford, Mischa Auer, Albert Dekker, Billy Gilbert, Anna Lee, Oscar Homolka, Samuel S. Hinds, Reginald Denny, Vince Barntree, James Craig.

A Man Betrayed (Republic, 1940) 83 minutes
Directed by John Auer, Screenplay by Isabel Dawn, Photographed by Jack Marta, Edited by Charles Craft.
With J.W., Frances Dee, Edward Ellis, Wallace Ford, Ward Bond, Harold Huber.

Lady from Louisiana (Republic, 1941) 84 minutes
Directed by Bernard Vorhaus, Screenplay by Vera Caspary, Photographed by Jack Marta, Edited by Edward Mann.
With J.W., Ona Munson, Ray Middleton, Henry Stephenson, Helen Westley, Jack Pennick, Dorothy Dandridge, Shimen Ruskin.

The Shepherd of the Hills (Paramount, 1941) 97 minutes
Directed by Henry Hathaway, Screenplay by Grover Jones and Stuart Anthony (from the novel by Harold Bell Wright), Photographed by Charles Lang, Edited by Ellsworth Hoaglund.
With J.W., Betty Field, Harry Carey, Beulah Bondi, James Barton, Samuel S. Hinds, Marjorie Main, Ward Bond, Marc Lawrence.

Lady for a Night (Republic, 1942) 87 minutes
Directed by Leigh Jason, Screenplay by Isabel Dawn and Boyce DeGaw, Photographed by Norbert Brodine, Edited by Ernest Nims.
With J.W., Joan Blondell, Ray Middleton, Phillip Merivale, Blanche Yurka, Edith Barrett, Leonid Kinsky, Hattie Noel, Montague Love.

Reap the Wild Wind (Paramount, 1942) 124 minutes; Color
Directed by Cecil B. DeMille, Screenplay by Alan LeMay, Charles Bennett and Jesse Lasky, Jr. (based on a *Saturday Evening Post* story by Thelma Strabel), Photographed by Victor Milner and William V. Skall, Edited by Anne Bauchens.
With J.W., Ray Milland, Paulette Goddard, Susan Hayward, Raymond Massey, Robert Preston, Lynn Overman, Louise Beavers, Walter Hampden, Elizabeth Risdon, Hedda Hopper, Martha O'Driscoll, Victor Kilian, Monte Blue, Charles Bickford, Janet Beecher, Barbara Britton, Mildred Harris, Victor Varconi, Julia Faye, Oscar Polk, Ben Carter, Lane Chandler, Milburn Stone.

The Spoilers (Universal, 1942) 84 minutes

Directed by Ray Enright, Screenplay by Laurence Hazard and Tom Reed, Photographed by Milton Krasner, Edited by Andy Buchanan.

With *J.W.*, Marlene Dietrich, Randolph Scott, Margaret Lindsey, Harry Carey, Richard Barthelmess, William Farnum, George Cleveland, Samuel S. Hinds, Russell Simpson, Jack Norton.

In Old California (Republic, 1942) 88 minutes

Directed by William McGann, Screenplay by Gertrude Purcell and Frances Hyland, Photographed by Jack Marta, Edited by Howard O'Neill.

With *J.W.*, Binnie Barnes, Albert Dekker, Helen Parrish, Patsy Kelly, Edgar Kennedy, Dick Purcell, Harry Shannon, Charles Halton.

Flying Tigers (Republic, 1942) 101 minutes

Directed by David Miller, Screenplay by Kenneth Gamet and Barry Trivers (from a story by Gamet), Photographed by Jack Marta, Edited by Ernest Nims.

With *J.W.*, John Carroll, Anna Lee, Paul Kelly, Gordon Jones, Mae Clarke, Addison Richards, Edmund MacDonald, Bill Shirley.

Reunion in France (MGM, 1942) 104 minutes

Directed by Jules Dassin, Screenplay by Jan Lustig, Photographed by Robert Planck, Edited by Nick Toper.

With *J.W.*, Joan Crawford, Phillip Dorn, Reginald Owen, John Carradine.

Pittsburgh (Universal, 1942) 98 minutes

Directed by Lewis Seiler, Screenplay by Kenneth Gamet and Tom Reed, Photographed by Robert DeGrasse, Edited by Robb Luehr

With *J.W.*, Marlene Dietrich, Randolph Scott, Frank Craven, Louise Albritton, Thomas Gomez, Ludwig Stossel, Shemp Howard.

A Lady Takes a Chance (RKO Radio Pictures, 1943) 86 minutes

Directed by William Seiter, Screenplay by Robert Ardrey, Photographed by Frank Redman, Edited by Theron Warth.

With *J.W.*, Jean Arthur, Charles Winninger, Phil Silvers, Mary Field.

Alternate title: *The Cowboy and the Girl*.

War of the Wildcats (Republic, 1943) 102 minutes

Directed by Albert S. Rogell, Screenplay by Ethel Hill and Eleanor Griffin, Photographed by Jack Marta, Edited by Ernest Nims.

With *J.W.*, Martha Scott, Albert Dekker, Gabby Hayes, Marjorie Rambeau, Dale Evans, Grant Withers, Sidney Blackmer, Paul Fox.

Alternate title: *In Old Oklahoma*.

The Fighting Seabees (Republic, 1944) 100 minutes

Directed by Howard Lydecker and Ed Ludwig, Screenplay by Borden Chase and Aeneas MacKenzie (based on a story by Chase), Photographed by Robert de Grasse, Edited by Phillip Martin, Jr.

With *J.W.*, Ella Raines, Ward Bond, Gabby Hayes, Audrey Long.

Flame of the Barbary Coast (Republic, 1945) 91 minutes
Directed by Joseph Kane, Screenplay by Borden Chase, Photographed by Frank de Grasse, Edited by Richard Van Enger.
With *J.W.*, Ann Dvorak, Joseph Schildkraut, William Frawley, Virginia Grey, Russell Hicks, Jack Norton, Paul Fix.

Back to Bataan (RKO Radio Pictures, 1945) 97 minutes
Directed by Edward Dmytryk, Screenplay by Ben Barzman and Richard Landau, Photographed by Nicholas Musuraca, Edited by Marston Fay.
With *J.W.*, Anthony Quinn, Beulah Bondi, Fely Franquelli, Leonard Strong, Richard Loo, Phillip Ahn, Laurence Tierney.

Dakota (Republic, 1945) 83 minutes
Directed by Joseph Kane, Screenplay by Laurence Hazard, Photographed by Jack Marta, Edited by Frederick Allan.
With *J.W.*, Vera Hruba Ralston, Walter Brennan, Ward Bond.

They Were Expendable (MGM, 1945) 136 minutes
Directed by John Lord, Screenplay by Lt. Commander Frank Wead (based on a story by William L. White), Photographed by Joseph H. August, Edited by Frank E. Hull.
With *J.W.*, Robert Montgomery, Donna Reed, Jack Holt, Ward Bond, Marshall Thompson, Paul Langton, Leon Ames, Arthur Walsh, Don Curtis, Cameron Mitchell, Jeff York, Murray Alper, Harry Tenbrook, Jack Pennick, Alex Havier, Charles Trowbridge.

Without Reservations (RKO Pictures, 1945) 107 minutes
Directed by Mervyn LeRoy, Screenplay by Andrew Solt, Photographed by Milton Krasner, Edited by Jack Ruggiero and Harold Stine.
With *J.W.*, Claudette Colbert, Don DeFore, Anne Triola, Phil Brown.

Angel and the Badman (Republic, 1947) 100 minutes
Directed by James Edward Grant, Screenplay by Grant, Photographed by A. J. Stout, Edited by Harry Keller.
With *J.W.*, Gail Russell, Harry Carey, Bruce Cabot, Irene Rich, Lee Dixon, Tom Powers.

Tycoon (RKO Radio Pictures, 1947) 126 minutes; color
Directed by Richard Wallace, Screenplay by Barbara Chase and John Twist (based on the novel by C. E. Scoggins), Photographed by Harry J. Wild, Edited by Frank Doyle.
With *J.W.*, Laraine Day, Sir Cedric Harwicke, Judith Anderson, James Gleason, Anthony Quinn.

Fort Apache (RKO Radio Pictures, 1948) 128 minutes

Directed by John Ford, Screenplay by Merian C. Cooper, Photographed by A. J. Stout, Edited by Jack Murray.

With *J.W.*, Henry Fonda, Shirley Temple, John Agar, Pedro Armendariz, Ward Bond, Irene Rich.

Red River (United Artists, 1948) 125 minutes

Directed by Howard Hawks, Screenplay by Borden Chase and Charles Schnee, Photographed by Russell Harlan, Edited by Christian Nyby.

With *J.W.*, Montgomery Clift, Walter Brennan, Joanne Drew, Harry Carey, John Ireland.

Three Godfathers (MGM, 1949) 106 minutes; Color

Directed by John Ford, Screenplay by Laurence Stallings and Frank Nugent, Photographed by Winton Hoch, Edited by Nick Toper.

With *J.W.*, Pedro Armendariz, Harry Carey, Jr., Ward Bond, Mae Marsh, Mildred Natwick, Jane Darwell, Guy Kibbee, Dorothy Ford, Ben Johnson, Charles Halton, Hank Worden.

Wake of the Red Witch (Republic, 1949) 106 minutes

Directed by Edward Ludwig, Screenplay by Harry Brown and Kenneth Gamet (based on the novel by Garland Roark), Photographed by Reggie Lanning, Edited by Richard L. Van Enger.

With *J.W.*, Gail Russell, Gig Young, Adele Mara, Luther Adler, Eduard Franz, Grant Withers.

She Wore a Yellow Ribbon (RKO Radio Pictures, 1949) 104 minutes; Color

Directed by John Ford, Screenplay by Frank Nugent and Laurence Stallings, Photographed by Winton Hoch, Edited by Jack Murray.

With *J.W.*, Joanne Dru, John Agar, Ben Johnson, Harry Carey, Jr., Victor McLaglen, Mildred Natwick, George O'Brien, Arthur Shields, Harry Woods, Chief Big Tree, Noble Johnson.

The Fighting Kentuckian (Republic, 1949) 100 minutes

Directed by George Waggoner, Screenplay by Waggoner, Photographed by Lee Garmes, Edited by Richard L. Van Enger.

With *J.W.*, Vera Ralston, Phillip Dorn, Oliver Hardy, Marie Windsor, John Howard, Hugo Haas.

Sands of Iwo Jima (Republic, 1949) 105 minutes

Directed by Allan Dwan, Screenplay by Harry Brown and James Edward Grant (from a story by Brown), Photographed by Reggie Lanning, Edited by Richard L. Van Enger.

With *J.W.*, John Agar, Adele Mara, Forrest Tucker, Wally Cassell, James Brown, Martin Milner.

Rio Grande (Republic, 1950) 105 minutes

Directed by John Ford, Screenplay by James Kevin McGuinness, Photographed by Bert Glennon, Edited by Jack Murray.

With *J.W.*, Maureen O'Hara, Ben Johnson, J. Carroll Naish, Victor McLaglen, Chill Wills, Harry Carey, Claude Jarman, Jr., Grant Withers, the Sons of the Pioneers.

Operation Pacific (Warner Bros., 1950) 111 minutes
Directed by George Waggoner, Screenplay by Waggoner, Photographed by Bert Glennon, Edited by Alan Crosland, Jr.
With *J.W.*, Patricia Neal, Ward Bond, Scott Forbes, Phillip Carey, Martin Milner, Jack Pennick.

Flying Leathernecks (RKO Radio Pictures, 1951), 102 minutes; Color
Directed by Nicholas Ray, Screenplay by James Edward Grant, Photographed by William Snyder, Edited by Sherman Todd.
With *J.W.*, Robert Ryan, Don Taylor, Janis Carter, Jay C. Flippen, William Harrigan.

The Quiet Man (Republic, 1951) 129 minutes; Color
Directed by John Ford, Screenplay by Frank Nugent, Photographed by Winton Hoch, Edited by Jack Murray.
With *J.W.*, Maureen O'Hara, Barry Fitzgerald, Ward Bond, Victor McLaglen, Mildred Natwick.

Big Jim McLain (Warner Bros., 1952) 90 minutes
Directed by Edward Ludwig, Screenplay by James Edward Grant, Edited by Jack Murray, Photographed by A. J. Stout.
With *J.W.*, Nancy Olsen, James Arness, Alan Napier, Gayne Whitman, Hans Conreid, Veda Ann Borg.

Trouble Along the Way (Warner Bros., 1953) 110 minutes
Directed by Michael Curtiz, Screenplay by Melville Shavelson and Jack Rose, Photographed by A. J. Stout, Edited by Owen Marks.
With *J.W.*, Donna Reed, Charles Coburn, Tom Tully, Marie Windsor, Sherry Jackson, Chuck Connors.

Island in the Sky (Warner Bros., 1953) 109 minutes
Directed by William Wellman, Screenplay by Ernest Gann (from his novel), Photographed by William Clothier, Edited by Ralph Dawson.
With *J.W.*, Lloyd Nolan, Walter Abel, James Arness, Andy Devine, Allyn Joslyn, James Lydon.

Hondo (Warner Bros., 1953) 84 minutes; Color
Directed by John Farrow, Screenplay by James Edward Grant, Photographed by Robert Burks and A. J. Stout, Edited by Ralph Dawson.
With *J.W.*, Geraldine Page, Ward Bond, Michael Pate, Lee Aaker, James Arness, Paul Fix.

The High and the Mighty (Warner Bros., 1954) 147 minutes; Color
Directed by William Wellman, Screenplay by Ernest K. Gann (from his novel), Photographed by A. J. Stout, Edited by Ralph Dawson.
With *J.W.*, Claire Trevor, Laraine Day, Robert Stack, Jan Sterling, Phil Harris, Robert Newton.

The Sea Chase (Warner Bros., 1955) 117 minutes; Color
Directed by John Farrow, Screenplay by Warren Bellah and John Twist (based on the novel by Andrew Geer), Photographed by William Clothier, Edited by William Ziegler.
With *J.W.*, Lana Turner, David Farrar, Lyle Bettger, Tab Hunter, James Arness, Paul Fix.

Blood Alley (Warner Bros., 1955) 118 minutes; Color
Directed by William Wellman, Screenplay by A. S. Fleischman (from his novel), Photographed by William Clothier, Edited by Fred McDowell.
With *J.W.*, Lauren Bacall, Paul Fix, Joy Kim, Mike Mazurki.

The Conqueror (RKO Radio Pictures, 1956) 110 minutes; Color
Directed by Dick Powell, Screenplay by Oscar Millard, Photographed by Joseph La Shelle, Leo Tover, Harry Wild, and William Snyder, Edited by Robert Ford and Kenneth Marstella.
With *J.W.*, Susan Hayward, Pedro Armendariz, Agnes Morehead, Thomas Gomez, John Hoyt, William Conrad, Ted de Corsia, Leslie Bradley.
Note: Atomic testing near the shooting of this film is said to have caused the cancer deaths of this film's director and many of its principal players.

The Searchers (Warner Bros., 1956) 119 minutes; Color
Directed by John Ford, Screenplay by Frank Nugent, Photographed by Winton Hoch, Edited by Jack Murray.
With *J.W.*, Jeffrey Hunter, Vera Miles, Natalie Wood, John Qualen, Olive Carey, Henry Brandon, Ken Curtis, Harry Carey, Jr., Antonio Moreno, Hank Worden, Lana Wood, Walter Coy, Dorothy Jordan, Pippa Scott, Pay Wayne, Ward Bond.

The Wings of Eagles (MGM, 1957) 118 minutes; Color
Directed by John Ford, Screenplay by Frank Fenton, Photographed by Paul Vogel, Edited by Gene Ruggiero.
With *J.W.*, Dan Dailey, Maureen O'Hara, Ward Bond, Ken Curtis.

Jet Pilot (RKO Radio Pictures, 1957) 112 minutes
Directed by Josef von Sternberg, Screenplay by Jules Furthman, Photographed by Winton Hoch, Edited by Michael McAdam.
With *J.W.*, Janet Leigh, Jay C. Flippen, Paul Fix, Richard Rober.

Legend of the Lost (United Artists, 1957) 109 minutes; Color
Directed by Henry Hathaway, Screenplay by Robert Presnell and Ben Hecht, Photographed by Jack Cardiff, Edited by Bert Bates.
With J.W., Sophia Loren, Rossano Brazzi, Kurt Kasznar, Sonia Moser.

The Barbarian and the Geisha (20th Century–Fox, 1958) 104 minutes; Color
Directed by John Huston, Screenplay by Charles Grayson, Photographed by Charles Clark, Edited by Stuart Gilmore.
With J.W., Eiko Ando, Sam Jaffe, So Yamamura, Norman Thomson.

Rio Bravo (Warner Bros., 1959) 141 minutes; Color
Directed by Howard Hawks, Screenplay by Jules Furthman, Photographed by Russell Harlan, Edited by Folmar Blangsted.
With J.W., Dean Martin, Ricky Nelson, Angie Dickinson, Walter Brennan, Ward Bond, John Russell, Pedro Gonzalez-Gonzalez.

The Horse Soldiers (United Artists, 1959) 119 minutes; Color
Directed by John Ford, Screenplay by John Lee Mahin and Martin Rackin, Photographed by William Clothier, Edited by Jack Murray.
With J.W., William Holden, Constance Towers, Hoot Gibson, Anna Lee.

The Alamo (United Artists, 1960) 199 minutes; Color
Directed by John Wayne, Screenplay by James Edward Grant, Photographed by William Clothier, Edited by Stuart Gilmore.
With J.W., Richard Widmark, Laurence Harvey, Richard Boone, Frankie Avalon, Patrick Wayne, Linda Cristal, Joan O'Brien, Chill Wills, Joseph Calleia, Ken Curtis, Veda Ann Borg, Guinn "Big Boy" Williams.

North to Alaska (20th Century–Fox, 1960), 122 minutes; Color
Directed by Henry Hathaway, Screenplay by John Lee Mahin, Photographed by Leon Shamroy, Edited by Dorothy Spencer.
With J.W., Stewart Granger, Ernie Kovacs, Capucine, Fabian.

The Comancheros (20th Century–Fox, 1961) 107 minutes; Color
Directed by Michael Curtiz, Screenplay by James Edward Grant and Clair Huffaker, Photographed by William Clothier, Edited by Louis Loeffler.
With J.W., Stuart Whitman, Ina Balin, Nehemiah Persoff, Lee Marvin.

The Man Who Shot Liberty Valance (Paramount, 1962) 123 minutes
Directed by John Ford, Screenplay by James Bellah and Willis Goldbeck, Photographed by William Clothier, Edited by Otto Irving.
With J.W., Jimmy Stewart, Vera Miles, Lee Marvin, Andy Devine.

Hatari (Paramount, 1962) 157 minutes
Directed by Howard Hawks, Screenplay by Leigh Bracket, Photographed by Russell Harlan, Edited by Stuart Gilmore.

With *J.W.*, Hardy Kruger, Elsa Martinelli, Red Buttons, Gerard Blaine, Michele Giradon.

The Longest Day (20th Century–Fox, 1962) 180 minutes
Directed by Ken Annakin, Screenplay by Cornelius Ryan (based on his book), Photographed by Jean Borgoin, Henri Persin and Walter Woritz.
With , Robert Mitchum, Henry Fonda, Robert Ryan, Rod Steiger Robert Wagner, Richard Beymer, Mel Ferrer, Jeffrey Hunter, Paul Anka, Sal Mineo, Roddy McDowell, Stuart Whitman, Steve Forrest, Eddie Albert, Edmund O'Brien, Fabian, Red Buttons, Tom Tryon, Alexander Knox, Richard Burton, Kenneth Moore, Peter Lawford, Richard Todd, Sean Connery, Curt Jergens, Paul Hartmann, Ray Danton, George Segal, Werner Hinz, Gert Froebe.

How the West Was Won (MGM, 1962) 162 minutes; Color
Directed by Henry Hathaway, John Ford, and George Marshall, Screenplay by James Webb, Photographed by William Daniels, Milton Krasner, Charles Lang, and Joseph LaShelle, Edited by Harold F. Kress.
With Carroll Baker, James Stewart, Lee J. Cobb, Henry Fonda, Carolyn Jones, Debbie Reynolds, Karl Malden, Gregory Peck, George Peppard, Robert Preston, *J.W.*, Eli Wallach, Richard Widmark, Walter Brennan, Andy Devine, Raymond Massey, Agnes Moorehead, Harry Morgan, Thelma Ritter, Mickey Shaughnessy, Russ Tamblyn, Lee Van Cleef, Joe Sawyer.
Note: Narrated by Spencer Tracy.

Donavan's Reef (Paramount, 1963) 112 minutes; Color
Directed by John Ford, Photographed by William Clothier, Edited by Otho Lovering.
With *J.W.*, Lee Marvin, Elizabeth Allen, Jack Warden, Cesar Romero, Dorothy Lamour.

McLintock! (United Artists, 1963) 127 minutes; Color
Directed by Andrew McLaglen, Screenplay by James Edward Grant, Photographed by William Clothier, Edited by Otho Lovering.
With *J.W.*, Maureen O'Hara, Patrick Wayne, Stefanie Powers, Yvonne DeCarlo, Jack Kruschen, Chill Wills, Jerry Van Dyke, Edgar Buchanan, Bruce Cabot, Strother Martin, Gordon Jones.

Circus World (Paramount, 1964) 131 minutes; Color
Directed by Henry Hathaway, Screenplay by Ben Hecht, Julian Halvey and Jamed Edward Grant, Photographed by Jack Hilyard and Claude Renoir, Edited by Dorothy Spencer.
With *J.W.*, Claudia Cardinale, Rita Hayworth, Lloyd Nolan, Richard Conte, John Smith.

The Greatest Story Ever Told (United Artists, 1965) 195 minutes; Color
Directed by George Stevens, Screenplay by Stevens and James Lee Barrett, Photographed by William Mellor and Loyal Griggs, Edited by Harold Kress.

With Max von Sydow, Dorothy McGuire, Robert Loggia, Charleton Heston, Michael Anderson, Robert Blake, Burt Brinckerhoff, John Considine, Jamie Farr, David Hedison, Peter Mann, David McCallum, Roddy McDowell, Gary Raymond, Tom Reese, David Sheiner, Ina Balin, Janet Margolin, Sidney Poitier, Carroll Baker, Pat Boone, Van Heflin, Sal Mineo, Shelley Winters, Ed Wynn, J.W., Telly Savalas, Angela Lansbury, Victor Buono, Nehemiah Persoff.

In Harm's Way (Paramount, 1965) 165 minutes; Color
Directed by Otto Preminger, Screenplay by Wendell Mayes, Photographed by Loyal Griggs, Edited by George Tomasini.
With J.W., Kirk Douglas, Patricia Neal, Tom Tryon, Paula Prentiss, Brandon de Wilde, Jill Haworth, Dana Andrews, Stanley Holloway, Burgess Meredith, Franchot Tone.

The Sons of Katie Elder (Paramount, 1966) 122 minutes; Color
Directed by Henry Hathaway, Screenplay by William Wright, Alan Weiss and Harry Essex, Photographed by Lucien Ballard, Edited by Warren Low.
With J.W., Dean Martin, Martha Hyer, Michael Anderson, Earl Holliman, Jeremy Slate, James Gregory.

Cast a Giant Shadow (United Artists, 1966) 142 minutes; Color
Directed by Melville Shavelson, Screenplay by Ted Berkman, Photographed by Aldo Tonti, Edited by Gene Ruggiero.
With J.W., Yul Brynner, Kirk Douglas, Senta Berger, Angie Dickinson, Luther Adler.

War Wagon (Universal, 1967) 101 minutes; Color
Directed by Burt Kennedy, Screenplay by Clair Huffaker (based on his book).
With J.W., Kirk Douglas, Howard Keel, Robert Walker, Keenan Wynn, Bruce Cabot, Valora Noland.

El Dorado (Paramount, 1967) 126 minutes; Color
Directed by Howard Hawks, Screenplay by Leigh Brackett (based on the novel *The Stars in Their Courses* by Harry Brown), Photographed by Harold Rossen, Edited by John Woodcock.
With J.W., Robert Mitchum, James Caan, Charlene Holt, Michele Carey, Arthur Hunnicut, Paul Fix.

The Green Berets (Warner Bros., 1968) 141 minutes; Color
Directed by John Wayne and Ray Kellogg, Screenplay by James Lee Barrett (from the novel by Robin Moore), Photographed by Winton Hoch, Edited by Otho Lovering.
With J.W., David Janssen, Jim Hutton, Aldo Ray, Raymond St. Jacques, Bruce Cabot, Jack Soo.

Hellfighters (Universal, 1968) 121 minutes; Color
Directed by Andrew McLaglen, Screenplay by Clair Huffaker, Photographed by William Clothier, Edited by Folmar Blangsted.
With *J.W.*, Katherine Ross, Vera Miles, Jim Hutton, Jay C. Flippen, Bruce Cabot, Barbara Stuart.

True Grit (Paramount, 1969) 128 minutes; Color
Directed by Henry Hathaway, Screenplay by Marguerite Roberts (from the novel by Charles Portis), Photographed by Lucien Ballard, Edited by Warren Low.
With *J.W.*, Kim Darby, Glen Campbell, Robert Duvall, Dennis Hopper, Strother Martin, Alfred Ryder.

The Undefeated (20th Century–Fox, 1969) 119 minutes; Color
Directed by Andrew McLaglen, Screenplay by James Lee Barrett, Photographed by William Clothier, Edited by Robert Simpson.
With *J.W.*, Rock Hudson, Antonio Aguilar, Roman Gabriel, Marian McCargo, Lee Meriwether.

Chisum (Warner Bros., 1970) 110 minutes; Color
Directed by Andrew McLaglen, Screenplay by Andrew Fenady, Photographed by William Clothier, Edited by Robert Simpson.
With *J.W.*, Forrest Tucker, Christopher George, Ben Johnson, Glen Corbett, Andrew Prine.

Rio Lobo (National General Pictures, 1971) 114 minutes; Color
Directed by Howard Hawks, Screenplay by Leigh Brackett and Burton Wohl, Photographed by William Clothier, Edited by Robert Simpson.
With *J.W.*, Jorge Rivero, Jennifer O'Neill, Jack Elam, Victor French, Chris Mitchum.

Big Jake (National General Pictures, 1971) 110 minutes; Color
Directed by George Sherman, Screenplay by Harry Julian Fink, Photographed by William Clothier, Edited by Harry Gerstad.
With *J.W.*, Maureen O'Hara, Richard Boone, Patrick Wayne, Chris Mitchum, John Ethan Wayne.

The Cowboys (Universal, 1972) 128 minutes; Color
Directed by Mark Rydell, Screenplay by Irving Ravetch, Harriet Frank, Jr., and William Dale Jennings, Photographed by Robert Surtees, Edited by Robert Swink and Neil Travis.
With *J.W.*, Roscoe Lee Browne, Bruce Dern, Colleen Dewhurst, Slim Pickens, Lonny Chapman.

The Train Robbers (Warner Bros., 1972) 91 minutes; Color
Directed by Burt Kennedy, Screenplay by Kennedy, Photographed by William Clothier, Edited by Frank Santillo.

With *J.W.*, Ann-Margret, Rod Taylor, Ben Johnson, Christopher George, Bobby Vinton.

Cahill, United States Marshal (Warner Bros., 1972) 102 minutes; Color
Directed by Andrew McLaglen, Screenplay by Julian Fink and R. M. Fink, Photographed by Joseph Biroc, Edited by Robert Simpson.
With *J.W.*, George Kennedy, Gary Grimes, Neville Brand, Clay O'Brien, Marie Windsor, Jackie Coogan.

McQ (Warner Bros., 1975) 116 minutes; Color
Directed by John Sturges, Screenplay by Lawrence Roman, Photographed by Harry Stradling, Jr., Edited by William Ziegler.
With *J.W.*, Eddie Albert, Diana Muldaur, Colleen Dewhurst, Clu Gulager, David Huddleston.

Brannigan (United Artists, 1975) 111 minutes; Color
Directed by Doug Hickox, Screenplay by Chris Trumbo, Mike Butler, William McGivern and William Norton, Photographed by Gerry Fisher, Edited by Willia Ziegler.
With *J.W.*, Richard Attenborough, Judy Geeson, Mel Ferrer, John Vernon, Donald Pilon.

Rooster Cogburn and the Lady (Universal, 1976) 107 minutes; Color
Directed by Stu Millar, Screenplay by Martin Julien, Photographed by Harry Stradling, Jr., Edited by Robert Swink.
With *J.W.*, Katharine Hepburn, Anthony Zerbe, Richard Jordan, John McIntyre, Paul Koslo.

The Shootist (Paramount, 1976) 115 minutes; Color
Directed by Don Siegel, Screenplay by Miles Hood Swarthout and Scott Hale (based on the novel by Glendon Swarthout), Photographed by Bruce Surtees, Edited by Douglas Stewart.
With *J.W.*, Lauren Bacall, Ron Howard, James Stewart, Richard Boone, Hugh O'Brien, Bill McKinney, Harry Morgan, John Carradine, Sheree North, Richard Lenz, Scatman Crothers, Gregg Palmer, Alfred Dennis, Melody Thomas, Kathleen O'Malley.

John Wayne made cameo appearances in **I Married a Woman** (RKO Radio Pictures, 1958) and on several television shows.

Opposite, left: Wayne as Rooster Cogburn in his Oscar-winning role for *True Grit* (Paramount, 1969). Right: Wayne with his real-life grandson in *Big Jake* (National General Pictures, 1971).

John Garfield

In his fine book on the Western, *They Went Thataway*, writer James Horowitz refers to John Garfield as "not a cowboy, but he could beat the pants off any tough guy in Hollywood. . . ." Garfield may not have been the greatest tough guy, as Horowitz asserts, but he certainly is among the most important, being the transitional character between the Cagney-Bogart school of yore and the Brando-Dean school that was to follow. While he was a product of the forties and often played an underworld figure, Garfield was much younger than Cagney or Bogart had been in their films and thus added a youthful zest to his characterizations. He brooded in character from the perspective of an angry young man who had just emerged from adolescence to find suppression and alienation in World War II America. He was not content with following the established norm in society and consequently was labeled a troublemaker in the same way that the Cagney characters were. Garfield was also a young punk, however, whose youthful vitality links him to the later, younger tough guys of the fifties, a sort of harbinger for the enduring presentations of postwar youthful alienation that James Dean would come to popularize.

Garfield's earliest roots initially established this persona, his ensuing roles perpetuating it. Even his early death, at the age of 39, kept him from straying too far from the youthful roles that were his forte — dying too soon was an eerily apt culmination to his abrupt and fascinating career. His dark appearance projected the same alluring qualities as George Raft, his youthful passion and vitality making him more sexual.

He glorified women, but still dismissed them as inferior even through his glorification. In glorifying women, the Garfield screen persona fantasized about their sexual appeal as well as their domestic appeal (the two extremes in womanhood as presented in the era's American cinema).

Garfield's first screen appearance of any notoriety was in the 1938 Warner Bros. drama, *Four Daughters*. In this film he's a rebellious hoodlum whose inability to suck up to family ideals makes him an outcast. He becomes involved in an unlikely romance with one of the Lane sisters (stars

John Garfield

of the film) who portray wholesome ladies suppressed by the strict conservatism in their home. The young lady taking up with Garfield is not doing so as an act of rebellion as much as an altruistic attempt to reform him into one of the many faceless conservatives in that society. Such a thing cannot happen to the Garfield screen persona, not even in the idealistic American cinema of the late thirties, and thus the character is killed off.

Not that the Garfield character was incapable of being believable as anything but a hoodlum. In *They Made Me a Criminal*, he portrays a prizefighter who is publicized as good and clean — typical of how the media promoted the era's athletic heroes. He was one who never drank and always dedicated fights to his mother, for example. A wild party that occurs just after one victory, however, shows a reporter otherwise. This leads to a drunken struggle and an accidental death. Garfield (known as Johnny in this section of the film) is knocked unconscious while his manager and girl escape in Johnny's car. There is an accident, the car is destroyed by fire as are the bodies therein, one of them presumably Johnny. When Johnny awakens days later he is startled to read that he not only is said to have committed murder, but is now dead. The advice of another unscrupulous friend has him roaming the country as a hobo, under the alias of Jack Dorney. He cannot get into fights as his prizefighting stance could be recognized (as a fighter he was a noted southpaw). This interesting rule suppresses his manhood, and thus Dorney must present himself as semitough in a world of tough men, backing down to pseudotough guys.

In the course of the narrative, Garfield (as Dorney now) is reformed by a wholesome woman who lives on a ranch with her tough grandmother (May Robson in a characteristic supporting role) and a group of juvenile delinquents who are being rehabilitated for petty crimes (the Dead End Kids in all of their energetic glory). The situations are somewhat hackneyed, and the climax is, predictably, a prizefight where Dorney cannot use his left-handed stance and is beaten soundly until finally switching toward the end (this is the only nonmusical directed by Busby Berkeley, his choreographical prowess presented in the fight scenes). Garfield is reformed through these hackneyed situations, but the believability stems from his having always perpetuated a wholesome image outside of his less wholesome self. He plays good guy while being a bad guy, and then is forced to become a good guy when he is abruptly shown how unscrupulous his peers have been in the fight game. That he is allowed to retain his identity gives the viewer a forgiving society in the form of a detective played by Claude Rains, who did recognize Dorney as Johnny at the fight. Now that Johnny no longer has to run, Dorney no longer has to back down and suppress his coveted manhood.

Garfield's abilities as an actor were shown in a screen persona that was very precise, thus limiting his screen roles. While always successful in performance, he was placed in a seemingly endless series of Warner Bros. programmers throughout the early and mid-forties, from the prison dramas *Blackwell's Island* and *Castle on the Hudson* to war sagas like *Air Force*. That he matured greatly during the late forties is a testament to his hooking meatier roles that better befitted his masculine image. Garfield was too sensual to be presented as a tough criminal in the Cagney fashion, and he was too young and "street" looking to play the sexual Clark Gable–type roles.

The perfect place for Garfield was in roles that fell just between the examples above. Perhaps the first important role was the pivotal one in Elia

Kazan's brilliant indictment of anti–Semitism titled *Gentleman's Agreement* (1947). It placed Garfield in the role of the falsely accused, only from the perspective that he was the innocent while the accusers were guilty of harsh bigotry. It is his plight that causes the lead character (Gregory Peck) to pose as a Jew and attempt to enjoy the same benefits as a Gentile (such as membership in exclusive clubs). That this film became one of the most idealistic statements against the bigotry of its time is enhanced by the fact that both Kazan and Garfield were ruined by their communist sympathies during the McCarthy witch-hunts a few years later (Kazan being one of the infamous "Hollywood Ten").

Garfield's telling part in *Gentleman's Agreement* was what led to his being cast opposite Lana Turner as the star of Tay Garnett's steamy screen adaptation of James M. Cain's *The Postman Always Rings Twice*. In spite of a tawdry remake in 1980, this original version, though victimized by then-prevalent censorship, managed to exhibit a strong emphasis on Garfield's character's sexuality as had been intimated in so many of his other screen roles. Garfield is perfectly cast in the role of a drifter whose presence overpowers the sexually repressed Turner, as the pair soon stumble into an affair and eventually plot to murder her sexless husband (Cecil Kellaway). As the film deals with empty lives, the film is presented as very dark and brooding, enhancing the performances and the flavor of the production.

Rather than the blatant sexuality that appears so forced in the remake (which featured Jack Nicholson and Jessica Lange), this original American version (the story was filmed twice before, in France and in Italy) is powerful in presenting the sexual angst that is overpowering Turner as well as the stereotypically masculine lust that propels Garfield to a victim of his own unceasing libido. The two look at each other and tremble on the inside, exhibiting their inner needs through the facial expression and body language that any good actor is endowed with. Garfield is not so complex a person as are his animal drives, which blend with his animal magnetism. He is a physical being, a sexy male whose almost spiritual presence is the personification of sensual Turner's fantasies. *The Postman Always Rings Twice* also enhances Garfield's eternal attachment to youth and young roles, as his character is presented as the young catalyst who fulfills Turner's needs in a way in which her older mate cannot. The emphasis on the sexual aspects of his persona stems from his playing a character out of steamy pulp fiction — a character that is honed to include traits of the established Garfield persona.

But if *The Postman Always Rings Twice* accentuated the sexual aspects of Garfield's screen presentation of masculinity, his other 1947 starrer, *Body and Soul*, focused on the athletic aspects. Garfield is again a boxer in yet another story regarding a tough kid with a good punch making it in the world of prizefighting. Garfield's character becomes a victim of this environment as his set of values decreases to that of a stereotypical pugilist whose most prized possessions are wealth and victory—two things that go together in this portrayal of the seedy business. That both can be obtained by inflicting physical injury is perhaps a perverse statement against the antithesis of the athletic world of the American male, that being the business world. In the late forties and early fifties, Hollywood approached businessmen for their sameness and established place in society. *The Man in the Gray Flannel Suit* (20th Century–Fox, 1956) is perhaps the best screen example from this period.

In *Body and Soul*, success is gained through hurting others just as it is in the business world, boxing instead taking a more blatant approach via physical pain. One character in the film, a washed up black boxer, deals with bigotry in the business and dies early due to injuries suffered in the ring. As Garfield's character sees this boxer used as a piece of meat, he questions his own existence and ultimately no longer has the security that he so self-centeredly started with. Garfield's idealism is that of a young man (further accenting the youthful aspects of his screen persona) who comes of age within the sport and finally realizes how it destroys lives. The business world that it parallels deals with older men who have left youth behind and are taking their place in society as per conservative structure.

That Garfield's screen persona presented masculinity through idealistic as well as sexual terms makes it all the more ironic that his career was ruined by the McCarthy witch-hunts. He did very little work of note after *Body and Soul*, succumbing to a heart attack in 1953 at the age of 39. It is somewhat fitting that he met an early end, as there seemed to be no place for a mature Garfield in the American cinema. As Garfield got older, the times became progressively more liberal and ultimately would have caught up with the persona that he best exhibited as a young man.

Garfield's brief career may have been only a small aspect of American film, but the impact he had on characterization had a profound effect on future tough guys from Marlon Brando and James Dean to Sylvester Stallone, whose *Rocky* drew several comparisons to *Body and Soul*. Garfield is important for presenting the initial aspects of the Hollywood tough guy from the perspective of sexuality and idealism as stemming from youthful vitality. The link between adolescence and adulthood that his performances conveyed was to find itself at the forefront of many important American films of the ensuing decades.

John Garfield Filmography

Four Daughters (Warner Bros., 1938) 90 minutes
Directed by Michael Curtiz, Screenplay by Julius Epstein, Photographed by Ernest Haler, Edited by Ralph Dawson.
With *J.G.*, Priscilla Lane, Rosemary Lane, Lola Lane, Gale Page, Dick Foran, Jeffrey Lynn, Frank McHugh.

Blackwell's Island (Warner Bros., 1939) 85 minutes
Directed by William McGann, Screenplay by Crane Wilbur, Photographed by Sid Hickox, Edited by Douglas Gould.
With *J.G.*, Rosemary Lane, Dick Purcell, Victor Jory, Stanley Fields, Morgan Conway, Granville Bates

Daughters Courageous (Warner Bros., 1939) 107 minutes
Directed by Michael Curtiz, Screenplay by Julius and Philip Epstein, Photographed by James Wong Howe, Edited by Ralph Dawson.
With *J.G.*, Rosemary Lane, Lola Lane, Priscilla Lane, Claude Rains, Fay Bainter, Donald Crisp, May Robson, Frank McHugh.

Dust Be My Destiny (Warner Bros., 1939) 88 minutes
Directed by Lewis Seiler, Screenplay by Robert Rossen, Photographed by James Wong Howe, Edited by Warren Lowe.
With *J.G.*, Priscilla Lane, Alan Hale, Frank McHugh, Billy Halop, Bobby Jordan, Charlie Grapewin.

Juarez (Warner Bros., 1939) 132 minutes
Directed by William Dieterle, Screenplay by John Huston, Photographed by Tony Gaudio, Edited by Warren Low.
With *J.G.*, Paul Muni, Bette Davis, Brian Aherne, Claude Rains, Donald Crisp, Gale Sondergaard.

They Made Me a Criminal (Warner Bros., 1939) 92 minutes
Directed by Busby Berkely, Screenplay by Sid Herzig, Photographed by James Wong Howe, Edited by Jack Kilifer.
With *J.G.*, Gloria Dickson, Claude Rains, May Robson, Billy Halop, Leo Gorcey, Huntz Hall, Bobby Jordan, Bernard Punsley, Gabe Dell.

Castle on the Hudson (Warner Bros., 1940) 76 minutes
Directed by Anatole Litvak, Screenplay by Seton Miller, Photographed by Art Edeson, Edited by Tom Richards.
With *J.G.*, Ann Sheridan, Pat O'Brien, Burgess Meredith, Henry O'Neill, John Litel.

East of the River (Warner Bros., 1940) 73 minutes
Directed by Alfred E. Green, Screenplay by Fred Niblo, Jr., Photographed by Sid Hickox, Edited by Thomas Pratt.
With *J.G.*, Brenda Marshall, Marjorie Rambeau, George Tobias, William Lundigan, Moroni Olsen.

Flowing Gold (Warner Bros., 1940) 82 minutes
Directed by Alfred Green, Screenplay by Kenneth Gamet, Photographed by Sid Hickox, Edited by James Gibbon.
With *J.G.*, Frances Farmer, Pat O'Brien, Raymond Walburn, Cliff Edwards, Tom Kennedy.

Saturday's Children (Warner Bros., 1940) 101 minutes
Directed by Vince Sherman, Screenplay by Julius and Philip Epstein, Photographed by James Wong Howe, Edited by Owen Marks.
With *J.G.*, Anne Shirley, Claude Rains, Lee Patrick, George Tobias, Roscoe Karns

Out of the Fog (Warner Bros., 1941) 93 minutes
Directed by Anatole Litvak, Screenplay by Robert Rossen and Jerry Wald, Photographed by James Wong Howe, Edited by Warren Low.
With *J.G.*, Ida Lupino, Eddie Albert, Thomas Mitchell, John Qualen, George Tobias.

The Sea Wolf (Warner Bros., 1941) 100 minutes
Directed by Michael Curtiz, Screenplay by Robert Rossen (based on the novel by Jack London), Photographed by Sol Polito, Edited by George Amy.
With *J.G.*, Edward G. Robinson, George Raft, Marlene Dietrich, Alan Hale, Frank McHugh, Eve Arden, Barton MacLane, Walter Catlett, Joyce Compton, Lucia Carroll, Ward Bond, Egon Brecher, Cliff Clark, Joseph Crehan.

Dangerously They Live (Warner Bros., 1942) 77 minutes
Directed by Robert Florey, Screenplay by Maria Parsonet, Photographed by L. William O'Connell, Edited by Harold McLeron.
With *J.G.*, Nancy Coleman, Raymond Massey, Moroni Olsen, Esther Dale, Lee Patrick.

Tortilla Flat (MGM, 1942) 105 minutes
Directed by Victor Fleming, Screenplay by John Lee Mahin (based on the novel by John Steinbeck), Photographed by Karl Freund, Edited by James Newsome.
With *J.G.*, Spencer Tracy, Hedy Lamarr, Frank Morgan, Akim Tamiroff, Sheldon Leonard, John Qualen.

Air Force (Warner Bros., 1943) 124 minutes
Directed by Howard Hawks, Screenplay by Dudley Nichols, Photographed by James Wong Howe, Edited by George Amy.

With *J.G.*, John Ridgely, Gig Young, Arthur Kennedy, Charles Drake, George Tobias.

Fallen Sparrow (RKO, 1943) 94 minutes
Directed by Richard Wallace, Screenplay by Warren Duff, Photographed by Nicholas Musuraca, Edited by Robert Wise.
With *J.G.*, Maureen O'Hara, Walter Slezak, Patricia Morrison, Martha O'Driscoll, John Banner.

Destination Tokyo (Warner Bros., 1944) 125
Directed by Delmer Daves, Screenplay by Al Metz and Daves, Photographed by Bert Glennon, Edited by Charles Nyby.
With *J.G.*, Cary Grant, Alan Hale, John Ridgely, Dane Clark, Warner Anderson.

Pride of the Marines (Warner Bros., 1945) 125 minutes
Directed by Delmer Daves, Screenplay by Al Metz, Photographed by Peverell Marley, Edited by Owen Marks.
With *J.G.*, Dane Clark, John Ridgely, Rosemary DeCamp, Eleanor Parker, Ann Doran.

Humoresque (Warner Bros., 1946) 123 minutes
Directed by Jean Negulesco, Screenplay by Clifford Odets, Photographed by Ernest Haller, Edited by Rudi Fehr.
With *J.G.*, Joan Crawford, Oscar Levant, J. Carroll Naish, Joan Chandler, Tom D'Andrea.

Nobody Lives Forever (Warner Bros., 1946) 100 minutes
Directed by Jean Negulesco, Screenplay by W. R. Burnett, Photographed by Arthur Edeson, Edited by Rudi Fehr.
With *J.G.*, Geraldine Fitzgerald, Walter Brennan, Faye Emerson, George Tobias, Robert Shayne.

The Postman Always Rings Twice (MGM, 1946) 113 minutes
Directed by Tay Garnett, Screenplay by Harry Ruskin (based on the novel by James Cain), Photographed by Sidney Wagner, Edited by George White.
With *J.G.*, Lana Turner, Cecil Kellaway, Hume Cronyn, Audrey Totter, Leon Ames.

Body and Soul (United Artists, 1947) 104 minutes
Directed by Robert Rossen, Screenplay by Abraham Polonski, Photographed by James Wong Howe, Edited by Robert Parrish.
With *J.G.*, Lili Palmer, Hazel Brooks, Anne Revere, William Conrad.

Gentlemen's Agreement (20th Century–Fox, 1947) 118 minutes
Directed by Elia Kazan, Screenplay by Moss Hart, Photographed by Arthur Millar, Edited by Harmon Jones.

With Gregory Peck, Dorothy McGuire, *J.G.*, Celeste Holm, Anne Revere, June Havoc, Albert Dekker.

Force of Evil (MGM, 1948) 78 minutes
Directed by Abraham Polonsky, Screenplay by Polonsky, Photographed by George Barnes, Edited by Walter Thompson.
With *J.G.*, Beatrice Pearson, Thomas Gomez, Howland Chamblind, Roy Roberts.

We Were Strangers (Columbia, 1949) 106 minutes
Directed by John Huston, Screenplay by Huston and Peter Viertel, Photographed by Russell Metty, Edited by Al Clark.
With *J.G.*, Jennifer Jones, Pedro Armendariz, Gilbert Roland, Ramon Navarro, Wally Cassell.

The Breaking Point (Warner Bros., 1950) 102 minutes
Directed by Michael Curtiz, Screenplay by Ranald MacDougall (based on the book *To Have and Have Not* by Ernest Hemingway which had been filmed two years before), Photographed by Ted McCord, Edited by Alan Crosland, Jr.
With *J.G.*, Patricia Neal, Phyllis Thaxter, Juano Hernandez, Wallace Ford, Edward Ryan, Ralph Dumke.

Under My Skin (20th Century–Fox, 1950) 86 minutes
Directed by Jean Negulesco, Screenplay by Casey Robinson (based on the Ernest Hemingway short story *My Old Man*), Photographed by Joseph Cashelle, Edited by Dorothy Spencer.
With *J.G.*, Michelle Presle, Luther Adler, Orley Lindgren, Noel Drayton, Paul Bryar.

He Ran All the Way (United Artists, 1952) 77 minutes
Directed by John Berry, Screenplay by Guy Endore and Hugo Butler, Photographed by James Wong Howe, Edited by Francis Lyon.
With *J.G.*, Shelley Winters, Wallace Ford, Selena Royle, Gladys George, Norman Lloyd

John Garfield also had bit roles or guest appearances in the following: **Footlight Parade, Four Wives, Hollywood Canteen, Thank Your Lucky Stars, Jigsaw.**

Marlon Brando

The actors John Garfield, Marlon Brando, and James Dean represent an interesting evolution of the new young tough guys that were found in postwar American movies. If Garfield was the virile young counterpart to Bogart's middle-aged tough guy, and Dean was the embodiment of adolescent toughness, Brando's screen image was one of the child and the adult wrestling for control. Brando was capable of exhibiting strong macho bravado while through the same character displaying the inarticulate, mumbling insecurities of the awkward postadolescent male who feels trapped by the suppressive society that was America of the fifties. Brando's screen persona revealed that the traditional masculine role and its various quirks were actually utilized to hide male insecurities rather than to present the masculine norm. It was always evident that he was acting tough in order to shield qualities that allowed his vulnerability to show through. This enigmatic personality caused Brando to become one of the most important antiheroes of the fifties counterculture as well as one of the most innovative movie tough guys.

His first important screen role was in the filmization of Tennessee Williams' *A Streetcar Named Desire* (1951). As Stanley Kowalski, Brando is described by Blanche Dubois (Vivien Leigh) as "an animal, subhuman, bearing raw meat home from the jungle." This destructive male animal is a vivid look at American screen toughness during the fifties from the perspective of the postwar American male filled with the feelings of alienation, nonconformity, and mistrust of the established social conventions. Stanley Kowalski is not a hero in his crudity as was John Wayne, but instead is a very insecure and ultimately powerless individual who used the most primitive sort of toughness to shield his insecurities and ultimate powerlessness. One can draw a direct comparison to Brando's first screen role, in Fred Zinneman's *The Men* (1950). As a paraplegic war casualty, Brando admits to being afraid of readjusting to life with these physical limitations. Where a John Wayne would have known no fear and instead would have overcome his handicap with the sort of macho bravado as he had displayed in all of his Westerns, Brando instead faces his fears head-on and accepts them as valid in a world that now features new, more gross limitations to his survival.

Stanley Kowalski is not physically handicapped, but his emotional and psychological handicaps are limiting enough to cause him to have the same fears of insecurity. He lives in a world of domestic passivity on the part of his wife Stella (Kim Hunter), heavy drinking, all-night card games, and a struggling for sexual conquest (a reiteration of his masculinity even if only to himself), using his sister-in-law as the victim (he ultimately arranges for her to be sent to an asylum). Stanley Kowalski's caveman sensibilities are a mask for his inner torment of self-doubt. Through Brando he is the embodiment of the lower-class American male—the sort of man that society accepts as tough through the crudest and most primitive means, complete with ripped T-shirt, bulging muscles, and the agonized cry of "Where's my woman? Stella! Stellaaa!!"

A true harbinger to James Dean's troubled adolescent of the fifties was Marlon Brando's portrayal of the alienated, leather-garbed biker in *The Wild One* (1954). Once again Brando's character was a sensitive sort whose compassion was masked by a necessary masculine surface in keeping with the accepted norm for a man in his position in a society's counterculture. Yet while presenting the rugged surface of the adolescent male, Brando perfectly allowed us to see how thinly veiled this image was and how tormented and anguished the real person was underneath the superficial facade. While rebelling against the established society, the biker group forms its own egalitarian subsociety in which the same basic establishment takes place, only it is an established order that is different than the masses, and thus is accepted within the subculture. Yet the group has a strict moral, ethical, and dress code that all must adhere to in order to belong, which exhibits very strongly the need for affiliation each of them does have, so strong in that it causes them to form their own inner society where they can comfortably live within the affiliation.

This role helped to establish Brando firmly as an actor whose roles presented the type of tough guy who, feeling trapped and alienated by society, withdrew into a world of his own where he could feel comfortable as an individual of importance, with ideas not to be dismissed or questioned. It is this sort of male who was not presented during the forties (there were no notable American films, for instance, dealing with the conscientious objectors who took a jail sentence rather than going to war in order to retain their pacifism). Brando's traditional masculine characterizations are facades that hide true feelings. Yet these feelings are brought out in his films. In *The Wild One* his defeated character sobs.

The consummate Brando portrayal of the fifties was as Terry Malloy in Elia Kazan's *On the Waterfront* (1954). Malloy is a defeated man, an

Marlon Brando as *The Wild One* (Columbia, 1953).

ex-boxer whose stratum in life has sunk to running cheap errands for union badmen. Sold out during his prizefighting career by his repugnant hoodlum brother, Terry is the ultimate working-class victim of American society. While he has tenderness and vitality, he is sorely lacking in any educational or professional skills that will enable him to achieve more than his present stratum. Time has passed him by. In his classic "could've been a contender" scene with his brother (Rod Steiger), Malloy actually states, in literal terms, where he's at and what he has amounted to as a result of corruption. His life parallels that of many working-class males of this period, calling forth images of postwar prosperity being cast asunder by the limitations of

Brando and Eva Marie Saint in *On the Waterfront* (Columbia, 1954).

idealists in a world run by a corrupt bureaucracy where threats of destruction loom overhead like a falling sword.

Malloy is the grown-up youth of the fifties, the young adult counterpart to the adolescent rebel of *The Wild One*. He needs not prove his masculinity as he was once a prizefighter, so he can be seen raising pigeons and caring for them, this hobby being just that, and not an idiosyncrasy. Malloy is powerful and brutal, as well as sensitive, caring, and vulnerable. This diversity presents a more honest male image and thus creates a newer, more detailed example of screen toughness. Brando's presentations of the sensitive tough guys of the fifties would culminate with James Dean's even more profound portrayals of this same theme through the perspective of the tortured adolescent.

Brando's screen career was as enigmatic as his characters. His established persona was used in several guises, from Zapata to Fletcher Christian to Chaplin's *A Countess from Hong Kong* and finally *Last Tango in Paris*. It culminates well in Francis Ford Coppola's *The Godfather* (1970), a serious look at the inner workings of a Mafia organization, with Brando in the lead role. This was the toughness that would mark the seventies, Brando again playing a role that was pivotal in the realm of the movie tough guy. The kingpin he portrays is soft-spoken and terrifying even if only for his total lack of emotion. The character exudes the narcissistic qualities of the stereotypical Sicilian patriarch while also allowing us to examine his ruthless cunning and tragically vindictive spirit. This was a character in total control, but unlike John Wayne's cowboy or Clint Eastwood's detective, Brando's kingpin was a tormented individual whose Neapolitan compassion and his sons' filial anguish only intensified his inner agony.

The Brando tough guy was not as complex or diverse as those portrayed by Bogart, but Marlon Brando gave American film its most important tough-guy image of the fifties. When this image was stretched and shaped, it succeeded far better than when it was shelved for the many other roles Brando played throughout his career. As enigmatic as his career may be, Marlon Brando's most important portrayals are the essence of fifties masculinity and what it meant to be a consummate tough guy in that period's American cinema.

Marlon Brando Filmography

The Men (United Artists, 1950) 87 minutes
Directed by Fred Zinneman, Screenplay by Carl Foreman, Photographed by Robert de Grasse.
With *M.B.*, Teresa Wright, Everet Sloane, Jack Webb, Richard Erdman.

A Streetcar Named Desire (Columbia, 1951) 121 minutes
Directed by Elia Kazan, Screenplay by Tennessee Williams (based on his play), Photographed by Harry Stradling.
With *M.B.*, Vivien Leigh, Kim Hunter, Karl Malden, Rudy Bond.

Viva Zapata! (20th Century–Fox, 1952) 113 minutes
Directed by Elia Kazan, Screenplay by John Steinbeck, Photographed by Joe MacDonald.
With *M.B.*, Jean Peters, Anthony Quinn, Joseph Wiseman, Arnold Moss.

Julius Caesar (MGM, 1953) 121 minutes
Directed by Joseph L. Mankiewicz, Screenplay: the play by William Shakespeare, Photographed by Joseph Ruttenberg.
With *M.B.*, James Mason, John Gielgud, Louis Calhern, Edmund O'Brien, Greer Garson, Deborah Kerr, George MacReady, Michael Pate.

The Wild One (Columbia, 1953) 79 minutes
Directed by Laslo Benedek, Screenplay by John Paston (based on the story by Frank Rooneyu), Photographed by Hal Mohr.
With *M.B.*, Mary Murphy, Robert Keith, Lee Marvin, Jay C. Flippen.

On the Waterfront (Columbia, 1954) 107 minutes
Directed by Elia Kazan, Screenplay by Buddy Schulberg (suggested by articles by Malcolm Johnson), Photographed by Boris Kaufman.

Brando and Vivien Leigh in Tennessee Williams' *A Streetcar Named Desire* (Columbia, 1951).

With *M.B.*, Eva Marie Saint, Karl Malden, Rod Steiger, Lee J. Cobb.

Désirée (20th Century–Fox, 1954) 110 minutes; Color
Directed by Henry Koster, Screenplay by Daniel Taradash (based on the novel by Annemarie Selinko), Photographed by Milton Krasner.
With *M.B.*, Jean Simmons, Merle Oberon, Michael Rennie, Cameron Mitchell, Elizabeth Sellers, Charlotte Austin, Cathleen Nesbit.

Guys and Dolls (MGM, 1955) 149 minutes; Color
Directed by Joseph L. Mankiewicz (based on the play by Jo Swerling and Abe Burrows which was adapted from the story by Damon Runyan), Photographed by Harry Stradling.
With Frank Sinatra, *M.B.*, Jean Simmons, Vivian Blaine, Stubby Kaye.

Teahouse of the August Moon (MGM, 1956) 123 minutes; Color
Directed by Daniel Mann, Screenplay by John Patrick (based on his play and the book by Vera Sneider), Photographed by John Alton.
With *M.B.*, Glen Ford, Machito Kyo, Eddie Albert, Paul Ford.

Sayonara (Columbia, 1957) 147 minutes, Color
Directed by Joshua Logan, Screenplay by Paul Osborn (based on the novel by James A. Michener), Photographed by Ellsworth Fredericks.

With *M.B.*, Miko Taka, Red Buttons, Patricia Owens, Ricardo Montalban, Myoshi Umecki, Kent Smith.

The Young Lions (20th Century–Fox, 1958) 167 minutes
Directed by Edward Dmytryk, Screenplay by Edward Anhalt (based on the novel by Irwin Shaw), Photographed by Joe MacDonald.
With *M.B.*, Montgomery Clift, Dean Martin, Hope Lange, Barbara Rush, May Britt, Maximillian Schell.

The Fugitive Kind (United Artists, 1960) 121 minutes
Directed by Sidney Lumet, Screenplay by Tennessee Williams and Meade Roberts (based on Williams' play *Orpheus Descending*), Photographed by Boris Kaufmann.
With *M.B.*, Anna Magnani, Joanne Woodward, Maureen Stapleton, Victor Jory, R. G. Armstrong.

One-Eyed Jacks (Paramount, 1960) 141 minutes; Color
Directed by Marlon Brando, Screenplay by Guy Trosper and Calder Willingham (based on the novel *The Authentic Death of Henry Jones* by Charles Neider), Photographed by Charles Lang, Jr.
With *M.B.*, Karl Malden, Pina Pelicer, Katy Jurado, Ben Johnson, Slim Pickens, Larry Duran.

Mutiny on the Bounty (MGM, 1962) Originally 185 minutes, edited to 178 minutes; Color
Directed by Lewis Milestone, Screenplay by Charles Lederer (based on the novel by Charles Nordhoff and James Norman Hall), Photographed by Robert L. Surtees.
With *M.B.*, Trevor Howard, Richard Harris, Hugh Griffith, Richard Hayden, Tim Seely, Percy Herbert.

The Ugly American (Rank, 1962) 120 minutes; Color
Directed by George Englund, Screenplay by Stewart Stern (based on the novel by William J. Lederer), Photographed by Clifford Stine.
With *M.B.*, Eiji Okada, Sandra Church, Pat Hingle, Arthur Hill, Jocelyn Brando, Kukrit Pramoj.

Bedtime Story (Rank, 1964) 99 minutes
Directed by Ralph Levy, Screenplay by Stanley Shapiro and Paul Henning, Photographed by Clifford Stine.
With *M.B.*, David Niven, Shirley Jones, Dody Goodman, Aram Stephan.

Morituri (20th Century–Fox, 1965) 122 minutes
Directed by Bernhard Wicki, Screenplay by Danie Taradash (based on the novel by Werner Jeorge Luedecke), Photographed by Conrad Hall.
With *M.B.*, Yul Brynner, Janet Margolin, Trevor Howard, Martin Berath, Hans Christian Blech.

The Chase (Columbia, 1965) Originally 133 minutes, edited to 122 minutes; Color

Directed by Arthur Penn, Screenplay by Lillian Hellman (based on the novel by Horton Foote), Photographed by Joseph La Shelle.

With *M.B.*, Jane Fonda, Robert Redford, E.G. Marshall, Angie Dickinson, Janice Rule, Miriam Hopkins, Martha Hyer, Richard Bradford, Robert Duvall, James Fox, Diana Hyland, Henry Hull.

The Appaloosa (Rank, 1966) 98 minutes; Color

Directed by Sidney J. Furie, Screenplay by James Bridges and Roland Kibbee (based on the novel by Robert MacLeod), Photographed by Russell Metty.

With *M.B.*, Anjanette Comer, John Saxon, Rafael Campos, Miriam Colon, Emilo Fernandez.

A Countess from Hong Kong (Rank, 1967) 120 minutes; Color

Directed by Charlie Chaplin, Screenplay by Chaplin, Photographed by Arthur Ibbetson.

With *M.B.*, Sophia Loren, Sydney Chaplin, Tippi Hedren, Patrick Cargill, Michael Medwin.

Candy (Ciro, 1968) 122 minutes; Color

Directed by Christian Marquand, Screenplay by Buck Henry (based on the novel by Terry Southern and Mason Hoffenberg), Photographed by Giuseppe Rotunno.

With Ewa Aulin, *M.B.*, Richard Burton, James Coburn, Walter Matthau, Ringo Starr, John Huston.

Night of the Following Day (Rank, 1968) 93 minutes; Color

Directed by Hubert Cornfield, Screenplay by Cornfield and Robert Phippeny (based on the novel *The Snatchers* by Lionel White), Photographed by Willy Kurant.

With *M.B.*, Richard Boone, Rita Moreno, Pamela Franklin, Jess Hahn, Gerald Buhr.

Burn! (United Artists, 1968) Originally at 132 minutes, edited to 112 minutes; Color

Directed by Gillo Pontecorvo, Screenplay by Franco Solinas and Giorgio Alorio (from a story by Pontecorvo), Photographed by Marcello Gatti and Giuseppe Bruzzolini.

With *M.B.*, Evaristo Marquez, Renato Salvatori, Norman Hill, Gianpiero Albertini.

Note: Alternate title: *Queimada!*

The Nightcomers (Avco-Embassy, 1971) 96 minutes; Color

Directed by Michael Winner, Screenplay by Michael Hastings, Photographed by Robert Paynter.

With *M.B.*, Stephanie Beacham, Thora Hird, Harry Andrews, Verna Harvey, Christopher Ellis.

The Godfather (Paramount, 1971) 175 minutes; Color
Directed by Francis Ford Coppola, Screenplay by Mario Puzo and Coppola (based on the novel by Puzo), Photographed by Gordon Willis.
With *M.B.*, Al Pacino, James Caan, Richard Castellano, Robert Duvall, Sterling Heyden, Diane Keaton, Abe Vigoda, Richard Conte, Talia Shire, Al Martino.
Note: Brando won an Oscar for his role in this film, which he refused to accept.

Last Tango in Paris (United Artists, 1972) 129 minutes; Color
Directed by Bernardo Betrolucci, Screenplay by Bertolucci and Franco Arcalli, Photographed by Vittorio Staoraro.
With *M.B.*, Maria Schneider, Darling Legitmus, Catherine Sola, Mauro Marchetti, Dan Diament.

The Missouri Breaks (United Artists, 1976) 126 minutes; Color
Directed by Arthur Penn, Screenplay by Thomas McGuane, Photographed by Michael Butler.
With *M.B.*, Jack Nicholson, Randy Quaid, Kathleen Lloyd, Frederic Forest, Harry Dean Stanton.

Superman (Warner Bros., 1978) 143 minutes; Color
Directed by Richard Donner, Screenplay by Mario Puzo, Robert Benton, David and Leslie Newman, Photographed by Geoffrey Unsworth.
With Christopher Reeve, Margot Kidder, Gene Hackman, Jackie Cooper, *M.B.*

Apocalypse Now (United Artists, 1979) 146 minutes; Color
Directed by Francis Ford Coppola, Screenplay by John Milius (based on the novel by Joseph Conrad).
With *M.B.*, Martin Sheen, Robert Duvall.

James Dean

When one analyzes a cinema figure that has been as studied as James Dean, one must take into account the results and theories of all previous analyses. Whenever Dean's character is approached as per its toughness, there is a tendency to point out that the character was an adolescent (or, in the case of *Giant*, an arrested adolescent) whose toughness was merely a facade to hide his juvenile angst. This persona is further enhanced by the actor's tragic early death; a chillingly fitting end to a life-style that allegedly emulated much of what we saw on screen.

Dean did more than emerge as the quintessential postwar adolescent icon. He, like Brando before him, managed to present a level of masculinity that stated it was all right to exude emotional qualities that had heretofore been associated strictly with passive female stereotypes. His tough-yet-tender persona added further depth to what was considered masculine in the American cinema, challenging the ways of earlier tough guys who felt it necessary to shield emotions in order to maintain that special element of toughness. Dean showed toughness in another guise, perhaps one that could only stem from the idealism of adolescence. He showed us how to be tough enough to care.

While the Dean personality was indeed that of a tough guy, he still could not help caring passionately for others, especially those whom he related to and those he felt a strong desire to impress. Consequently, this tough guy could not live an unthinking and unfeeling existence like John Wayne could; he instead felt it necessary to rage much like the Cagney tough guy did. Only Dean was far more openly compassionate than Cagney, having a more unabashed exhibition of his often blatant romantic nature.

Dean did a few bit parts in films like *Sailor Beware* (1952) with Dean Martin and Jerry Lewis before landing his first starring role, in Elia Kazan's somewhat bowdlerized version of John Steinbeck's *East of Eden* (1965). Dean's dynamic performance as a confused adolescent whose continual attempts to please his hardworking, spiritless father (Raymond Massey) immediately carved a niche for the young actor. Dean's character was

James Dean (center) struck a chord in American youth when he appeared with Burl Ives (left) and Raymond Massey in *East of Eden* (Warner Bros., 1955).

forced to deal with, from an adolescent perspective, a broken home, a favored older brother, discovering the sordid truth about his estranged mother, all while attempting to understand his own impulses and trying so desperately to please his seemingly unpleasable father.

The filial anguish expressed by Dean sounded a chord in the youth of America during the conservative fifties and immediately transformed the actor into an antihero for the American adolescent moviegoer who also felt the alienation Dean projected on the screen. Dean's toughness in this character stems from his steadfast refusal to deny the emotions he has that his father will deem too effeminate. He has the ability to show sorrow, to give love, and to exude the type of sensitivity that stereotypical tough males suppressed. This makes him attractive to his older brother's girl (Julie Harris) — the film presenting a young woman as the only character who can genuinely understand the significance of sensitivity in a young man. He shows toughness by taking the initiative to win his father's love and understanding, as well as to find the mother who he had presumed was dead. When he discovers she is alive, but a prostitute, he identifies with her inability to accept the suppressive farm life her husband (and his father) gave to them and understands her longing for greater adventure. He then sets out to seek the same understanding from his father.

Dean's relationship with his brother's girl shows that his screen character, like Brando's, is more interested in her kind, understanding attitude towards him than he is with the gaggle of fast-and-loose young ladies the attractive Dean has at his disposal, not being fully satisfied with women who offer little more than sexual gratification. When he steals a kiss from his brother's girl, he shows once again that this character is capable of exhibiting the tenderness that had been alien to tough guys in previous American films. This capacity to show tenderness and give love while still standing strong for what he believed in presented an infinitely more positive male image in American cinema.

East of Eden was such a sensation that Dean's status was tremendously enhanced as an actor, and he was quickly shunted into two other films before his tragic death in an auto crash on September 30, 1955. Although his subsequent two films, *Rebel Without a Cause* (1955) and *Giant* (1956), were both released posthumously, the impact of *Eden* was strong enough to create an orgy of nationwide mourning when the actor was killed. Lonely, alienated adolescents who identified with the Dean character in *East of Eden* felt a severe loss when their hero perished. Many of his most passionate fans committed suicide, not unlike the furor that met the death of Rudolph Valentino. The release of *Rebel* only enhanced his legend, as it displayed an even stronger case against suppressed adolescence.

As Jim Stark, Dean gave an eternal testament to alienated youth that has become an absolute staple of the American screen image of adolescence. He is first shown drunk, taken to the police station, giggling at the procedures of the officers, and finally attempting to display his capacity to give love by offering his jacket to a shivering younger boy in the station. When the boy does not take the jacket, Jim is offended: "Why didn't you take my jacket?"

The younger boy is Plato (Sal Mineo), a slight lad whose problems at home cause him to escape into a dream world inhabited by surrogate parental figures in the absence of his own. He has a photo of actor Alan Ladd on the inside door of his school locker. Ladd is a small but masculine screen male whom Plato could conceivably emulate. He is soon attracted to Jim Stark, and subsequently Jim replaces the intangible Ladd. A third member of the group is Judy (Natalie Wood), whose alienation stems from her father's flat refusal to show physical affection toward her as a result of her premature budding puberty now showing definite signs of young womanhood. The conservative father is so possessed by his sexually attractive daughter's appearance in ways that he feels he must suppress, he therefore is repulsed by her wanting to kiss him on the cheek—a reaction that causes her to believe he no longer loves her.

Dean with Sal Mineo and Natalie Wood as three alienated youngsters in *Rebel Without a Cause* (Warner Bros., 1955).

Jim's problem is equally typical. His mother is overbearing and domineering while his father is weak and passive, catering to his wife's every whim. Their constant bickering, the mother's steady badgering of the father, and both parents' overzealous attempts to put on a "front" to appear emotionally successful in the familial perspective to others, puts tremendous pressure on Jim's overactive adolescent emotions. At one point he screams: "You're tearing me apart! You say one thing, he says another, and then everybody changes back again!" As a result of the turmoil at home, Dean must escape into another world. His attempts to make friends are also unsuccessful.

Realizing that he must be his own man, Jim accepts when challenged by a teenage gangleader to what they call a "chickie-run." This act has both boys, in separate cars, racing toward a cliff. The first to brake or escape the auto is the chicken — a name that Jim particularly abhors as he realizes how accurately it describes his passive father. Jim escapes in time from his vehicle during the "chickie-run," but the other boy's sleeve is caught on the inside door handle and he is stuck in the car. He plummets to his death. Jim believes he should go to the police, but upon reporting this accident to his parents finds that they vehemently disagree.

MRS. STARK:	Did anybody see you, did anyone recognize you there?
JIM:	No.
MRS. STARK:	Then how do they know it was you?
JIM:	But it WAS me, I was there!
MRS. STARK:	But if nobody saw you . . .
JIM:	It doesn't matter, it doesn't matter, it doesn't matter...
MR. STARK:	You can't be idealistic all your life, Jimbo.
MRS. STARK:	It isn't good to get involved.
JIM:	I AM INVOLVED, WE ARE ALL INVOLVED! Mom— Dad—just once I want to do something right!

Mrs. Stark's attempts to end the argument by triumphantly announcing that the family is moving. "No!" cries Jim, "you're not going to use me as an excuse to move!" Jim's patience is eventually pushed to the limit as he lunges as his father and out the door into the night.

The parents of all three leading adolescent figures in the story—Jim, Judy, and Plato—alienate them in different ways. Plato's parents are never there, virtually nonexistent. He is being brought up by a black cleaning woman who understands the plight of these oppressed youths as a result of her own culture's history. Judy's parents are perhaps the most typical— strong father figure and passive mother—but her attempts to please her father continually ruined: "The other night he thought I was wearing too much lipstick. He scrubbed it off so hard I thought he was going to rub my lips off!"

The film culminates with all three youngsters setting up their own egalitarian subsociety inside an old abandoned mansion. Jim and Judy are the parent figures while Plato is the child. As he sleeps on the floor at Judy's feet, she reaches down and strokes his hair. When Jim and Judy notice that he is wearing two different-colored socks, they giggle and say to each other, "I've done that, though, haven't you?" The parental figures we have seen in the film up to this point would more conceivably have belittled the child for his haste and stupidity.

With Plato asleep, Jim and Judy walk around the mansion exploring its many rooms. Plato, left alone, is awakened with a start by a group of rough gang members who are after Jim for causing the death of their leader in the "chickie-run." Plato, who is carrying a gun, shoots and injures one of the boys, runs away, and hides in a nearby observatory. Soon the observatory is surrounded by police as well as Jim's parents, who are notified by police that a description of one of the youths matches that of their son.

Jim goes to Plato, speaking to him inside the dark observatory. Plato, having felt abdandoned once again by people he loves, asks, "Why did you and Judy leave me?" Jim explains that they did not leave him and also informs him that he must now leave the observatory. Jim then arranges that the police surrounding the building lower their weapons and turn off their searchlights so that he can coax the frightened Plato out. Jim asks for Plato's gun, promising to return it. He secretly removes the bullets and gives it back. Plato then slowly leaves the observatory with Jim. An overzealous police officer notices the youngster's gun and shoots him dead. There is a close-up of Jim, hand outstretched, screaming, "I've got the bullets!" Jim's father runs up to his sobbing son, embraces him and promises, "I'll try to be as strong as you want me to be." He gives Jim his jacket.

So the rebels in this film did have a cause, which was their reaction to a diseased society that manifested itself within their family structures. Jim Stark realizes that no matter how sensitive a male chooses to be, he must still face a brutal real world and thus retain enough toughness not to be "chicken." To Jim, strength meant being able to recognize and accept weakness. As a result, he was the strength for the frail Judy and the timid Plato.

Recent studies have also analyzed the latent homosexuality between the Jim Stark and Plato characters, these studies the result of James Dean's alleged bisexuality and Sal Mineo's notorious homosexual life-style offscreen. Plato is no doubt very attracted to Stark, but their relationship, though arguably more important than the one between Jim and Judy, is less a homosexual relationship than a testament to male bonding. It is true Jim Stark comes from the typical family structure that is said to foster homosexuality (weak, passive father and strong, domineering mother), while Plato is at the age of intense sexual awakening. But Dean's important presentation of a man having the traditionally effeminate feelings of love and tenderness would not have the proper impact on the American movie tough guy unless that character was fiercely heterosexual. To give a homosexual these attributes would be to explain stereotypically feminine traits as only belonging to men who are gay. Giving said attributes to a fully heterosexual character is to add these traits to the traditional screen male and, hence, come up with a more complex and more positive image of movie manhood. That Jim Stark was heterosexual is what makes Dean's contribution to the struggle against sex role stereotyping in the American cinema so substantial.

With George Stevens' *Giant*, Dean's last film, we see the first attempts at allowing his characterization to mature with him. It is difficult to comprehend just how successfully a fully matured James Dean would have fared in the American cinema, but his performance as Jett Rink in *Giant* had him in transition, displaying late adolescence crowding confused adulthood. But within the film, Jett Rink evolves from a compassionate Jim Stark type of character to a ruthless alcoholic capitalist—a state the film's narrative will have us believe is inevitable for such an idealist. During the film's opening moments Rink is the preferable male image, in contrast to Rock Hudson, who forces a screaming four year old to ride a pony he's terrified of, stating, "He'll stay on that pony if I have to tie him on!" What *Giant* gives the viewer

Elizabeth Taylor, Rock Hudson, and Dean in the latter's final film, *Giant* (Warner Bros., 1956).

is a glimpse at what James Dean would have presented in ensuing roles had he lived.

    In an extremely short film career, James Dean gave us a pivotal characterization that changed the way young men were shown in movies. The rebellious youth became a new folk hero for contemporary society as John Wayne had been for an earlier generation—the generation represented by the adult figures in *Rebel Without a Cause* and *East of Eden*. James Dean is the emblem of a major social attitude that soon bled into a full-fledged counterculture amidst rock and roll music, a generation gap, and an ensuing parade of confused and alienated American adolescents who latched onto subsequent hero figures (from Elvis Presley to John F. Kennedy to the Beatles to Ozzy Osbourne) in an effort to better understand themselves and their direction. Dean's tragic death was an ugly harbinger for future tragedies involving similar counterculture heroes like Presley and John Lennon. Although we have had several very important counterculture superstars in the wake of James Dean, their massive popularity would have been inconceivable without his original example of adolescent rebellion in a suppressive adult society.

James Dean Filmography

East of Eden (Warner Bros., 1955) 115 minutes; Color
Directed by Elia Kazan, Screenplay by Paul Osborne (based on the novel by John Steinbeck), Photographed by Ted McCord, Edited by Owen Marks.
With *J.D.*, Julie Christie, Raymond Massey, Jo Van Fleet, Burl Ives, Robert Davales, Albert Dekker.

Rebel Without a Cause (Warner Bros., 1955) 111 minutes; Color
Directed by Nicholas Ray, Screenplay by Stewart Stern (based on a story by Ray), Photographed by Ernest Haller, Edited by William Ziegler.
With *J.D.*, Natalie Wood, Sal Mineo, Jim Backus, Ann Doran, William Hopper, Edward Platt, Corey Allen, Dennis Hopper, Nick Adams, Rochelle Hudson.

Giant (Warner Bros., 1956) 201 minutes; Color
Directed by George Stevens, Screenplay by Fred Guiol and Ivan Moffat (based on the novel by Edna Ferber), Photographed by William C. Mellor, Edited by William Hornbeck.
With Rock Hudson, Elizabeth Taylor, *J.D.*, Carrol Baker, Jane Withers, Dennis Hopper, Sal Mineo, Paul Fix, Earl Holliman.

Dean had bit parts in the following films: **Fixed Bayonets, Sailor Beware,** and **Has Anybody Seen My Gal.**

Elvis Presley

Since his death in 1977, Elvis Presley has been examined by two schools: the serious intellectuals who write on rock music and the passionate fans who refuse to believe Presley guilty of the slightest aberration. The former group is objective in their praise of Presley's contribution to American popular culture and his impact on so many areas, while the latter group sees him as a messiah more than a show-biz phenomenon, and approach everything he did with uncritical zeal.

The Presley films are very weak for the most part, but they were nevertheless important even if only as outlets for a tough-guy persona that is among the most important in entertainment. The persona that Presley developed through his raucous rock music used its medium to establish the various stages of adolescent angst. His manic gyrations and blatant shouting and wailing combined to provide the perfect fantasy outlet for hyperactive adolescents in the suppressive fifties. The persona that developed from this was so strong it literally changed the world, being the mainspring from which stemmed virtually every counterculture phenomenon thereafter, from the Beatles to Sid Vicious.

The one aspect of Presley's long and often tragic career that has been given little attention is his screen work. Presley worked with directors as diverse and important as Michael Curtiz, who directed both *Angels with Dirty Faces* and *Casablanca*, and Norman Taurog, whose work went back as far as silent comedy. And although his management saw Presley as a commodity rather than a creative artist—forcing him into a seemingly endless series of mindless pop musicals with titles like *Fun in Acapulco*—when left alone to his own resources and given the freedom to draw from his own influences, Presley proved himself to be a genuinely creative artist. His management's bad decisions hampered his film career beyond repair, but since his films were indeed representations of his rock and roll persona—and his screen character virtually anthropomorphizes the very essence of rock and roll music—they are important to assess as essential examples of yet another type of movie tough guy.

Presley came to a rather inauspicious start with his first film, *Love Me Tender* (1956), despite its being a major box-office success. While it wasn't a truly bad film, this pedestrian Western with a narrative that dealt closely with sibling rivalry was perhaps a very effective adolescent drama of its period. Western films and television shows were very strong commodities at this time. Adolescents were the largest audience for either medium, and thus the Western setting for Presley was familiar territory to his target audience. Plus, the film's dealing with romance and sibling rivalry—two of the more predominant adolescent topics—also adds to its teen market value. Elvis is not only allowed to exhibit passion, pain, frustration, love, and defiance; he is also granted a death scene, which is yet another in a series of presentations from this period that symbolizes the mortality of youth.

Loving You (1957) was more familiar for Presley and his fans, as well as being a rather uncomfortable harbinger for what was ahead. It remains the best of his flighty pop musicals, with better songs and a more terse dramatic narrative dealing with the rise of a nobody (Elvis) to a somebody in the pop music world, despite protests from parents. Had the film dealt more seriously with parental reaction (the initial rumblings of the coming generation gap) as well as Presley's attempts to deal with his image once fame had been thrust upon him, *Loving You* could have been a rather important effort. What we have is a musical that is every bit as unimaginative as Presley's Western debut had been, with a few interesting ingredients saving it from the depths of the truly wretched.

The film that many Presley enthusiasts consider to be his most important is the 1957 musical drama *Jailhouse Rock*, which is loosely based on the now legendary hit song from the period. This film features Presley as the quintessential adolescent tough guy of the period (although he is not playing an adolescent), with a black leather jacket, a guitar, and a snarl. The title song is presented in a number choreographed by Presley himself, his indelible stamp of hard, masculine dance steps evident rather than the more effeminate, overly produced numbers he would soon grow accustomed to, making it the most impressive of all musical scenes in his films.

The plot of *Jailhouse Rock* has Presley in the characteristic role of a singer whose talents were matched only by his cocky self-assuredness. As with a previous film, *Loving You*, Presley rarely smiles. In later interviews he stated that the actors he studied in order to gain a perspective on screen acting did little smiling. These actors included Humphrey Bogart, Marlon Brando, and James Dean. Thus Presley used noted tough guys in the American cinema as the foundation for his own performances on film. This toughness is most evident in *Jailhouse Rock* not only because of the film's tough prison setting, but because it is the film that most closely associates with the image Presley had created through his music.

When the short-fused Presley character is jailed for manslaughter, the

Elvis Presley

film presents the singer's impulsive actions as being destructive. Presley's manic gyrations on television even before he embarked on a film career caused much outrage from parents who feared this teen idol was inflicting emotional wounds on their children that were every bit as dangerous as the physical wounds his *Jailhouse Rock* character inflicted upon his victim in the manslaughter incident. The character eventually does make it as a singer, but feels alienated by the critics who attempt to analyze what he feels are his natural instincts, as well as the record company big shots who stifle his creative control. As a tough guy, Presley's *Jailhouse Rock* character is a very emotional being who can only express his passions through his music. His suppression at exhibiting these emotions is shown by his violent reactions to the bureaucrats that run the music business which he would like to join if only he is given full creative freedom (how art imitates life!). Presley worked quite well in this setting and showed that he could successfully hone his acting style to a point where some impressive ability was evident. That he could successfully transcend his rock and roll persona into those of his screen characters is also impressive, especially in subsequent films where that image would conceivably seem out of place.

Presley made headlines for being inducted into the army in 1958, but not until he had finished the Michael Curtiz–directed adaptation of Harold Robbins' seamy book *A Stone for Danny Fisher,* which was retitled *King Creole* to capitalize on yet another Presley hit. It was to remain Presley's greatest film and finest performance, a James Deanesque story of a tough punk whose embarrassment at his father's inability to be a "real man" is so affecting that it causes him to drop out of school and eventually become hooked up with a local gangster (Walter Matthau) at whose club Presley sings for the extra money his father does not make.

Presley is allowed to exhibit all of the emotions that most befit troubled youths, and he does so with the sincerity that was absent from his sub-sequent roles in mindless musicals. Director Curtiz uses the dark dinginess of the slum environment effectively in an effort to present the general toughness of Presley's world, while Presley draws upon his own poverty-stricken roots to exhibit the fierce loyalty and unflinching manhood that must accompany slum life. His father's passive existence keeps him from surviving, and when Presley sees his parent being verbally accosted by his employer, he is disgusted and wallows still deeper in his own filial anguish. *King Creole* is the Presley film in which the singer is allowed to be a tough guy for the sake of toughness, something he believes essential to survival. Although he is attracted to the tough demeanors of the gangsters he even-tually gets mixed up with, he exudes compassion toward his gangster boss's girl friend (Carolyn Jones), a prostitute whom the gangster belittles and simply uses for sexual gratification. Presley soon discovers that the stereotypically feminine feeling of love and compassion are important aspects of full-fledged masculinity. Presley becomes a man when, by the end of the film, he recognizes his own capacity to give love and understands its importance.

When Presley returned from the army, he was shunted into a series of rapidly made musicals that turned a profit on the Presley name. Whatever acting abilities the singer had indicated in his prearmy films were stifled in virtually all of his postarmy efforts. Especially during the sixties, when the British rock and roll invasion that gave us the Beatles and the Rolling Stones was in full swing, Presley shrugged off his ability with whatever weak films and songs his management thrust upon him. That Presley was indirectly responsible for the British rock invasion was beside the point (many of the incoming Brit-rockers cited Elvis as their major influence). He seemed a has-been at 25 despite the fact that his films, no matter how awful, turned a healthy profit.

At Presley's insistence, his management allowed him one escape from the quagmire of silly musical nonentities, and *Flaming Star* (1961) was a welcome throwback to his prearmy works. In this intense Western directed by Don Siegel, Elvis is a half-breed who is forced to deal with period bigotry from both whites and native Americans. It was one of the first successful attempts to deal with that period's racism, thus making it an important as well as a good film. Presley sings the title song, and no others thereafter. It was successful enough to allow Elvis the freedom of making more dramatic pictures.

Presley's tough guy exhibited the same qualities in *Flaming Star* as he did in his earlier films, but *Follow That Dream* (1962) presented him as a shy, reserved country boy whose toughness somehow blended with his own perverse naiveté. It was successful, but the similar *Wild in the Country* (1962) had more trouble sustaining the same basic image. In the latter film Elvis plays a gifted writer whose talents are dismissed, as he is considered no more than a hillbilly punk. A teacher (Hope Lange) believes in him, but he then is forced to deal with the jealousy of his girlfriend (Tuesday Weld).

With these dramas it seemed filmmakers were having trouble finding roles for a more mature Presley, while still somehow maintaining examples of this rock and roll tough-guy image. The attempts at giving the singer a meaningful role only made him look pretentious after the pop musicals that so quickly became his trademark. The audiences stayed away, and Elvis was again relegated to films with titles like *Tickle Me* (1965) and *Paradise—Hawaiian Style* (1966). The Presley tough guy was a mere caricature throughout the sixties: sexually attractive, a good singer, able to throw a few good punches and subsequently win the girl. He had very few deviations from this basic image (*Charro!*, *Change of Habit*), and these few were not successful artistically or commercially. Presley's comeback occurred, not coincidentally, through his music. A 1968 TV special, on which he was given full creative control while the producers sidetracked his dollar-happy management, was a veritable celebration of all that he, or rock music, had ever stood for.

Elvis Presley's importance to film is not minimal, despite a wealth of terrible star vehicles. He managed to create a media image that altered American musical personalities in unfathomable ways, and parlayed this image into a film career where another aspect of the tough guy was

Presley proved he could indeed act in films like *Flaming Star* (20th Century–Fox, 1960).

presented. While his musicals often showed him as a simple crooner languishing within a bourgeois society, his handful of substantial films is a testimony to his important contributions. He was a tough guy whose toughness personified the inner feelings of adolescence as well as emotions of working-class Americans in a conservative society.

Elvis Presley Filmography

Love Me Tender (20th Century–Fox, 1956) 94 minutes
   Directed by Robert Webb, Screenplay by Robert Buckner, Photographed by Leo Tover, Edited by Hugh Fowler.
   With *E.P.*, Richard Egan, Debra Paget, Robert Middleton, Neville Brand.

Loving You (Paramount, 1957) 101 minutes; Color
   Directed by Hal Kanter, Screenplay by Herbert Baker, Photographed by Charles Lang, Edited by Howard Smith.
   With *E.P.*, Lizabeth Scott, Wendell Corey, Dolores Hart, James Gleason.
   Note: Elvis' parents can be seen in one sequence as audience members. When his mother died, Elvis refused to ever screen this picture again.

Jailhouse Rock (MGM, 1957) 96 minutes
   Directed by Richard Thorpe, Screenplay by Guy Trosper, Photographed by Robert Bronner, Edited by Ralph Winters.
   With *E.P.* Jennifer Holden, Anne Neyland, Mickey Shaughnessy, Dean Jones, Percy Helton.
   Note: Presley choreographed the "Jailhouse Rock" dance sequence.

King Creole (Paramount, 1958) 116 minutes
   Directed by Michael Curtiz, Screenplay by Herbert Baker and Michael Gazzo (based on the Irving Wallace novel *A Stone for Danny Fisher*), Photographed by Russell Harlan, Edited by Warren Low.
   With *E.P.*, Walter Matthau, Dean Jagger, Dolores Hart, Jan Shepard, Vic Morrow, Carolyn Jones.

G.I. Blues (Paramount, 1960) 115 minutes; Color
   Directed by Norman Taurog, Screenplay by Edmund Beloin and Henry Garson, Photographed by Loyal Griggs, Edited by Warren Low.
   With *E.P.*, James Douglas, Robert Ivers, Juliet Prowse, Leticia Roman.

Flaming Star (20th Century–Fox, 1960) 92 minutes; Color
   Directed by Don Siegel, Screenplay by Clair Huffaker and Nunnally Johnson (based on a novel by Huffaker), Photographed by Charles C. Clarke, Edited by Hugh S. Fowler.
   With *E.P.*, Barbara Eden, Steve Forrest, Dolores Del Rio, John McIntyre, Karl Swenson.

Blue Hawaii (Paramount, 1961) 90 minutes
Directed by Norman Taurog, Screenplay by Hal Kanter, Photographed by Charles Lang, Edited by Warren Low.
   With *E.P.*, Joan Blackman, Nancy Walters, Roland Winters, Angela Lansbury, Howard McNear.

Wild in the Country (20th Century–Fox, 1961) 112 minutes; Color
Directed by Philip Dunne, Screenplay by Clifford Odets, Photographed by William Mellor, Edited by Dorothy Spencer.
With *E.P.*, Hope Lange, Tuesday Weld, Millie Perkins, Rafer Johnson.

Follow That Dream (United Artists, 1962) 107 minutes; Color
Directed by Gordon Douglas, Screenplay by Charles Lederer, Photographed by Leo Tover, Edited by William Murphy.
With *E.P.*, Arthur O'Connell, Anne Helm, Joanna Moore, Jack Kruschen, Simon Oakland, Alan Hewitt.

Girls! Girls! Girls! (Paramount, 1962) 109 minutes; Color
Directed by Norman Taurog, Screenplay by Ed Anhalt and Allan Weiss, Photographed by Loyal Griggs, Edited by Stanley Johnson.
With *E.P.*, Stella Stevens, Jeremy Slate, Laurel Goodwin, Benson Fong, Robert Strauss.

Kid Galahad (United Artists, 1962) 95 minutes; Color
Directed by Phil Karlson, Screenplay by William Fay, Photographed by Barnett Guffey, Edited by Stuart Gilmore.
With *E.P.*, Gig Young, Lola Albright, Jan Blackman, Charles Bronson, Ned Glass.

Fun in Acapulco (Paramount, 1963) 100 minutes; Color
Directed by Richard Thorpe, Screenplay by Allan Weiss, Photographed by Daniel Fapp, Edited by Stanley Johnson.
With *E.P.*, Ursula Andress, Elsa Cardenas, Paul Lukas, Larry Domain, Alejandro Rey.

It Happened at the World's Fair (MGM, 1963) 103 minutes; Color
Directed by Norman Taurog, Screenplay by Si Rose, Photographed by Joe Ruttenberg, Edited by Fred Steinkamp.
With *E.P.*, Joan O'Brien, Gary Lockwood, Vicki Tiu, H. M. Wynant.

Kissin' Cousins (MGM, 1964) 96 minutes; Color
Directed by Gene Nelson, Screenplay by Gerald Drayson Adams, Photographed by Ellis Carter, Edited by Ben Lewis.
With *E.P.*, Arthur O'Connell, Tommy Farrell, Jack Albertson, Pamela Austin, Yvonne Craig.

Roustabout (Paramount, 1964) 101 minutes; Color
Directed by John Rich, Screenplay by Paul Nathan and Allan Weiss, Photographed by Lucien Ballard, Edited by Warren Low.
With *E.P.*, Barbara Stanwyck, Joan Freeman, Leif Erickson, Sue Ann Langdon, Pat Buttram.

Viva Las Vegas (MGM, 1964) 85 minutes; Color
  Directed by George Sidney, Screenplay by Sally Benton, Photographed by Joe Biroc, Edited by John McSweeney, Jr.
  With *E.P.*, Ann-Margret, Cesare Danova, William Demarest, Jack Carter.

Girl Happy (MGM, 1965) 96 minutes, Color
  Directed by Boris Segal, Screenplay by Harvey Bullock, Photographed by Philip Lathrop, Edited by Rita Roland.
  With *E.P.*, Shelley Fabares, Harold J. Stone, Gary Crosby, Judy Baker, Nita Talbot.

Harum Scarum (MGM, 1965) 95 minutes; Color
  Directed by Gene Nelson, Gerald Drayson Adams, Photographed by Fred Jackman, Edited by Ben Lewis.
  With *E.P.*, Mary Ann Mobley, Fran Jeffries, Michael Ansara, Jay Novello.

Tickle Me (Allied Artists, 1965) 90 minutes; Color
  Directed by Norman Taurog, Screenplay by Edward Bernds and Ellwood Ullman, Photographed by Loyal Griggs, Edited by Archie Marshak.
  With *E.P.*, Jocelyn Lane, Julie Adams, Jack Mullaney, Merry Anders.

Frankie and Johnny (United Artists, 1966) 87 minutes; Color
  Directed by Fred De Cordova, Screenplay by Alex Gottlieb, Photographed by Jacques Marquette, Edited by Grant Whytock.
  With *E.P.*, Donna Douglas, Harry Morgan, Sue Ann Langdon, Nancy Kovack, Robert Strauss.

Paradise — Hawaiian Style (Paramount, 1966) 91 minutes; Color
  Directed by Michael Moore, Screenplay by Allan Weiss, Photographed by Wallace Kelley, Edited by Warren Low.
  With *E.P.*, Suzanna Leigh, James Shigeta, Donna Butterworth, Marianna Hill.

Spinout (MGM, 1966) 102 minutes; Color
  Directed by Norman Taurog, Screenplay by Theodore J. Flicker, Photographed by David Fapp, Edited by Rita Roland.
  With *E.P.*, Shelley Fabares, Diane McBain, Deborah Walley, Dodie Marshall, Jack Mullaney.

Clambake (United Artists, 1967) 100 minutes; Color
  Directed by Arthur Nadel, Screenplay by Arthur Brown, Jr., Photographed by William Margulies, Edited by Tom Rolf.
  With *E.P.*, Shelley Fabares, Will Hutchins, Bill Bixby, James Gregory, Gary Merrill.

Easy Come, Easy Go (Paramount, 1968) 95 minutes; Color
  Directed by John Rich, Screenplay by Allan Weiss and Anthony Lawrence, Photographed by William Margulies, Edited by Archie Marshek.

With *E.P.*, Dodie Marshall, Pat Priest, Pat Harrington, Skip Ward, Frank McHugh.

Live a Little, Love a Little (MGM, 1968) 89 minutes; Color
Directed by Norman Taurog, Screenplay by Michael Hoey and Dan Greenberg, Photographed by Fred Konekamp, Edited by John McSweeney, Jr.
With *E.P.*, Michele Grey, Don Porter, Rudy Vallee, Dick Sargent, Sterling Holloway.

Speedway (MGM, 1968) 92 minutes; Color
Directed by Norman Taurog, Screenplay by Philip Shuken, Photographed by Joe Ruttenberg, Edited by Russell Farrell.
With *E.P.*, Nancy Sinatra, Bill Bixby, Gale Gordon, William Schalbert.

Stay Away Joe (MGM, 1968) 101 minutes; Color
Directed by Peter Tewsbury, Screenplay by Burt Kennedy, Photographed by Fred Konekamp, Edited by George Brooks.
With *E.P.*, Burgess Meredith, Joan Blondell, Katy Jurado, Thomas Gomez, Henry Jones, Quentin Dean.

The Trouble with Girls (And How to Get into It) (1969, MGM) 97 minutes; Color
Directed by Peter Tewksbury, Screenplay by Arnold and Lois Peyser, Photographed by Jacques Marquette, Edited by George Brooks.
With *E.P.*, Marilyn Mason, Nicole Jaffee, Sheree North, Edward Andrews, John Carradine, Vincent Price.

Change of Habit (Universal, 1969) 93 minutes; Color
Directed by William Graham, Screenplay by James Lee and Eric Bercovici, Photographed by Paddy Schweitzer and Russell Metty, Edited by Douglas Stewart.
With *E.P.*, Mary Tyler Moore, Barbara McNair, Jane Elliot, Leorna Dana, Ed Asner, Regis Toomey.

Charro! (Universal, 1970) 98 minutes; Color
Directed and and writted by Charles Marquis Warren, Photographed by Ellsworth Fredericks, Edited by Al Clark.
With *E.P.*, Ina Balin, Victor French, Lynn Kellogg, Barbara Werle, Solomon Sturges.

Presley also appeared in the following documentaries: **Elvis: That's the Way It Is** (1970), **Elvis on Tour** (1972), **This Is Elvis** (1981).

Clint Eastwood

The infusion of sensitive qualities in males of the fifties American cinema like James Dean and Marlon Brando, and the rebellious, generally liberal spirit of the rock and roll myth as exemplified by Elvis Presley, leads us to Clint Eastwood. Through his roles, from the Sergio Leone spaghetti Westerns of the sixties to the Dirty Harry Callahan series of the seventies, Eastwood presented the style of toughness that some filmmakers felt was necessary to revive the sagging male image. He was quiet, stoic, and presented the same unflinching masculinity of John Wayne, only sans the morals. Wayne would never shoot a man in the back, nor would his films imply that corruption was inherent in the establishment. Wayne's code of honor allowed him the same stereotypical toughness; however, staples like Mom, apple pie, and patriotism were forever lauded, never questioned. Eastwood was a loner in a world where everything around him seemed evil and confusing. In his Westerns this was due to various forms of savage man. In his detective films it was due to the counterculture that right-wing Americans were unable to comprehend. Eastwood solved his problems with a gun—a surrogate penis which enhanced his asexual manliness as it remained totally under his control.

To young men of the sixties who somehow did not formulate an opinion about Vietnam or the prevailing politics or social causes, Eastwood gave them a throwback to the stereotypical authoritarian male: superiority from one who deals with essentially traditional values. The insecurities of working-class males (layoffs, unemployment) could be what caused them to latch onto the Eastwood character who remained in total control without budging.

To young men of the sixties who did become involved in the counter-culture, Eastwood's character embodied that subculture's outlook upon authority and the status quo. They related to the alienation of the Eastwood character and secretly admired his having the gall to battle such forces so unflinchingly, not realizing that the forces he was essentially battling were those of the very counterculture these young men represented.

Clint Eastwood as the "man with no name."

The Sergio Leone–directed spaghetti Westerns *A Fistful of Dollars* (1964), *For a Few Dollars More* (1965), and *The Good, the Bad, and the Ugly* (1966), as well as their American cousins *Hang 'em High* (1968) and *Coogan's Bluff* (1968), all presented Eastwood as a quiet, alienated loner ("the man with no name") who does not trust society and uses violence as self-protection. He does not care about any codes of the West which limit the times and places for shootings. He kills without remorse, believing that

Eastwood disrupts a robbery attempt as Dirty Harry in *Sudden Impact* (Warner Bros., 1983.

impulsive action without introspection is most effective. In these earlier films he can be accused of a now almost traditional, or legendary, wooden performance, but his violent outbursts aren't quite as offensive as in his later films, given the corruption he is surrounded by. His impassive demeanor is shown as necessary in a lawless region. Once this impassive demeanor was presented as belonging to a modern-day law enforcement official, however, it was used for a perverse kind of antiyouth propaganda which applauded the very "me decade" qualities that pervaded the seventies.

Don Siegel's *Dirty Harry* (1971) and its sequels present a wealth of negative stereotypes amidst a maelstrom of mindless violence. These films assert that the social order has been ruined by the formerly suppressed minorities: racial groups, lower social classes, young people. In order to regain control over this national hubbub, a hero is needed. Harry Callahan is that hero, wreaking havoc on all those who dare expect a voice in the prevailing system. His method of law enforcement is to destroy his victims with no thought to such "unmasculine" things as civil rights.

In the Dirty Harry series, college-age persons with long hair are whining psychopaths; blacks are pimps, bank robbers or cops; wealthy people are blown away in their swimming pools. No explanation is given for the stereotypes, other than that these groups are evil simply because it is inherent within their racial group, age group, or social class. The films

assert that the world is an evil place filled with inexplicably awful t̲e̲
(who all just so happen to be minorities), without even the slightest e̲.
tion of the poor and oppressed and just what it is that leads them to
of crime. Eastwood's Harry Callahan is the embodiment of a neo–Fascist
leader who destroys these evil forces, his flagrant disregard for their civil
rights being necessary to succeed in ridding the world of such vermin.

In *Dirty Harry* we are introduced to a dangerous game of cat and
mouse that Harry enjoys playing with his victims. Holding a gun on them,
he asks whether they can recall if he spent five or six shots. If they guess
incorrectly, they are gunned down. One black bank robber has the opportunity to kill Harry, but does not take the chance that Harry has spent his
six shots. Hence the white man's intellectual superiority to the black in this
case. We are also introduced to further exhibitions of prejudice as Harry
makes snide remarks about his Hispanic partner not only for his ethnic
background, but also for his having gone to college. Intellectuality is
equated with impotence as the robot killing machine Harry Callahan
grumbles, "Just what I need, a college boy!"

Of course Harry's chief adversary is a long-haired hippie type who is
presented as a wholly repugnant evil force, eerily representing right-wing
views of left-wing liberals during this period. Harry approaches his
adversary as Hitler approached the Jews—believing him to be vermin and
that he should be wiped out without remorse. Harry shoots and then tor-
tures his victim in spite of his superiors' pleading to "avoid a bloodbath."
Harry is relentless in his persecution of this side of society that goes against
the suppressive norm. That the young man is presented as a vicious sniper
(without explanation of course) allows the audience to feel hatred as well.
Thus the propaganda of *Dirty Harry* serves its purpose well and demon-
strates the ugliness of vigilantism while applauding and even glorifying the
same.

Magnum Force (1973) is another Harry Callahan vehicle, this time
presenting three young people as adversaries. These are college-age rookie
cops who become overzealous in their killing, battling corruption by
slaughtering those involved with drugs, pornography, prostitution, et al.
Harry is called out to stop these evil youngsters—so he slaughters them in
the same fashion that they slaughtered the others, reprimanding them by
utilizing those same methods that they are being reprimanded for. Such
methods are more inconsistent than they are ironic.

Eastwood retained this persona in all of his subsequent films, including
the odious "comedy" *Every Which Way but Loose* (1979), in which one of
the key scenes features Eastwood attempting to get his pet orangutan
laid. This persona was popular in spite of bad material—the working-class
American male overcoming his feelings of insecurity by escaping into the
omnipotent, powerful Eastwood character. The films spawned many

imitations, most notably Michael Winner's *Death Wish* and its sequels, in which the liberalism of Paul Kersey (Charles Bronson) was shown as impotent when his wife and daughter are brutally raped. Kersey fights back by casually gunning down all dissenters on the streets, fighting injustice usually perpetrated by young people and the poor. Vigilantism was definitely in vogue.

By the time he made *Heartbreak Ridge* (1986), Eastwood's screen persona was very firmly established. Playing a tough military officer in the pro-war eighties seemed a natural. What we get here is enhanced sexism as well as the other undesirable qualities of Eastwood's previous pictures. Eastwood directed himself, presenting women in the stereotypical, often demeaning positions of secretaries or waitresses. His ex-wife (Marsha Mason) has decided that she will achieve security only if she remarries a wealthy bar owner.

Heartbreak Ridge also reestablishes Eastwood's antiintellectual status. All career men in the army who have a scholastic background are presented as wimpy thinkers, while the true masculine image is one like Eastwood's — an old army veteran who paid his dues in Korea and Vietnam, something that deserves tremendous respect in a film of this sort. He whips his young male recruits into shape (unlike his previous films, they are not adversaries in the traditional sense, but are again in his total control), and of course they learn to respect his murderous military toughness once they are assigned to invade a Central American country (we aren't told why). This was the last film Eastwood made before being elected mayor of Carmel, California.

The films of Clint Eastwood contain a tough-guy image that embodies most of the traditional elements, using them to assert many pro–Fascist sensibilities, especially that of the tough cop who restores law and order without incorporating proper laws into his own system of enforcement. The films also reinforce many negative stereotypes in an effort to present a very extreme form of evil so that the Eastwood character comes off as heroic in spite of his repugnant practices. The Eastwood films are actually very dangerous items in spite of any claims of technical competence. That they present the predominant image of male toughness in the American cinema from the late sixties onward makes them as influential as they are offensive. In any case, they are very important films for careful analysis.

Eastwood as Marine Gunnery Sergeant Tom Highway leads his platoon in a training scene from *Heartbreak Ridge* (Warner Bros., 1987).

Clint Eastwood Filmography

A Fistful of Dollars (United Artists, 1964) 100 minutes
Directed by Sergio Leone, Screenplay by Leone, Duccio Tessari, Victor Catena, G. Schock, Photographed by Jack Dalmos, Edited by Roberto Cinguini.
With *C.E.*, John Welles, Marianne Koch, Pepe Calvo, Wolfgang Lukschy.
Note: Original title: **Per un Pugno di Dollaro** (based on Kurosawa's *Yojimbo*).

For a Few Dollars More (United Artists, 1965) 130 minutes
Directed by Sergio Leone, Screenplay by Leone and Luciano Vincenzoni, Photographed by Massimo Dallamano, Edited by Giorgio Ferralonga.
With *C.E.*, Lee Van Cleef, John Welles, Rosemary Dexter, Klaus Kinski, Mara Krup.
Note: Original title: **Per Qualche Dollaro in Piu.**

The Good, the Bad, and the Ugly (United Artists, 1966) 161 minutes
Directed by Sergio Leone, Screenplay by Leone and Luciano Vincenzoni, Photographed by Tonino Delli Colli, Edited by Nino Bargali.
With *C.E.*, Lee Van Cleef, Eli Wallach, Aldo Giuffre, Mario Brega.
Note: Original title: **Il Buono, il Brutto, il Cattivo.**

Hang 'Em High (United ARtists, 1968) 125 minutes
Directed by Ted Post, Screenplay by Leonard Freeman and Mel Goldberg, Photographed by Leonard South and Richard Kline, Edited by Gene Fowler, Jr.
With *C.E.*, Ed Begley, Pat Hingle, Inger Stevens, James MacArthur, Arlene Golonka.

Coogan's Bluff (Universal, 1968) 93 minutes
Directed by Don Siegel, Screenplay by Herman Miller, Dean Riesner, Howard Rodman, Photographed by Bud Thackery, Edited by Sam Waxman.
With *C.E.*, Lee J. Cobb, Susan Clark, Tisha Sterling, Don Stroud, Betty Field, Tom Tully.

Where Eagles Dare (MGM, 1969) 155 minutes
Directed by Brian G. Hutton, Screenplay by Alastair MacLean, Photographed by Arthur Ibbetson, Edited by John Jympson.
With *C.E.*, Richard Burton, Mary Ure, Patrick Wymark, Michael Hordern, Donald Houston.

Paint Your Wagon (Paramount, 1969) 166 minutes
Directed by Joshua Logan, Screenplay by Alan Jay Lerner and Paddy

Chayefsky, Photographed by William Fraker and Loyal Griggs, Edited by Robert C. Jones.

With *C.E.*, Lee Marvin, Jean Seberg, Harve Presnell, Ray Walston.

Two Mules for Sister Sara (Universal, 1970) 114 minutes

Directed by Don Siegel, Screenplay by Albert Maltz, Photographed by Gabriel Figueroa, Edited by Robert Shugrue.

With *C.E.*, Shirley MacLaine, Manolo Fabregas, John Kelly, Alberto Morin, Armando Silvestre.

Kelly's Heroes (MGM, 1970) 148 minutes

Directed by Brian G. Hutton, Screenplay by Troy Kennedy Martin, Photographed by Gabriel Figueroa, Edited by John Jympson.

With *C.E.*, Telly Savalas, Don Rickles, Donald Sutherland, Carroll O'Connor, David Janssen.

The Beguiled (Universal, 1971) 100 minutes

Directed by Don Siegel, Screenplay by John B. Sherry and Gary Grimes, Photographed by Bruce Surtees, Edited by Carl Pingatore.

With *C.E.*, Geraldine Page, Elizabeth Hartman, Jo Anne Harris, Mae Mercer.

Play Misty for Me (Universal, 1971) 102 minutes

Directed by Clint Eastwood, Screenplay by Joe Heims and Dean Riesner, Photographed by Bruce Surtees, Edited by Carl Pingatore.

With *C.E.*, Jessica Walter, Donna Mills, John Larch, Jack Ging, Irene Hervey.

Dirty Harry (Warner Bros., 1971) 102 minutes

Directed by Don Siegel, Screenplay by Harry and Rita Fink, Dean Riesner, Photographed by Bruce Surtees, Edited by Carl Pingatore.

With *C.E.*, Harry Guardino, Reni Santoni, Andy Robinson, John Bernon, John Larch, John Mitchum.

Joe Kidd (Universal, 1972) 87 minutes

Directed by John Sturges, Screenplay by Elmore Leonard, Photographed by Bruce Surtees, Edited by Ferris Webster.

With *C.E.*, Robert Duvall, John Saxon, Don Stroud, Stella Garcia.

High Plains Drifter (Universal, 1972) 105 minutes

Directed by Clint Eastwood, Screenplay by Ernest Tidyman, Photographed by Bruce Surtees, Edited by Ferris Webster.

With *C.E.*, Verna Bloom, Mariana Hill, Mitchell Ryan, Billy Curtis, Jack Ging.

Magnum Force (Columbia, 1973) 122 minutes

Director by Ted Post, Screenplay by John Mileus and Michael Cimino, Photographed by Frank Stanley, Edited by Ferris Webster.

With *C.E.*, Hal Holbrook, Felton Petty, Mitch Ryan, David Soul, Tim Matheson.

Thunderbolt and Lightfoot (United Artists, 1974) 114 minutes
Directed by Michael Cimino, Screenplay by Cimino, Photographed by Frank Stanley, Edited by Ferris Webster.
With *C.E.*, Jeff Bridges, George Kennedy, Geoffrey Lewis.

The Eiger Sanction (Universal, 1975) 128 minutes
Directed by Clint Eastwood, Screenplay by Hal Diesner and Warren Murphy, Photographed by Frank Stanley, Edited by Ferris Webster.
With *C.E.*, George Kennedy, Vonetta McGee, Jack Cassidy.

The Outlaw Josey Wales (Warner Bros., 1976) 140 minutes
Directed by Clint Eastwood, Screenplay by Phil Kaufman and Sonia Chernus, Photographed by Bruce Surtees, Edited by Ferris Webster.
With *C.E.*, Chief Dan George, John Vernon, Bill McKinney, Sam Bottoms, Sondra Locke.

The Enforcer (Universal, 1976) 96 minutes
Directed by Jim Fargo, Screenplay by Stirling Silliphant and Dean Riesner, Photographed by Charles Short, Edited by Joel Cox.
With *C.E.*, Bradford Dillman, Harry Guardino, John Mitchum, Tyne Daly.

The Gauntlet (Universal, 1977) 110 minutes
Directed by Clint Eastwood, Screenplay by Michael Butler and Dennis Shyrock, Photographed by Rexford Metz, Edited by Ferris Webster.
With *C.E.*, Sondra Locke.

Escape from Alcatraz (Paramount, 1978) 110 minutes
Directed by Don Siegel, Screenplay by Richard Tuggle, Photographed by Bruce Surtees, Edited by Ferris Webster.
With *C.E.*, Patrick McGoohan, Roberts Blossom, Jack Thigeau, Fred Ward, Paul Benjamin.

Every Which Way but Loose (Warner Bros., 1979) 112 minutes
Directed by James Fargo, Screenplay by Jeremy Joe Kronsberg, Photographed by Rexford Metz, Edited by Ferris Webster.
With *C.E.*, Sondra Locke, Ruth Gordon, Geoffrey Lewis, John Quade, Clyde.

Bronco Billy (Warner Bros., 1980) 119 minutes
Directed by Clint Eastwood, Screenplay by Dennis Hackim, Photographed by David Worth, Edited by Ferris Webster.
With *C.E.*, Sondra Locke, Geoffrey Lewis, Sam Bottoms, Scatman Crothers.

Eastwood behind bars in *Escape from Alcatraz* (Paramount, 1978).

Any Which Way You Can (Warner Bros., 1981)
    Directed by Buddy Van Horn, Screenplay by Stanford Sherman, Photographed by David Worth, Edited by Ferris Webster.
    With *C.E.*, Sondra Locke, Geoffrey Lewis, Ruth Gordon, Harry Guardino, William Smith, Clyde.

Firefox (Warner Bros., 1982) 137 minutes
    Directed by Clint Eastwood, Screenplay by Alex Lasker, Photographed by Bruce Surtees, Edited by Ferris Webster.
    With *C.E.*, Freddie Jones, David Huffman, Warren Clarke, Ron Lace, Kenneth Colley.

Honky Tonk Man (Warner Bros., 1982) 122 minutes
Directed by Clint Eastwood, Screenplay by Clancy Carlisle, Photographed by Bruce Surtees, Edited by Ferris Webster.
With *C.E.*, Klye Eastwood, John McIntire, Alexa Kenin, Verna Bloom, Matt Clark, Barry Corbin.

Sudden Impact (Warner Bros., 1983) 117 minutes
Directed by Clint Eastwood, Screenplay by Joe Stuntson, Photographed by Bruce Surtees, Edited by Joel Cox.
With *C.E.*, Sandra Locke, Pat Hingle, Bradford Dillman, Paul Drake, Audrie J. Neenan.

City Heat (Warner Bros., 1984) 97 minutes
Directed by Richard Benjamin, Screenplay by Sam O. Brown (Blake Edwards), Photographed by Nick McLean, Edited by Jacqueline Cambas.
With *C.E.*, Burt Reynolds, Jane Alexander, Madeline Kahn, Rip Torn, Irene Cara, Richard Roundtree.

Tightrope (Warner Bros., 1984) 114 minutes
Directed and written by Richard Tuggle, Photographed by Bruce Surtees, Edited by Joel Cox.
With *C.E.*, Genevieve Bujold, Dan Hedaya, Alison Eastwood, Jennifer Beck, Marco St. John.

Pale Rider (Warner Bros., 1985) 122 minutes
Directed by Clint Eastwood, Screenplay by Michael Butler and Dennis Shyrack.
With *C.E.*, Michael Moriarty, Carrie Snodgrass, Christopher Penn, Sydney Penny.

Heartbreak Ridge (Warner Bros., 1987) 130 minutes
Directed by Clint Eastwood.
With *C.E.*, Marsha Mason, Everett MacGill, Moses Gunn, Eileen Heckart, Bo Svenson, Boyd Gaines, Mario Van Peebles, Arlen Dean Snyder.

The Dead Pool (Warner Bros., 1988) 91 minutes
Directed by Clint Eastwood, Written by Steven Sharon.
With *C.E.*, Patricia Clarkson, Evan C. Kim, Liam Neeson, David Hunt, Michael Currie, Michael Goodwin, Guns & Roses.

Eastwood directed but did not appear in **Bird** (1988), which starred Forrest Whittaker as jazz saxophonist Charlie "Bird" Parker.

Eastwood had brief roles in the following films: **Francis in the Navy** (1955, also David Janssen's film debut), **Lady Godiva** (1955), **Revenge of the Creature** (1955), **Tarantula** (1955), **The First Traveling Saleslady** (1956), **Never Say**

Goodbye (1956), **Star in the Dust** (1956), **Escapade in Japan** (1957), **Ambush at Cimmaron Pass** (1958), **LaFayette Escadrille** (1958).

Eastwood also appeared as Rowdy Yates on 144 episodes of the CBS TV series **Rawhide** (1959–1966).

Sylvester Stallone

Sylvester Stallone's immense popularity with American moviegoers during the seventies and eighties had a great deal to do with his shrewd marketing abilities. He knew how to capture the public's fancy and did so with incredible success. As a tough guy, he presented his persona under the guise of whatever tough guy type the public would presumably appreciate the most, be it the underdog Rocky Balboa or the impassionate killing machine John Rambo. The toughness of either character is important to contrast since the former began as a compassionate lower-class nobody who modified his character once success was thrust upon him, while the latter is a stereotypical hard-as-nails serviceman, capable of feats that would make Superman envious.

Stallone appeared in a series of films with brief bit roles as a tough mug with little or no character distinction. Writing and starring in *Rocky* (1976) is what made him a household word. This old-fashioned boxing drama, a rehash of any one of a dozen "B" pictures from the forties, captured the public fancy that Stallone was aiming for. His Rocky was an underdog, an insecure small-time prizefighter who supplemented his income as a collector on the docks for a sly loan shark. Rocky is surrounded by losers, none of whom are nearly as philosophical about their position as he is. The rest all fantasize about get-rich-quick schemes, while Rocky never considers making much of a mark.

It is perhaps rather implausible for Rocky to be picked as the opponent for world heavyweight champion Apollo Creed (Carl Weathers), but this is only because Stallone's script is constructed so that we are introduced to Rocky and his world prior to Creed making his selection. Such exhibition matches do exist in prizefighting. The story has Rocky being selected, hence it is important for the script to let us know Rocky. Perhaps it would not have seemed implausible had Stallone's script featured the Creed sequences and followed them with a look at Rocky, but then the rhythm of the film would have been hampered. Soon Rocky slowly realizes he is being dismissed as a laughingstock by the media during publicity for this

Sylvester Stallone as "Rocky," with Talia Shire (United Artists, 1976).

exhibition, while his most dubious acquaintances now insist that they are his cherished friends.

Of course Rocky does not win the fight, but he does manage to last the entire fifteen rounds, a major feat in itself. Thus a new tough guy is presented to the American moviegoer in the form of a fantasy hero, one who can capably pull off a personal victory in spite of his not managing to win the fight itself. The toughness of Rocky embodies the all–American never-say-die spirit. He has nothing but power in his favor. He cannot outbox the champion; he is not as intelligent nor as wealthy, nor is he as charismatic.

The battle here is between a nobody and a somebody, and since in this context the nobody can prove himself to be a somebody, then the moviegoers who are haunted by their own insecurities can relate to, and be exhilarated by, these circumstances. Stallone continued to play upon audience sympathies in the same fashion with subsequent Rocky features (from *Rocky II* to *Rocky IV* as of this writing), but gradually had to modify the character in order to fit changing times.

Before embarking on *Rocky II*, Stallone attempted to utilize his stardom in two non–Rocky features: *Fist*, based very loosely on the life of Jimmy Hoffa, and *Paradise Alley* (both 1978), based on Stallone's novel *Peacock Alley* and which he directed as well as starred in. This latter film is most interesting in that not only is Stallone's writing more layered than *Rocky*, but his direction contains a clear understanding of how to depict street life (the story is set in the slums just after World War II) so that it properly sets the tone and mood for each sequence. Stallone carefully fills each scene with evil-looking types so as to enhance the tragic atmosphere, while most of the action takes place at night. Even the indoor shots are dark and murky.

Stallone is not Rocky in *Paradise Alley*, but a shifty draft-dodger whose get-rich-quick schemes are the antithesis of Rocky's philosophical acceptance of his position in life. Stallone's character in this film becomes involved, with his two brothers, in the shady world of small-time professional wrestling. We get a glimpse at many things outside of the sibling rivalry that is the focus of the film. Stallone surrounds the narrative's major conflict with interesting subplots that display the small-time hood activity prevalent in these areas, including petty theft, muggings, prostitution, veiled homosexuality among the gang members. We also see the racism that pervaded the era, as the wrestler whom Stallone's brother beats to gain prominence in the ring is a black man whose grappling talents are abused by shady employers, this wrestler having virtually nowhere to go to complain. *Paradise Alley* has so many interesting touches that it could well be considered Stallone's most impressive work. It did not, however, capture the public fancy, thus forcing the business-minded Stallone to sacrifice art for artifice.

Rocky II (1979) was little more than a rehash of its predecessor, interesting mostly for the fact that Rocky does win the championship this time. *Rocky III* (1982) is more interesting in that it presents another element of the character, that being his naive attempts to deal with such sudden, massive success after living so long, and accepting, life as a small-time boxer. The conflicts of wealth and his championship status are studied in a somewhat streamlined fashion (Mr. T appearing as a big, intimidating contender against whom Rocky must again prove himself), but Stallone does attempt here to use his character in a context less familiar than the two previous ventures.

Stallone wrote, directed, and starred in *Paradise Alley* (Universal, 1978).

Rocky IV (1985) is the film in which Stallone transforms Rocky into a veritable cartoon character. His standard formula is used as anticommunist propaganda, Rocky battling an evil Soviet fighter, in the U.S.S.R., amidst a series of hopeless clichés. The Soviet fighter is announced as being "in the *red* corner." Rocky is cheered midway through the match by the onlooking Soviet spectators, his sense of fair play far too attractive for them. Rocky, upon defeating his opponent, manages to hush the entire packed arena so that he can make a speech about relations between their country and the United States — a speech so moving that the Soviet dignitaries in the audience stand and applaud along with the casual fans. Thus Rocky manages to accomplish more with his speech than past presidents had managed with various peace talks.

Stallone as "Rambo": the mass-market sensation of the 1980s (Orion, 1985).

Rocky IV is not, however, as appalling as *Rambo* (also 1985), made immediately prior. A sequel to *First Blood* (1982), *Rambo* is prowar propaganda at its most feverish, with Stallone's title character returning to Vietnam alone in an effort to rescue P.O.W.s from the evil North Vietnamese. This is "Dirty Harry Goes to War" as Rambo polishes off the enemy quite handily, despite their efforts to get him first (the enemy in these films constitutes some of the worst marksmen who ever held a gun).

The significance of *Rambo* stems once again from Stallone wanting to present a tough guy that catches the public's fancy. *Rambo* was an incredibly successful film on a commercial level, as it was released during a time when many Americans decided that being vindictive against all threatening forces was the answer to victory, even peace. Vietnam, the most glaring blight on our nation's recent past, is the best area to stage a film of this sort. That John Rambo is no more than an impassionate mercenary does not hinder the character's success. In a subsequent marketing explosion as eerie as any in recent memory, Rambo became a hero among small children who were presumably too young to see the R-rated film. There were dozens of Rambo toys on the market, from guns to knives, allowing children to playfully reenact such scenes of destruction as shooting or stabbing a friend who is playing the enemy. Compassion was far from popular, as the popularity of Rambo outdid even Dirty Harry's.

It is then not surprising that Stallone eventually made *Cobra* (1986), in which he is a detective with the same coldheartedness as Clint Eastwood's Harry Callahan or Charles Bronson's Paul Kersey. The only thing that distinguishes *Cobra* from the Dirty Harry or Death Wish series is that it is even more bloody and violent than those films it chose to emulate. It was another box-office smash.

Sylvester Stallone is perhaps lacking in original ideas, his tough guys being no more than incarnates of previous styles. His shrewd marketing sensibilities, however, give us the most stated example of what had happened to the presentation of toughness and masculinity in the American cinema by the eighties. To be tough, we must not only believe that it is unmasculine to display emotion, but that we must also rely on violence in order to solve any of our conflicts. The importance of Stallone stems from the massive popularity of his interpretations of what it means to be a tough American male as according to its cinema. His Rambo and Cobra characters are cold, heartless, brutal, vindictive killers who do not bother reasoning, as such methods are dismissed as time-consuming and ultimately fruitless.

There have been many diverse examples of male toughness presented in the American cinema. It is rather unfortunate that this study culminates with the most primitive and mindless examples as prevalent.

Sylvester Stallone Filmography

Lords of Flatbush (Columbia, 1974) 86 minutes
Directed by Martin Davidson, Screenplay by Davidson, Stallone, and Stephen Verona, Photographed by Joseph Mangine, Edited by Stan Siegel.
With S.S., Perry King, Henry Winkler, Paul Mace, Susan Blakely, Maria Smith, Renee Paris.

Stallone as the ultra-violent "Cobra" (Cannon, 1986).

Rocky (United Artists, 1976) 119 minutes

Directed by John Avildsen, Screenplay by Stallone, Photographed by James Crabe, Edited by Richard Halsey.

With S.S., Talia Shire, Burgess Meredith, Burt Young, Thayer David, Carl Weathers.

F.I.S.T. (United Artists, 1978) 145 minutes
Directed by Norman Jewison, Screenplay by Joe Eszterhas and Stallone, Photographed by Laszlo Kovacs, Edited by Graeme Clifford.
With S.S., Rod Steiger, Peter Boyle, Melinda Dillon, David Huffman, Tony La Bianco, Kevin Conway.

Paradise Alley (Universal, 1978) 107 minutes
Directed and written by Stallone, Photographed by Laszlo Kovacs, Edited by Eve Newman.
With S.S., Lee Canalito, Armand Assante, Frank McRae, Anne Archer, Kevin Conway, Terry Funk.

Rocky II (United Artists, 1979) 119 minutes
Directed and written by Stallone, Photographed by Bill Butler and Danford B. Greene, Edited by Standford Allen.
With S.S., Talia Shire, Burgess Meredith, Burt Young, Carl Weathers, Janice Hampton.

Nighthawks (Universal, 1981) 99 minutes
Directed by Bruce Malmuth, Screenplay by David Shaber, Photographed by James Cotner, Edited by Christopher Holmes.
With S.S., Billy Dee Williams, Lindsey Wagner, Persis Khambatta, Nigel Davenport, Rutger Hauer.

Victory (Paramount, 1981) 117 minutes
Directed by John Huston, Screenplay by Yobo Yablonski, Photographed by Gerry Fisher, Edited by Roberta Silvi.
With S.S., Michael Caine, Pepe, Bobby Moore, Osvaldo Ardilies, Paul Van Himst.

First Blood (Orion, 1982) 105 minutes
Directed by Ted Kotchett, Screenplay by Michael Kozoll and William Sackheim, Photographed by Andrew Laszlo, Edited by Tom Noble.
With S.S., Richard Crenna, Brian Dennehy, David Caruso, Jack Starrett, Michael Talbott.

Rocky III (MGM, 1982) 99 minutes
Directed and written by Stallone, Photographed by Bill Butler, Edited by Don Zimmerman.
With S.S., Talia Shire, Burgess Meredith, Burt Young, Carl Weathers, Mr. T., Hulk Hogan.

Rhinestone (20th Century–Fox, 1984) 111 minutes
Directed by Bob Clark, Screenplay by Phil Alden Robinson, Photographed by Timothy Glafos, Edited by Stan Cole.
With S.S., Dolly Parton, Richard Farnsworth, Rob Liebman, Tim Thomerson, Steven Apostle.

Top: A flag-waving Rocky Balboa in *Rocky IV* (United Artists, 1985). Bottom: Stallone arm-wrestles Rick Zumwalt in *Over the Top* (Cannon, 1986).

Rambo; First Blood II (Orion, 1985) 117 minutes
Directed by George Cosmatos, Screenplay by Stallone and James Cameson.
With S.S., Richard Crenna, Charles Napier, Samuel Berkoff.

Rocky IV (United Artists, 1985) 118 minutes
Directed and written by Stallone, Photographed by Bill Butler, Edited by Don Zimmerman.
With S.S., Talia Shire, Carl Weathers, Burt Young, Dolph Lundgren, Brigitte Nielson.

Cobra (Cannon, 1986) 87 minutes
Directed by George Cosmatos, Screenplay by Sylvester Stallone (based on the novel *Fair Game* by Paula Gosling), Photographed by Ric Waite, Edited by Don Zimmerman.
With S.S., Brigitte Nielsen, Reni Santoni, Andy Robinson, Lee Garlington, John Herzfeld, Art Le Fleur, Brian Thompson, David Rasche, Val Avery.

Over the Top (Cannon, 1986) 100 minutes
Directed by Menahem Golan, Screenplay by Stallone and Stirling Silliphant, Photographed by David Gurfinkel, Edited by Don Zimmerman.
With S.S., Robert Loggia, Susan Blakely, David Mendenhall, Rick Zumwalt, Terry Funk.

Rambo III (Tri-Star, 1988) 101 minutes
Directed by Peter MacDonald, Written by Sylvester Stallone.
With S.S., Richard Crenna, Mark de Jonge, Kurtwood Smith, Spiros Forcas, Sasson Gabai, Doudi Shoua, Randy Raney.

Stallone also made small appearances in the following: **Capone, Death Race 2000, Farewell My Lovely, No Place to Hide, Prisoner of Second Avenue, Cannonball, Staying Alive** (which he wrote, produced and directed).

Bibliography

Barbour, Alan. *Humphrey Bogart* (NYC: Pyramid Press, 1973).

Basinger, Jeanine. *The World War Two Combat Film* (NYC: Columbia University Press, 1986).

Benchley, Nathaniel. *Humphrey Bogart* (Boston: Little, Brown & Co., 1975).

Bergeman, Andrew. *We're in the Money* (NYC: New York University Press, 1971).

_____. *James Cagney* (NYC: Pyramid Press, 1973).

Cagney, James. *Cagney by Cagney* (Garden City, NY: Doubleday, 1976).

Carr, Roy, and Mike Farren. *Elvis: The Illustrated Record* (NYC: Harmony, 1982).

Cavett, Dick, and Christopher Porterfield. *Eye on Cavett* (NYC: Arbor House, 1983).

Essoe, Gabe. *The Films of Clark Gable* (NYC: Citadel Press, 1970).

Fenin, George, and William K. Everson. *The Western* (NYC: Bonanza Books, 1962).

Gallagher, Tag. *John Ford; The Man and His Films* (Berkeley, CA; University of California Press, 1986).

Grant, Barry Keith, ed. *Film Genre Reader* (Austin, TX: University of Texas Press, 1986).

Kapf, Stephen Louis. *The Gangster Film (1930–1940)* (NYC: Arno Press, 1973).

Mellen, Joan. *Big Bad Wolves* (NYC: Pantheon Press, 1977).

Poague, Leland. *Howard Hawks* (Boston: Twayne, 1982).

Presley, Priscilla. *Elvis and Me* (NYC: Putnam, 1985).

Robinson, Edward G., and Leonard Spigelgass. *All My Yesterdays* (NYC: Hawthorne, 1973).

Schickel, Richard. *James Cagney; A Celebration* (Boston: Little, Brown & Co., 1985).

Sultanick, Aaron. *Film; A Modern Art* (NY: Cornwall, 1986).

Tuska, Jon. *The American West in Film* (Westport, CT: Greenwood Press, 1985).

Yablonski, Lewis. *George Raft* (NYC: McGraw-Hill, 1974).

Index

The names of actors with individual chapters appear in boldface. Names and films in the filmographies are not listed here.